THE FUTURE OF
POLITICAL SCIENCE

This book contains some of the newest, most exciting ideas now percolating among political scientists, from hallway conversations to conference room discussions. To spur future research, enrich classroom teaching, and direct non-specialist attention to cutting-edge ideas, a distinguished group of authors from various parts of this sprawling and pluralistic discipline has each contributed a brief essay about a single novel or insufficiently appreciated idea on some aspect of political science. The 100 essays are concise, no more than a few pages apiece, and informal. While the contributions are highly diverse, readers can find unexpected connections across the volume, tracing echoes as well as diametrically opposed points of view. This book offers compelling points of departure for everyone who is concerned about political science—whether as a scholar, teacher, student, or interested reader.

Gary King is David Florence Professor of Government at Harvard University.

Kay Lehman Schlozman is J. Joseph Moakley Professor of Political Science at Boston College.

Norman H. Nie is Research Professor of Political Science at Stanford University and Professor Emeritus at the University of Chicago.

D1089433

THE FUTURE OF POLITICAL SCIENCE

100 Perspectives

Edited by
Gary King, Harvard University
Kay Lehman Schlozman, Boston College
Norman H. Nie, Stanford University

Routledge
Taylor & Francis Group

NEW YORK AND LONDON

First published 2009
by Routledge
270 Madison Ave, New York, NY 10016

Simultaneously published in the UK
by Routledge
2 Park Square, Milton Park, Abingdon, Oxon OX14 4RN

Routledge is an imprint of the Taylor & Francis Group, an informa business

©2009 Taylor & Francis

Typeset in Garamond 3
by Keystroke, 28 High Street, Tettenhall, Wolverhampton
Printed and bound in the United States of America on acid-free paper
by Walsworth Publishing Company, Marceline, MO

Library of Congress Cataloging in Publication Data
The future of political science:100 perspectives/Gary King,
Kay Lehman Schlozman, and Norman H. Nie, editors.
    p. cm.
    Includes bibliographical references and index.
    1. Political science.   I. King, Gary, 1958–   II. Schlozman, Kay Lehman,
    1946–   III. Nie, Norman H.
    JA71.F89 2009
    320—dc22   2008035563

ISBN10: 0–415–99700–3 (hbk)
ISBN10: 0–415–99701–1 (pbk)
ISBN10: 0–203–88231–8 (ebk)

ISBN13: 978–0–415–99700–3 (hbk)
ISBN13: 978–0–415–99701–0 (pbk)
ISBN13: 978–0–203–88231–3 (ebk)

CONTENTS

CONTENTS

vi

CONTENTS

CONTENTS

CONTENTS

ACKNOWLEDGMENTS

Any project involving so many authors, especially one involving 102 academics, is bound to be complicated. We are grateful to them for (mostly!) having eased the job by answering our repeated communications, following our rules, honoring the deadlines and, most importantly, producing thoughtful and stimulating essays. We thank Beverly MacMillen for superb assistance in keeping in touch with the authors, following who owed what when, and tracking various parts of the manuscript in bringing this book to fruition. We also thank our students, including Justin Grimmer at Harvard, who assisted in the development of our automated text analysis routines, Daniel Geary and Kathryn Smith of Boston College for assistance in copy-editing and specifying links between individual essays, and Curtiss L. Cobb and Daniel Butler at Stanford for helping make an initial hand-categorization of the essays into rubrics familiar to political scientists. Finally, our thanks go to Michael Kerns, our editor at Routledge who immediately saw the potential in our unconventional book proposal, and to his expert team, including Felisa Salvago-Keyes, Siân Findlay, and Heidi Cormode.

GK
KLS
NHN
July, 2008

AN INTRODUCTION TO THE FUTURE OF POLITICAL SCIENCE

Gary King, Kay Lehman Schlozman, Norman H. Nie

This book highlights many new ideas about possible future research directions in the discipline of political science. Unlike most books, the ideas presented here are intended to be at the earliest, most formative stage before sustained research backs them up or knocks them down. Some may be completely wrong, but all are worth considering. To identify and evaluate ideas like these is crucial to our enterprise—to scholars considering promising directions for their next research projects, graduate students searching for dissertation topics, undergraduates seeking a subject for an honors thesis, teachers looking for innovative courses to add to the curriculum, colleagues proposing faculty slots, deans evaluating those proposals, and anyone seeking a differentiated, expansive, and thoughtful view of where the discipline of political science is headed. In that rare moment when your routine academic responsibilities are not consuming every waking moment, you are alone at your desk, and you have a moment to consider your future intellectual direction, perhaps you will find something in these 100 essays to move your agenda along.

The Future of Political Science: 100 Perspectives presents brand new or insufficiently appreciated ideas about some aspect of the discipline. Many of these ideas represent what at least one author thinks other political scientists should know but may not: because it derives from another subfield, has gotten lost in the publication onslaught, has not before appeared in print, or has been published but overlooked. Some of the ideas represent what at least one author thinks *non*political scientists should know, that is, something that is well known, at least to some political scientists, of which policymakers, journalists, or the public at large would do well to take note and that, in turn, should also cause other political scientists to pay attention.

More specifically, we posed the following two questions and asked a group of political scientists each to choose one of them to answer in a brief essay:

- To what as-yet-unanswered question should your area of political science devote more effort?
- What is one finding, substantive or methodological, from political science (or a specified subfield within political science) that you wish were more widely known—by, for example, the media, public officials, voters, academics in another discipline, or other political scientists?

We encouraged each contributor to write a brief, informal, risky speculation instead of a formal, documented analysis, and we limited each contribution to about 1000 words. Our goal is to present and spark new thinking and inquiry, not to summarize the discipline as it is today. The authors we selected represent biased views of the discipline, both individually and collectively, but it is precisely these biases about the future that we hope to convey. Other authors would certainly focus on a different set of ideas. Since the point of this book is to incubate and discover emerging ideas in political science, we did not dictate the agenda by choosing a series of topics and, then, selecting authors to expound on our pre-conceived themes. Instead, we selected the authors first and they generated the essays, which constitute one group of answers to the questions we posed to them.

So, what did we find? What are the common themes? What will you find if you read these essays? As befits a pluralistic academic discipline—with no single, universally accepted, core paradigm and with numerous internal disagreements that have somehow not led to disciplinary divorce—the essays themselves are highly diverse. They argue, persuasively, for the significance of an astonishing array of variables for understanding politics, including individuals, families, demographic and social groups, laws, institutions, communities, nations, opinions, psychological orientations, and interests. Taken in pairs, essays sometimes make equally compelling cases for diametrically opposed points of view. Many of the essays propose intellectual bridges, bringing together elements usually considered in isolation from one another: for example, linking institutions to political behavior or yoking rational choice to several approaches to which it is usually deemed antagonistic—the political power of emotions, ethical values, or culture. Many of the essays take us in novel directions—suggesting innovative perspectives, urging us to investigate the consequences of little-noticed trends, proposing new methodologies, and incorporating new forms of evidence. Others remind us of something significant that we once knew but too often forget. And a few argue, usually with justice, that the subjects of their own research merit greater attention.

With 100! possibilities, placing these essays in some kind of order posed an obvious challenge. Every pair of essays we put together had many explicit or implicit commonalities. We grouped and ordered the essays, producing various types of organizing schemes. Given the great number of possibilities, relatively few of which would be obviously wrong, we resisted the suggestions of friendly readers, and the importunes of editors, each of whom posed a perfectly reasonable—but utterly different—organizing scheme complete with Roman numerals and hierarchically ordered topic headings. We also tried sitting on the floor and putting the essays in logical piles, but this too was uncertain. We turned instead to an automated procedure to assist us in locating an organizing scheme to present here. After trying various existing clustering algorithms that work on unstructured text, we ultimately developed one that seemed most useful for our purposes. The algorithm searches for a small number of essays in the collection, each of which is closest in substance to a cluster of other essays.

Figure 1 gives both a hand coding by our graduate students (see numbered categories at the top and numbers in the figure), who used familiar categories from political science related to the subject matter, as well as our automated representation of the similarities among the essays (in the clustering solutions). The bold name at the center of each cluster is the author whose essay has most in common in terms of its content with a group of other essays. Any essay within a cluster has more in common with the essay at the center of its cluster than with essays outside of that cluster. Essays within a cluster are ordered in terms of similarity with the central (emboldened) essay, starting with the essay with the most in common, appearing 12 noon (in the largest font) and continuing for those less and less in common ordered clockwise (with gradually smaller fonts). The positioning of the clusters on the page indicates how much the essays in each cluster have in common with essays in another cluster: the closer any two clusters are to one another, the more similar they are in content. To clarify the substantive ideas that the essays within each cluster have in common, Table 1 lists the exemplar document at the center of each cluster, a topic label we came up with, and a list of automatically generated words that best represent what is unusual about the essays within a cluster. (We developed a related algorithm to order the essays to print in this book and then hand-tooled it to reflect our understanding of the content of the essays.)

It is interesting that the hand and machine codings convey different information about the multiple layers of information in the themes of the essays. For example, our graduate students' scheme for categorization made the distinction, one well known within the discipline, between comparative politics and the various categories of American politics. However, the essays by authors from these usually separate fields touch one another in many ways. For another example, elections are a major motivating interest among our contributors (see the Hansen cluster), missed by our hand coders. For still another, the hand-coded "culture" category obscured work on beliefs and attitudes exemplified by a cluster that probes the origins of personal political choice (the Carpenter cluster). These are only a few examples of the dense web of interrelationships among the essays.

Figure 1 Similarities among the Essays

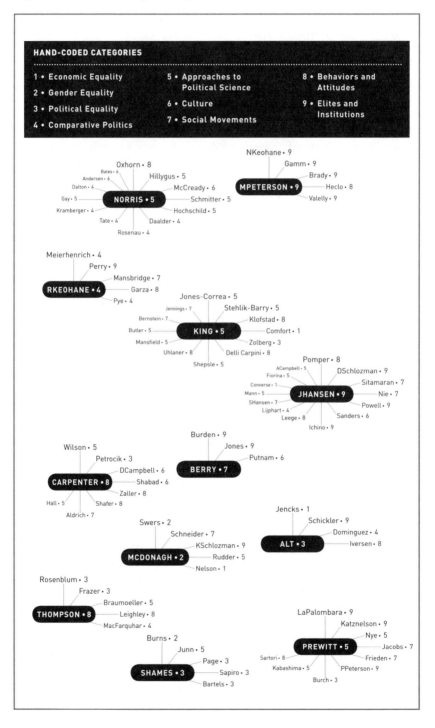

Having decided to forgo conventional organizing rubrics, we opted to give readers a hand in locating groups of essays that have something in common. At the end of each essay, we list other essays that are "of possible related interest." The essays listed (by number) have something in common with the specified essay—although they do not all have something in common with one another. We assembled these lists on the basis of the electronically generated clusters described earlier as well as two "human-based" techniques: the categorization based on traditional political science rubrics devised by our graduate students; and an effort by three close readers of the essays who proceeded essay by essay in search of links to other individual essays. (To evaluate the alternative methods used to find links among essays, we conducted an informal experiment. We generated a list of 100 pairs of essays: 25 were randomly selected from the essays that had been linked by the clustering algorithm; 25 randomly selected from the pairs generated by the humans looking for links between individual essays; 25 from the categories generated by the research assistants who used political science rubrics; and 25 randomly linked pairs. The 100 pairs were listed in a random order. Without specifying what it means to be "closely related," we asked two research assistants to use a three-point scale to rank each pair with respect to how closely related the two essays are. We were interested to learn that the clustering algorithm performed best in matching pairs of related essays, followed in descending order by the essay-by-essay approach, the political science categories, and random selection.)

The typeface on the list indicates how an essay was selected for inclusion on the list of essays that might also be of interest to a reader who wanted to pursue the themes in a particular essay: when the number of the essay is in the ordinary type font, it was specified by at least one person; when it is in *italics*, it was chosen by the clustering algorithm as close to the essay in question; when it is **emboldened**, it was specified through both means. You can use these alternative recommendations as you might movie reviewers who have specific tastes.

In keeping with the informal and spontaneous nature of the essays, we have kept such scholarly accoutrements as footnotes to a minimum.

Figure 1 opposite Similarities among the Essays
The bold name at the center of each cluster is the author whose essay has most content in common with the group of other essays connected to it by a dotted line. Any essay within a cluster has more in common with the essay at the center of its cluster than any essay outside of that cluster. Essays within a cluster are ordered according to similarity with the central (emboldened) essay, starting with the essay with the most in common, appearing at 12 noon (in the largest font) and continuing for those less and less in common ordered clockwise (with gradually smaller fonts). The set of clusters are oriented on the page so that those with greater substantive similarity to each other are plotted closer to one another in the figure. The numbers after the names refer to an attempt at hand coding into the categories listed at the top.

Table 1 Subject Matter of the Essay Clusters
This table lists, for each cluster, a title we devised and an automatically generated set of words that best convey what the essays in the cluster have in common.

Exemplar document	*Topic label*	*Words*
John Mark Hansen	Campaigns & Elections	voter, campaign, election, candidate, politician, social, partisan, electorate, journalist, scholar
Daniel Carpenter	Origins of Personal Choice	religion, belief, family, identify, conceptual, notion, simplify, influence, conservative
James E. Alt	Income Inequality	income, inequality, higher, money, affect, fall, distribution, high, reason, economy
Pippa Norris	Measuring and Studying Society	collect, sociological, comparison, culture, integral, develop, intern, design, survey, community
Shauna L. Shames	Social Inequality	gender, race, account, analyze, income, women, class, data, analysis, agenda
Gary King	Data used to Study Politics	public, influence, democrat, question, vote, consider, collect, govern, institute, area
Jeffrey M. Berry	Representation and Class	representation, constitution, lack, outcome, represent, religious, primary, white, dramatic, deserve
Mark A. Peterson	History, Elites, and Politics	historical, movement, perspective, thought, course, life, like, train, directly, recognition
Dennis F. Thompson	Positive and Normative Theory	theoretical, reality, empirical, theory, deserve, form, add, human, American, concept
Kenneth Prewitt	Policy Implications and Political Science	cost, process, pay, affect, modern, impact, function, opposite, decade, shift
Robert O. Keohane	Legal Studies and Politics	international, law, potential, regime, suggest, country, ground, rise, domestic, short
Eileen McDonagh	Gender Inequality	men, private, gender, right, experience, women, contemporary, ideological, focus, traditional

However, as an additional aid to anyone venturing onto unfamiliar intellectual terrain, a majority of the authors have appended references to a few works that interested readers might also wish to consult.

The occasion for assembling this particular group of 102 political scientists is Sidney Verba's retirement after a distinguished career that spanned a half-century; tenured appointments at Princeton, Stanford, the University of Chicago and, beginning in 1973, Harvard; and scholarship that ranged widely while retaining a thematic coherence in its focus on the role of the citizen in a democracy. It is traditional to honor the retirement of an academic of Sidney's stature with a festschrift. Because festschrifts, once published, are so rarely bought or read, we introduce in this volume what might be thought of, from the perspective of political science, as a new literary genre. By informal count, the resulting set of authors comprises 17 co-authors, 19 current and former research assistants, 27 students, 44 past and present departmental colleagues, and 102 friends and colleagues of Sidney Verba's—whose collective gratitude, esteem, and affection meant that they needed no convincing to contribute to this volume. This group represents a large fraction of the best places to study political science. It encompasses distinguished emeritus professors as well as current graduate students, two of whom embarked on their lives as scholars when they worked on Sidney's research projects as undergraduates. It includes a former research assistant who worked with Sidney and Gabriel Almond on *The Civic Culture* nearly a half-century ago, nine presidents of the American Political Science Association (and, we would wager, a number of future ones), and winners of every single major prize given in political science— but no one who has matched Sidney's record by winning them all.

However, as we made clear to the contributors, this volume is intended to honor Sidney Verba, not to be about him. (To assist readers who might wish to acquaint themselves with the range and power of Verba's scholarship, and to understand the mainsprings of his formidable academic reputation, we have listed a dozen of his most significant books, along with essays reviewing his work, in a separate bibliography at the end of the book.) With 102 authors writing very brief essays, we also sought to establish a boundary on the space devoted to biographical details about the authors and their personal comments about Sidney. Hence, we set ground rules that limited authors to two sentences (which we collect at the end of the book): one listing their current professional position and the other indicating when they met Sidney. The latter make clear the qualities that have inspired such respect and affection among all who have had the opportunity to work closely with Sidney in one capacity or another: intellect, curiosity, generosity, good judgment, empathy, warmth, and, above all, humor. Together, the three of us have been privileged to know Sidney for more than a century. We join with the other 99 authors in saluting a legendary career and a remarkable human being. But nothing will honor

Sidney Verba more than the ideas you come up with after reading the essays herein.

Finally, we expect that no one will find all the essays in this volume to be equally intriguing, and few will find the same essays to be especially intriguing. In fact, during the peer-review process for this book, even enthusiastic reviewers made the usual point about edited volumes that the essays are not uniform in quality. However, when asked to identify the best and worst essays, not only did no two anonymous referees choose the same essays for their lists, but several essays chosen as the *best* in the volume by one or more reviewers were singled out by other reviewers as the *worst*! Fortunately, the goal here is not to ensure that all readers like all the essays equally or, even, like most of the essays; it is only to try to spark innovation and improvement in thinking, teaching, researching, and reporting about politics. Thus, we encourage readers to approach this volume much as Chaucer recommended almost seven centuries ago in the "Prologue" to "The Miller's Tale" in *The Canterbury Tales* where he wrote:

> I moot reherce
> Hir tales alle, be they bettre or werse,
> Or elles falsen som of my mateere.
> And therfore, whoso list it nat yheere,
> Turne over the leef and chese another tale.

1

THE UNITED STATES: A DIFFERENT DEMOCRACY

Arend Lijphart
University of California, San Diego

One of the significant advances that American political science has made in the last few decades is that the fields of American politics and comparative politics are no longer as isolated from each other as they once were. Comparativists often include the U.S. in their analyses, and Americanists are much more aware of comparable institutions and practices in other countries. Several prominent political scientists, like Robert Dahl and Sidney Verba, have done outstanding work in both fields.

Generally, whenever the U.S. is compared with other countries, the emphasis is on contrasts rather than similarities. Nevertheless, I would argue that even among political scientists there is insufficient recognition of how radically different American democracy is: it is different not just in *many* respects, but in *most* respects! And politicians, journalists, and the attentive public are almost completely unaware of these differences, with the exception of a few policy questions. For instance, the fact that the U.S. is the only industrialized democracy without national health insurance and with highly permissive gun laws is occasionally mentioned in the media. But other salient differences, like our big income inequalities, relatively low tax burden, and extremely large prison populations usually escape attention. And there is little recognition of, and interest in, the many contrasts between the operation of democracy in the U.S. and that in other countries. Even as well informed a politician as President Bill Clinton apparently did not know that proportional representation (PR) is widely used in democracies around the world—and that the U.S. is the deviant case—when he commented in 1993 that Lani Guinier's advocacy of PR was "very difficult to defend" and even "antidemocratic."

In collaboration with Bernard Grofman and Matthew Shugart, I have been working on a book-length study tentatively entitled *A Different Democracy: American Government and Politics in Comparative Perspective*. It entails a systematic comparison of all of the major political institutions, rules, and practices in the U.S. with those in 28 other democracies: all of the countries that have been continuously democratic since the early 1990s and that have a minimum population of 5 million. (We exclude the many very small democracies in today's world because it does not make sense to compare a large democracy like the U.S. with countries that are so much smaller.) Of the 28 other democracies, five are in the Americas: Canada, Mexico, Brazil, Argentina, and Chile. Six are in Africa, Asia, and the Pacific: South Africa, India, Japan, South Korea, Israel, and Australia. The others are in Europe: the five large West European countries (UK, Germany, France, Italy, and Spain), three Nordic countries (Sweden, Denmark, and Finland), six other small West and South European countries (the Netherlands, Belgium, Switzerland, Austria, Portugal, and Greece), and three countries in Central Europe (Poland, Hungary, and the Czech Republic).

Across the board, when there are differences in democratic institutions and practices, the U.S. is almost always in the minority, usually a small minority, and frequently a minority of one. Our constitution is among the two or three that are the most difficult to amend. We have a presidential system, whereas most other democracies are parliamentary. Our House of Representatives is elected for the uniquely short term of two years; other lower (or only) houses are elected for at least three, and usually four or five years. We use juries in criminal trials more often than any other country, and only in Canada is the unanimity rule as prevalent as it is here. Our two-party system is unique in that it is an almost exclusive two-party system in which third parties are virtually absent; other so-called two-party systems tend to have significant numbers of small parties participating in elections and represented in legislatures. Our interest group system is rated by the experts to be either the least or among the least corporatist.

The contrasts are especially striking with regard to elections and election rules. Our Electoral College is unique; among the other countries with powerful presidents, only Argentina and Finland had electoral colleges in the recent past, but these were abolished in the 1990s. Our election method for the House of Representatives—plurality in single-member districts (SMDs)—is used by only three other democracies for lower-house elections (Britain, Canada, and India); France and Australia use SMDs but not plurality, and the other 23 use PR or partly proportional methods. In no other country is partisan and pro-incumbent gerrymandering as prevalent a problem as it is here. Press reports often refer to "primary elections" in other countries, but those are quite unlike American primaries which have three distinctive characteristics: they are imposed on the parties by the state; they are conducted by public officials; and they allow any voter who declares himself or herself to be a member of a party to vote in that party's primary. So-called primaries in other democracies fail to conform to one or more of these criteria; in this respect, too, the U.S. is unique.

2

The U.S. is not the only democracy with voluntary voter registration, but unique in making it a burdensome task. Turnout in our most important national elections, presidential elections, is lower than voter participation in the key national elections in all other democracies except Switzerland. The American "long ballot," on which the voter has to decide on as many as 30 or 40 different elections and referendums, is unique; in all other democracies, most ballots contain just one, or at most two or three, choices to be made in a single day. Our usual election day is Tuesday, a weekday; seven other democracies also use weekdays, but the other 21 conduct their elections on Sundays or a weekday that is declared a national holiday. Our entire system of election rules and administration is extremely decentralized, in contrast with the uniform rules in all other democracies with the partial exception of Switzerland. There are some 10 months between the first presidential primary in January and the election in November—in contrast with all other democracies that use two-stage elections, like majority-runoff elections, in which the two stages are usually only two, and at most five, weeks apart. We are the only democracy where many ex-felons are permanently disenfranchised—an especially serious limitation of voting rights because we put more people in prison than any other democracy. The above is obviously not an exhaustive list; for instance, no fewer than 43 unique or unusual characteristics of American parties and elections are addressed in our draft chapters for *A Different Democracy*.

More work needs to be done on the interactions among these variables and on the origins of the many American exceptionalisms. But the basic facts are clear and deserve to be much more widely recognized. Different does not necessarily mean worse, of course, but the knowledge that we are a very different democracy should make us more self-critical, more willing to consider political and constitutional reforms, and less eager to advocate American-style democracy for other countries.

Of possible related interest: Chapters **2**, 8, *68*, **74**.*

Suggested additional reading

Dahl, Robert A. *How Democratic is the American Constitution?* New Haven, CT: Yale University Press, 2001.
Hill, Steven. *10 Steps to Repair American Democracy*. Sausalito, CA: PoliPointPress, 2006.
Lipset, Seymour Martin. *American Exceptionalism: A Double-Edged Sword*. New York: W.W. Norton & Company, 1996.

*In this essay, and all others, numbers in ordinary font are chapters of possible interest suggested by a human coder, in *italics* are suggested by our automated algorithm, and **emboldened** are suggested by both.

2

TAKING PORTRAITS OR GROUP PHOTOS?

Russell Dalton
University of California, Irvine

If one enters a photography studio, the differences between people in the portraits are striking. Each person is unique. However, when one looks at the group photos, the commonalities between people dominate.

It is much the same in many features of mass political behavior. If we look at one nation, we are struck by its uniqueness—the institutions of democracy are different, and political groups and citizens have their distinct traits. For instance, Americanists stress the unique aspects of U.S. political institutions. However, the German political system is also unique among Western parliamentary democracies—with a federal system, a strong bicameral national legislature, the *konstruktives Misstrauensvotum*, and other institutional particulars. Similarly, Britain, Japan, and each established democracy also have their unique elements. The fundamental democratic structure of these nations and the basic principles of mass political behavior display many commonalities, and often these are lost in the search for detail and uniqueness.

The editors of this festschrift asked us to identify one finding from political science that we wish were more widely known outside the academy. I would not cite a specific finding, but a general dictum for American political science: *we are not alone*. For instance, as U.S. researchers struggle to address many of the political and social challenges facing our nation, the response of American academic and political experts is often to emphasize the uniqueness of the American political system. Voting turnout is declining; this must reflect problems such as registration or the organization of campaigns that should be reformed. Partisanship is weakening; this must arise from the poor performance of parties or the unique structure of American elections. Trust in government is decreasing; this must reflect a need to reform Congress, or the presidency, or the media. America seems highly polarized; this must reflect the structure of campaigns and party financing. This list could go on ad infinitum. I would argue that all these

4

trends now occurring within the American public are also occurring in other advanced industrial democracies. These other democracies do not share our unique political history or institutional structures—so we share something in common that can be missed in nation-centric analyses.

Similarly, one might stress the different patterns in citizen participation, voting choice, or the actions of political elites across nations—but this occurs mostly when we take close-up portraits, rather than ask about general processes, such as the influence of social structure on participation, the common elements of voting choice, or the commonalities of elite behavior. Political science includes both portraiture and group photos—but only the latter is likely to generate a real understanding of the phenomenon of interest.

Such introspection is a normal part of political research, and is not limited to the study of American politics. However, it is more difficult to be introspective when one studies a small nation, linked to others through institutions such as the European Union. Thus, to think in a comparative framework is a greater challenge for American political science.

Certainly there are important institutional differences in the structures of democracies that are worthy of comparison, and significant in their political outcomes. Yet, my suggested lesson is that human beings are the key element of all these systems, and people are perhaps more similar to one another than the institutions in which they function. People do act differently in different institutional contexts, but their goals, motivations and skills may be more comparable than we realize. This leads to functionally equivalent patterns, if we stand back and view the group picture and not the individual photograph. And contemporary democracies may share the effects of modernization, technological change, and social changes that transform mass politics across nations—which are not unique to single nations.

Thus, thinking about America in comparative context—in a Verba sort of way—should provide insights into the source and implications of mass politics that we miss by taking introspective views of these issues.

Of possible related interest: Chapters **1**, 15, 57, **71**.

3

WHY POLITICAL THEORISTS SHOULD THINK MORE CAREFULLY ABOUT LEADERSHIP

Nannerl O. Keohane
Princeton University

Leadership is a pervasive phenomenon in our society—and indeed in most societies we know anything about. Journalists and biographers often write about leadership. So do scholars from several disciplines—public policy, sociology, psychology, history, management theory—and those who labor in the vineyard that has come to be called "leadership studies."

"Leadership" is of course a central issue in government and politics. But relatively few political scientists have explored it with the care they have given to other issues. James MacGregor Burns, Richard Neustadt, James David Barber, Fred Greenstein, and Jim March are among those who have done so, with impressive results. Political theorists—in the sense of "political philosophers"—have paid even less attention to this topic. When they have considered leadership, it is almost always in the context of *limiting* the exercise of power or *channeling* it in directions that are desirable for the subjects of that power. Rarely has a political philosopher pondered leadership from the perspective of the leader, and written about the activities leaders engage in, or the kinds of skills that are needed for successful leadership in different kinds of situations, the impact the exercise of power has on the power-holder, or how leaders could be encouraged and prepared.

There are a few exceptions to this rule, including most notably Machiavelli and Max Weber, as well as Plato and Aristotle in a different vein. But most political philosophers, both past and present, are more interested in other issues, such as justice, liberty, equality, the legitimacy of authority, the elements of citizenship, forms of constitutions, the definition of sovereignty, or the requirements for effective democratic self-government.

I would argue that this neglect of leadership by political philosophers has left unfortunate gaps in our understanding of this crucial political activity. The "leadership" provided by men and women in any political community becomes a kind of black box in political philosophy, admired or feared, ignored or unexplored, but rarely analyzed or thoughtfully described. This is particularly true of the leadership provided by heads of governments, chief executive officers of corporations and others who have significant responsibility in the executive branches of governments and large private organizations.

What would it mean to take leadership so defined as a topic for political philosophy? Among the significant issues that would come in for more scrutiny than they have received over the years are the exercise of judgment by leaders; the relationship between leaders and the subordinates to whom responsibility has been delegated; questions about ethics and politics; and the distinctive characteristics of good decision-making on the part of those most centrally responsible for directing the activities of a political community, or for carrying out the will of others in a democratic system.

Understanding "judgment" is an especially pressing topic, and one for which political philosophers are particularly well equipped. Only a few political philosophers—including Aristotle, Hobbes, Kant, and Hannah Arendt—have explored this topic in any depth. Yet surely the quality of a leader's judgment, and how it is exercised in particular situations, is a factor that is crucial to the health or impairment of a political community.

A related topic is the way in which information is gathered and used by a leader, and how this is connected to a leader's way of making decisions, appointing subordinates, and taking responsibility for his or her actions. What does it mean to be a good listener, as we are told many successful leaders have been? And how is this related to being persuasive and visionary, which are also among the attributes ascribed to those who have made a significant impact as leaders?

Political philosophers are also particularly well placed to explore questions about the relationship between ethics and politics, given the kinds of issues we are trained to explore and understand. Are there differences between the kind of virtue appropriate to private life and the standards that a leader should follow in achieving the good for a larger community, as quite a few thoughtful people across the ages have contended? How do we understand those differences, and how do we ensure that this distinction does not lead to or excuse abuses of power, or prompt vices that are antithetical to political responsibility? What do we mean when we refer to the phenomenon of "dirty hands"? Not only Machiavelli and Weber, but several contemporary theorists—including Michael Walzer and Dennis Thompson—have provided useful insights into this set of issues, but much remains to be done.

It's time for us to get over the assumption prevalent in some quarters that "leaders" are no more than the creatures of their "followers"; or the view held by some scholars that leadership is unimportant or uninteresting compared with questions that concern individual citizens more directly; or the preference for addressing only questions that can be approached more abstractly. Political philosophers (like everybody else) need to notice how important leadership is in shaping all our lives. And a thoughtful assessment deeply rooted in the wisdom that is the heritage of political philosophy has much to contribute to the exploration of the many dimensions of leadership as a human phenomenon.

Of possible related interest: Chapters **4**, **11**, *12*, 67.

Suggested additional reading

Burns, James MacGregor. *Leadership*. New York: Harper and Row, 1978.
Machiavelli, Niccolò. *The Prince*. Boston, MA: St. Martin's Press.

4

THE LEADERSHIP GAP

Mark A. Peterson
University of California, Los Angeles

Leaders are pervasive in politics. When politics and policymaking are being discussed at any level of government or organizational setting, leaders are probably the most significant topic of conversation. Political and organizational leaders, and those who wish to rise into positions of leadership, dominate media coverage and become the subjects of best-selling biographies. Although most of what actually transpires in politics and policymaking is the product of diverse factors beyond the control or even influence of particular individuals, leaders hold more sway than any other participants in the system. They are the ones rewarded or punished for what is accomplished, or not. Failures in governing, policymaking, and institutional performance are often—perhaps usually—ascribed to failures of leadership. While John Lennon may have been able to imagine "no countries," few of us could imagine political life devoid of leaders.

And yet the extant political science literature conveys preciously little of sustained note about the relevant qualities of leaders and the systematic mechanics of leadership. To be sure, leaders abound in our scholarship, from presidents to prime ministers, legislative party or coalition leaders to committee chairs, social movement instigators to policy entrepreneurs. An entire section of the American Political Science Association—the Presidency Research Group—is devoted to the study of the single most prominent leadership institution in the U.S. and, arguably, the world. But search through all of this fine, often truly distinguished, work and one will look fruitlessly for conceptually well-defined, empirically established, repeatedly affirmed, and systemically robust conclusions about what attributes are meaningfully related to being a successful leader or that identify the qualities of efficacious leadership processes. Our work in the field has been quite effective at establishing the boundaries of leadership agency, the constraints that rein in the choices and influence of leaders, and the contextual forces that compel sometimes nearly robotic leaders to move in certain predictable directions. Demonstrating the contingency of leadership—and countering the overemphasis of the media and popular imagination on the consequentiality of individual leader actions—is one of the discipline's worthy accomplishments. But typically the impact of individual leaders and the role of leadership dynamics are cast as the figurative or literal residuals of the analysis. Total spending on the 2008 presidential primary and general election campaigns exceeded $1 billion. All to get elected to a residual. Let us just hope that the error term is normally distributed.

At least three reasons are frequently cited to explain the dearth of progress in the social scientific understanding of leaders and leadership. The field should take on these challenges directly, and recognize them as potential fallacies rather than unrelenting barriers to analysis. The first explanation for the leadership gap in political science suggests that, to the extent that leaders even make a difference, the effectiveness of leaders is highly dependent on their natural endowments, especially perceptiveness and personality. Thus leadership attributes are idiosyncratically attached to individuals and beyond the reach of systematic analysis by political scientists. They are not conducive to being learned and adopted. A quick review of U.S. presidential history, however, would reveal the tenuous relationship between personality types and individual effectiveness. Chief executives with divergent personalities have both succeeded and failed, and the same individuals in office—presumably governed by persistent personality traits—have experienced considerable variations in accomplishments beyond what can be explained by changes in the larger political, institutional, and social environment.

A second rationale for shying away from the more rigorous study of leaders and leadership is the so-called "small N" problem. At the extreme, for example, the U.S. has just one president at a time, only 44 since the founding of the republic, and each has served during arguably unique periods. There is no analytical leverage to be had. This perspective, however, misses the multiple types of actions with very large Ns that permeate single presidencies and only grow when assembled across administrations: legislative initiatives, executive orders, appointments, and any number of other decisions. These points of choice or action, where leadership could make a substantial difference at the margin, are the topics of voluminous research, but without yet fully exploiting the opportunities to home in on the instrumental characteristics of leaders and their import. The empirical challenges confronting this kind of research are substantial, but they should not be determinative.

Finally, and in a sense the upshot of combining the previous two explanations, meaningful leadership studies are thought to be enfeebled by being inherently atheoretical. There can be no conceptualization of N = 1 leaders bearing the gift or curse of particular personality traits. Break free of those perceived constraints, however, and the expansion of cases with meaningful forms of variation invites model building. Currently the field offers a good deal of theory that ignores the individual contributions of leaders, treating their differences as analytical noise and, at best, fodder for engaging stories. We need serious attention to be given to deriving concepts that posit how approaches to leadership can and do matter under varying sets of circumstances.

Although certainly relevant to the further analytical maturation of the discipline, these are issues of far more weight than just intellectual intrigue. Students in public policy programs are in training to serve the public—they are future policymakers and, not uncommonly, future leaders. The political science literature provides them with the conceptual and analytical tools to develop better strategic sensibilities by enhancing their understanding of political processes and the institutions in which policy is made or blocked. Many of these students, unsurprisingly, want to learn about how to become effective leaders. Myriad programs purport to teach them. Their courses too often rely on anecdotes and war stories, and, even worse, on the thematic fads and consultant-speak that infuse what passes as the leadership literature. By concentrating the conceptual and empirical firepower of political science on leaders and leadership, the discipline cannot only invigorate our knowledge of a central feature of politics, it can even contribute to an improved politics and policymaking.

Of possible related interest: Chapters **3**, 44, 45, *89*.

Suggested additional reading

Burns, James MacGregor. *Leadership*. New York: Harper & Row, 1978.

Jones, Bryan, ed. *Leadership and Politics: New Perspectives in Political Science*. Lawrence, KS: University Press of Kansas, 1989.

Rejai, Mostafa, and Kay Phillips. *Leaders and Leadership: An Appraisal of Theory and Research*. Westport, CT: Praeger Publishers, 1997.

5

INSTRUMENTAL VALUE OF ELITE MEMORIES ON PAST VIOLENCE DURING THE EMERGENCE OF A NEW STATE

Slovenian Experience

Anton Kramberger, Ana Barbič, Katja Boh
University of Ljubljana

Because of their infrequency, revolutionary times possess the characteristics of quasi-experiment. The independence of Slovenia from Tito's Yugoslavia and the emergence of the new Slovenian state (including nationwide referenda on withdrawal from Socialist Yugoslavia, in December, 1990, and the formal declaration of the new state, June, 1991) constitute an example.

Building a new state has been carried out by the old and newly emerged elite groups with strong support from the international political community. During the transition, the members of the old elite were engaged in skirmishes with their descendents and, above all, with the newly emerging elites in a struggle to (re)gain political power within the framework of a multi-party political system. In explaining such a struggle during a period of political transition, social scientists usually rely on structural determinants while neglecting less visible, but not less decisive, factors. We touch upon one of those factors, the trauma of emerging from subordination to the past regime of some members of the new Slovenian elite. Their traumatic experiences have been in many cases the key factor for entering political life during the transition period. That is, some members of the new Republic of Slovenia political, but also economic and cultural, elite were—due to their inclination toward the independence of a socialist republic of Slovenia within the Federal Socialist Republic of Yugoslavia, or their lack of loyalty to the federal state official regime, or other reasons—marginalized and subjected to two kinds of observable pressures: first, to direct pressure from former Yugoslavian repressive bodies; and, second, to pressure from official authorities of the Republic of Slovenia who were loyal to the socialist regime.

The subordination of the Slovenian formal and informal/marginalized elite within the former Yugoslavia led to unprocessed, partial, and hence contradictory "historical" conflicts that have been preserved in memories and are still felt in present days. Thus, it is essential to take them into consideration not only during the regime change but also in any analysis of contemporary Slovenian political situation, for these memories are rather regularly triggered in the public sphere, framing contemporary political culture and feeding today's discernable distrust of political authorities in Slovenia.

The data collected in face-to-face interviews in 1995* with 1041 elite members belonging to the Slovenian elite in 1988 (before the change in the political system), to the elite in 1995 (after the political regime change), or to both help us to understand this situation:

First, the rate of elite retention during the period 1988–1995 in Slovenia was between 70 and 80 percent. The 1988 outflow rate was 23 percent; the 1995 inflow rate was 31 percent. The highest was in the economic sphere and the lowest in politics, with culture somewhere in between. These rates seem high in comparison to other Southeast European transition countries, and it might be an artifact due to nonrandom sample designs across countries, nonresponses, field-work limitations, funding restrictions and the size of overall population of each country. Remember that Slovenia has only 2 million residents! Nevertheless, the substantive reason for the rate magnitude was probably a strong situational pressure before the regime change. Accomplishing a unique historical mission—the establishment of a new independent state of Slovenia—required a rapid consolidation of opposing elite groups. This initial elites' union was soon broken, and political struggles for power brought about many hot public disputes on the elite retention issue, especially around elections.

Second, 37.3 percent (or 389) of the elite individuals who were interviewed reported injury in their lives accompanied by violent political memories of political maltreatment, imprisonment, or confiscation of their assets and/or property. Deeply affronted, they may have wanted revenge upon the people (or their descendants) who were linked to the political regime that had caused injury to them or their families. In particular, this collective trauma has been recollected within the noncentral cultural elite

*A. Kramberger, V. Rus, H. Iglič, and A. Rus, *Survey of 1041 Slovenian Elite Members – In Office in 1988 and in 1995*. Ljubljana: Faculty of Social Sciences, University of Ljubljana, 1995, inspired by I. Szelényi and D. J. Treiman, *Social Stratification in Central and Eastern Europe – Elite Survey, Common Questionnaire for an International Comparative Survey in Six CEE Countries*. Los Angeles: Columbia University & Consortium of National Teams, 1993.

(by 47 percent in 1988 and 44 percent in 1995). In an atmosphere imbued with (past) political violence, it is not difficult to find a fair amount of hidden resentment.

Third, the self-image of the injured/maltreated elite members was harmed due to their subordination and the sad memories of past violence, possibly yielding a latent tendency for a more radical political change. The interviewed elite members showed a strong reluctance even to name themselves "elite." On the average, only four out of 10 (38 percent) identified themselves as members of an elite. The proportion was higher among the members of cultural elites because their accomplishments tend to be individual and personal (45 to 48 percent), and least among the members of economic elites (28 to 31 percent).

Fourth, in 1995, a majority, 85 percent, of elite members opted for relatively moderate social change while only 14 percent opted for radical change. The share of the latter was considerably higher among those who had experienced some type of political violence within the socialist political system. Obviously, only a part of those tensions has been resolved by initial building of a democratic state.

The unresolved part of "trauma" still exists. Its inherent public and personal distrust orients towards the past—instead of to the possibly less traumatic future of the young state—many of the current elite maneuvers, predominantly on domestic grounds. At the international level, Slovenia has reached enviable results: it became a member of the European Union in 2004, entered the EURO monetary system in 2007, and chaired the EU in the first half of 2008. The fear of losing some of the sovereignty recently gained has been "diminished" (or doubled) by inclusion into security alliances, including the North Atlantic Treaty Organization (NATO) in 2004.* This often contested issue has been frequently pointed out in the Central and East European (CEE) countries and is usually interpreted as a historical replication of an older track of foreign (vassalage) dependence. So hidden psychological and social mechanisms of the past violent discourse are still potent and may again determine/cause the burst of past "traumas" some time in the future.

Therefore, a deeper study of instrumental value of such traumatic elite memories is required in order to understand (or even predict) an irregular but periodic appearance of this vulnerable layer of political culture. Unresolved violent tensions among elite factions are especially characteristic of unstable political regimes, for which the building of a stable polity and state requires a longer period of time. Even though, in Slovenia,

---

* See Ana Barbič, "Izzivi in priložnosti podeželja." *Challenges and Opportunities of Rural Areas*. Ljubljana: Založba FDV, 2005.

the temptation for the re-opening of violent memories might be less manipulative than in other transition countries, the elite factions with NO history and those with THE history are a strong signal that a desired elite settlement has not been achieved yet. Thus, Slovenia still lacks a deeper and more complex human reading of its own history. Further research in this area may stimulate the formulation of a general theoretical framework on national conflict emergence and its possible escalation, which may help the key international actors to develop better tools for peaceful management of such conflicts.

Of possible related interest: Chapters 3, **7**, 52, 57.

Suggested additional reading

Adamski, W.W., P. Machonin, W. Zapf, eds. "Structural Change and Modernization in Post-Socialist Society." *Sisyphus Social Studies*. Vol. XV. Warsaw: Institute of Philosophy and Sociology of Polish Academy of Science, 2001.

Kramberger, A., and V. Vehovar. "Regime Change and Elite Dynamics in Slovenia during the 1990s: What Can the Elite Reproduction Rates Tell Us?" *Družboslovne razprave* 16 (2000): 143–180. Available online at: http://dk.fdv.uni-lj.si/dr/dr32-33KrambergerVehovar.PDF

Szelényi, S., and I. Szelényi. "Interests and Symbols in Post-Communist Political Culture: The Case of Hungary." *American Sociological Review* 61 (1996): 466–477.

6

POLITICIANS ARE
PEOPLE TOO

Philip Edward Jones
Harvard University

Understanding the links—or lack of links—between the public's prefer-ences and government policy is one of the central motivators for many of us who study American politics. Aside from constituency opinion, we know many of the factors that influence what lawmakers think and do. Broad ideological positions offer guidelines, political parties supply information and structure, and other political actors like interest groups try to persuade. But as political scientists, we tend to forget that legislators are people, too—with values, interests, and habits that are shaped by their experiences from life outside of politics, and that are unlikely to be cast aside once in office.

Barry Burden's recent research on the factors influencing how members of Congress behave suggests that this is a major limitation on our understanding of representative democracy. Across several issue areas, he shows that lawmakers' personal experiences have a direct effect on how they make policy, over and above the influences of party, constituency, or political ideology.

For example, Burden compares lawmakers who use tobacco to their colleagues who don't, and finds that smokers are more likely to vote, speak, and organize against proposals for tobacco control (such as restrictions on advertising, or ending government subsidies for tobacco farms). This finding is compelling and robust, holding even controlling for the "usual suspects" of constituency and party influence, or the legislator's ideological leanings. Rather than just faithfully doing what their constituents want, party leaders demand, or political ideologies predict, representatives are also guided by their own experiences and circumstances.

Similar results emerge in domains other than tobacco use. Being the parent of a school-aged child makes a representative more likely to be active on educational issues—and if the child attends public school, more likely to be active in opposition to proposed school voucher programs. Knowing the religious faith of lawmakers helps predict the positions they take (and how actively they pursue them) on complex ethical issues such as embryonic stem-cell research and the legal protection of religious freedoms.

Of course, demonstrating that elected representatives do not always act in accordance with their constituents' preferences or interests is not new. Principal-agent models of representation demonstrate how shirking can arise from voters' inability to effectively monitor and sanction every action their representatives take. But these models have been relatively silent on why representatives might want to shirk in the first place. In contrast, Burden's research opens the black box of legislative preferences to show that the experiences and interests that make politicians people also help them make national policy. In doing so, it raises two major challenges to the way we evaluate political representation in a mass democracy like America.

First, it challenges us to re-evaluate politicians' behavior. Rather than packages of ideological positions or placeholders for the median voter, the people we send to D.C. are real individuals, with real skills, experiences, and values acquired long before being elected. What are we to think of them when they act on these personal interests? From one viewpoint, these are the selfish actions of people who are in a position of power to better their own situation. From another, these are further proof of the links between descriptive and substantive representation, and of the need to have a government that "looks like America." Passing judgment on congressional behavior is somewhat simpler if we assume that legislators can either represent their party or their district, can do so descriptively or substantively, can be a delegate or a trustee, and so on. After Burden's research, these dichotomizations seem oversimplified, and in need of serious reconsideration.

Second, we are also challenged to re-evaluate constituents' behavior. A bleak caricature of the past 60 years of survey research would be that ordinary Americans do not know enough, do not care enough, and do not have the capacity to hold their representatives accountable for policy decisions. But if, as Burden writes in *Personal Roots of Representation*, "the limits of policy representation are often found in the representative himself," it seems time to re-examine our expectations about citizens' decision-making. Are voters who cast their ballots on the basis of a candidate's family or faith more or less informed than those who vote on the basis of her policy platform? More or less rational? More or less close to some democratic ideal?

Of course, these findings can be overstated: Burden's nuanced research shows that the effect of personal interests on congressional behavior varies by issue area, by the institutional setting, and whether the member is seeking to defend or overturn the status quo. Nonetheless, demonstrating that nonpolitical personal habits shape policy outcomes serves as a call to re-evaluate our expectations about the links between constituents and representatives in the U.S. and beyond—a call that is sure to be answered as more people learn about these findings.

Of possible related interest: Chapters 8, 14, 41, 89.

Suggested additional reading

Burden, Barry C. *Personal Roots of Representation*. Princeton, NJ: Princeton University Press, 2007.

7

ELITE TOUGH TALK AND THE TIDES OF HISTORY

Henry E. Brady
University of California, Berkeley

At Princeton University in March 1996, I heard James Baker III, Jack Matlock Jr., Brent Scowcroft, and others expand on how their efforts in the Reagan and Bush administrations led to the downfall of the Soviet Union and the end of the Cold War. Reagan's military build-up (especially his anti-ballistic missile "star-wars" program) and Reagan's "Mr. Gorbachev tear down this wall" speech in Berlin were credited with the collapse of the Soviet Union. We were told that most political change results from elite challenges and tough talk. Even political scientists studying democratic transitions have fallen victim to this with an overemphasis upon the role of elite negotiation and "elite pacting." In studying the collapse of the Soviet Union this perspective leads inevitably to an overemphasis on Gorbachev and Yeltsin's interactions and to a tale about how their cat-fighting tore the Soviet Union apart.

Leaders (and their followers) often seriously overestimate the impact their tough talk and pugnacious tactics have on their targets. They seriously underestimate the impacts of domestic forces—the economy, demography, public opinion, history, and culture—on the histories of nations.

We naturally focus on the dramatic moment when Reagan directly challenges Gorbachev or when Yeltsin challenges Gorbachev, but these episodes may be largely political theater symptomatic of deeper forces. Surely elite actions matter, but they do not matter in a way that is unfettered by the many forces which shape human actions, and the dramatic moments may be less important than the tides of fortune which cause elites to bump into one another at crucial moments. In a storm, ships hitting one another are mostly at the mercy of the waves.

Virtually no serious academic discussion of the collapse of the Soviet Union puts very much emphasis upon Reagan's pugnacious actions. But there is debate between structuralists who find the seeds of its destruction in long-standing features of the regime and the state, and elite theorists who focus on the inter-play between Mikhail Gorbachev and Boris Yeltsin. In research on the collapse of the Soviet Union, Cynthia Kaplan and I show that elites were highly constrained by public opinion and other institutional factors that operated against the background of large-scale structural characteristics such as the command economy and the structure of the political system. Elite actions were not strictly determined by these constraints, but they were hedged in, and successful maneuvers were often the result of recognizing exactly what was possible in a difficult and highly constrained situation.

Long-standing structural weaknesses in the command economy and the ethno-federal system of 15 Soviet republics (in which republics were named after a nationality that typically was demographically predominant) determined the fault-lines along which troubles could occur if enough stress developed. Perestroika's attempt to transform the system was undermined by domestic economic problems due to poor harvests and low oil prices, and glasnost's openness provided political opportunities for new voices. Nationalist movements in the Baltic States took these opportunities and directly challenged Gorbachev's policies. Yeltsin, through a series of brilliant political moves that appealed to public opinion also took advantage of these political opportunities, formulating a Russian populism that fused political grievances on the left and right and gained popular support. Eventually, these grievances and the reaction to them put so much stress on the system that it fell apart after the failed coup attempt of August 1991. This story says a lot about the relationship between large-scale structural factors and the machinations of leaders as they appeal to their constituencies, but it says little about Reagan's build-up and it does not lead to the conclusion that Gorbachev and Yeltsin alone can explain the break-up. Larger forces were at play.

The mistake of giving too much credit to elite actions is endemic in thinking about foreign policy and even domestic events. Because John Foster Dulles, for example, thought that his "containment" policy led to Khrushchev's famous Twentieth Party Congress speech of 1956 criticizing Stalin, he felt that keeping the pressure on Khrushchev and continuing the Cold War was a good idea. Opponents of Nixon's détente took the same perspective. More recently, neo-conservatives, partly emboldened by their belief that Reagan had ended the Cold War through his truculence, began to believe that they could have similar impacts on the Middle East through a bold policy of intervention in Iraq.

So how can elites matter? They can chart the currents of the time and launch their efforts at the right moment to catch the waves of public opinion or political opportunity. Nixon did this with his opening to China. Yeltsin did this with his series of moves against Gorbachev. But to do these things, elites must have a much greater understanding of what is going on when they intervene. They must become much better social scientists who eschew grand ahistorical strategies. And social scientists who teach courses in universities must make sure that this point is made clear to future leaders.

An aphorism and some agenda items for research follow from these observations. Elites cannot simply will history to be what they want it to be. They must understand the social forces they try to affect. My own corner of research is trying to understand how public opinion and political participation move over time and how they affect the options available to leaders. The research agenda requires developing a better understanding of when and how leaders can jump onto the waves of history and ride them to some destination. Reagan intuitively understood how to do this when he decided to placate his right-wing with his Berlin Wall speech while working with Gorbachev. Yeltsin did too when he harnessed Russian public opinion to his own career, and my research with Cynthia Kaplan attempts to understand exactly how Yeltsin did this. More grandly, it might be said that much of social science is an attempt to do this in one way or another.

Of possible related interest: Chapters 3, **4**, **5**, *81*.

Suggested additional reading

Brady, Henry E., and Cynthia S. Kaplan. *Gathering Voices: Political Mobilization and the Collapse of the Soviet Union*. New York: Cambridge University Press, forthcoming.

Etheredge, Lloyd. *A World of Men: The Private Sources of American Foreign Policy*. Cambridge, MA: MIT Press, 1978.

Roeder, Philip G. *Where Nation States Come from: Institutional Change in the Age of Nationalism*. Princeton, NJ: Princeton University Press, 2007.

8

REPRESENTATION AS
A FIELD OF STUDY

Barry C. Burden
University of Wisconsin

I hope that in future years political scientists give more attention to questions of representation. Representation is a fundamental issue in politics and deserves to be at the center of disciplinary scholarship. To be fair, there are literatures that address the degree to which citizens are well represented, and even what we mean by the term "representation." But this work can be scattered, is typically framed in other terms, and despite its heft still lacks the weight that the concept demands.

Part of this failing has to do with the way the discipline is divided into fields and subfields. Those studying American politics and those studying other countries—known as comparativists—frequently work in a parallel fashion rather than interact with each other directly. In the field of American politics, there is a further tendency to categorize research as "behavioral" or "institutional." As a result, the best scholars of public opinion and voting behavior often miss opportunities to interact with those studying legislatures and bureaucracies, and vice versa. To take one subfield as an example, in my view it would be enlightening to recast studies of public policymaking as examinations of representation, bringing in ideas from pluralism to budgeting to the spatial model to understand it.

Divisions among scholars are troubling because representation is judged precisely at the intersection of elite institutions and mass behavior. In other words, it is only by crossing subfield boundaries that one can get a clear look at the phenomena we value. We will naturally differ in the degree to which we believe the important variables are institutional or societal, but without considering both we cannot say terribly much about the representativeness of elites and governmental bodies.

It is telling that political theorists do not subject themselves to these subfield constraints and subsequently have made more direct headway on normative questions around representation. If we wish to assess how well the government does at representing its constituents, empiricists will need to disregard these subfield borders as well. This approach will encourage research driven by puzzles, normative concerns, and theoretical questions about representation while still providing results that will resonate in a variety of fields.

Of possible related interest: Chapters 1, **6**, 20, 41.

Suggested additional reading

Fenno, Richard F., Jr. *Home Style: House Members in Their Districts*. Boston: Little, Brown, 1978.

9

POLITICAL SCIENCE

What Should We Know?

David Butler
Nuffield College, Oxford

I have spent 60 years as a practicing political scientist, watching the expansion and transformation of the profession. Although much involved in election statistics and opinion polling, I have become more and more troubled at the takeover of our trade by mathematicians and game theorists at the expense of historians.

Politics is about the behavior of people living day by day in a historical context, following or breaking the rules or habits of their predecessors. Everything happens in a historical context. It is wise to be sceptical about articles on politics that never mention individual politicians. Specific leaders do make a difference. What if Gore not Bush had been adjudged the winner in 2000? What if Blair had yielded precedence to Brown in 1994? No numerical approach will explain the impact of Churchill in 1940 or of Kennedy in the early 1960s. The run of history is not inevitable.

Of course political scientists must not be mere journalists, reporting events and, of course, sophisticated mathematical approaches that produce new insights must be welcomed. But description will usually yield more than number-crunching in helping to understand political phenomena.

Of possible related interest: Chapters **3**, 25, 35, 36.

10

DYNAMIC CATEGORIES AND THE CONTEXT OF POWER

Jane Junn
Rutgers University

Categorization of ideas, people, institutions, and nations continues unabated as an intellectual force in political science. Categories of analysis run the gamut from mutually exclusive groupings to more complex constructions such as distinctions between people based in ideological positions. Groupings by race and gender are most often treated as static traits located toward the beginning of the causal chain, yet even these apparently high face-validity categories have broken down. The political dynamism accompanying globalization, democratization, and international migration suggests a reconfiguration of both analytic starting points and interpretive strategies for political science. In the study of political behavior in the U.S., scholars need to consider categories of analysis much more carefully, specifying and disentangling why and how the categories are created, what purpose the distinctions serve, why the "default" category is defined as it is, and how categories intersect with one another. Substantively, this kind of analysis is linked with a normative concern with inequality.

Many of the most politically salient categories closely track distinctions in social status and class, mirroring marginalization based in categorical imperatives. Hierarchies constructed from these distinctions create and reinscribe structural inequalities in institutions, culture, and the practice of politics, resulting in unjust outcomes. Justified by the categories themselves, inequalities have become both persistent and pernicious. What are the political roots, processes, and consequences of differentiation, stratification, and marginalization based on status and identity? How do systems or patterns of inequality operate in political frameworks? How do social movements and mass political participation address these issues and to what effect?

In order to build a better theory of political action at the individual level, political scientists need to step away from a pair of methodological presuppositions about the individual as unit of analysis combined with a normative position on political action that assumes equality of agency among individuals. In its most common form, analysis of political action in the mass public is accomplished by aggregating empirical observations taken from individuals. Characteristics of respondents are taken as given—as exogenously determined—and then aggregated into static and one-dimensional categories. For example, synchronic analyses of the effect of gender on political action observe different rates of political participation between women and men. Studies utilizing data over time show the divergence in political engagement by gender has narrowed dramatically, but despite the diminution in difference, the inequalities that do remain add up to many fewer women's voices in politics.

The analytic strategy of static categories in individuals as the unit of analysis not only impedes our ability to disentangle the roots of political inequality embedded in gender, but it also creates other undesirable consequences. One consequence for the tradition of the study of political behavior in the U.S. is the identification of the "puzzle of participation"—the observation of stagnant rates of political activity despite substantial increases in formal educational attainment over time. The most important explanatory variable for political action at the individual level is some mix of the socio-economic status (SES) duet of education and income. The problem with this most venerable of social scientific models is its application to explain change over time. If indicators of SES, particularly education, are critical antecedents to participation, and if formal education has risen dramatically and monotonically over time, why hasn't political activity increased in a commensurate rate? Taken together these findings create, at best, a puzzle and, at worst, an embarrassment for scholarship in this tradition. When categories are constructed from static accounts—woman, African American, poor—analyses most often look for the independent effect of one category against another. Race may be a more important predictor than gender for one dependent variable, whereas class might overwhelm the effects of race for a different outcome. Results structured by this perspective are meaningful when the default categories are assumed to be male, white, and middle class. But why continue to assume this? What is the inferential utility of arguing, for example, that race is more visible or more important than gender? How does this generalization apply to women of color?

Beyond acknowledging the complexity of categories and fashioning analytic strategies to accommodate this shift, individual-level approaches need to re-evaluate in a radical way another assumption driving the design of research questions and the interpretation of empirical results. The current state of knowledge in the political behavior literature based in individual-level approaches has been built substantially on an analytic triumvirate of synchronic data, the SES model, and a mainstream definition of political participation as voluntary legal acts directed at government officials toward policy outcomes. Undergirding this perspective is the assumption that individuals have equal agency. Inferential models estimated with the data belie this bias: one more year of education or one more mobilization request will increase political participation among people regardless of the particularities of their social and political context. The starting position that makes this assumption defensible is that the system itself—whether political, social, or economic, is neutral, not favoring one or another for any particular characteristic. But if we are suspicious that political responsiveness varies systematically by race, class, gender, or some other category, we must scrutinize the assumption and devise strategies to test the validity of the starting claim. There is ample evidence within political science and other disciplines to document pervasive inequalities inside the political, economic, and social systems of the U.S. This should serve as a stark reminder to political scientists that one cannot assume all individuals have equal ability and desire to influence the political system, and further, that the return on that investment in time and resources will be the same for all who take part. Instead, agency or individual rights in the liberal democratic vernacular, operate in both a social context of power relations as well as a structural context of democratic political institutions where actors deploy accumulated capital in pursuing their interests. The context of democratic politics itself is not neutral, not level, not fair. It matters who got there first and set up the rules of the game. In analyzing political behavior, we must account for power that is manifested in the political state as institutional structure and practice.

Treating categories dynamically and considering the context of power has to have a substantive end, and in this case, it is the enhancement of equality. From the perspective of individual-level behavioral research, the strong normative prior privileging equality of individual agency would force us to ask what we want from political action. Let us take the plunge and ask ourselves the biggest counterfactual for U.S. politics: what would things be like if everyone were equal? How should institutions be different? How could democratic practices and political culture work to enhance equality? We need to begin by assessing the extent to which the political system as we know it is good enough to create equality across domains, categories, and time.

Of possible related interest: Chapters 42, **43**, **61**, **65**.

11

POLITICS AS LEARNING

Hugh Heclo
George Mason University

When politics is happening, what is happening? The answer, of course, is that many different things can be happening, and political scientists are quite adept at dividing themselves into different camps around those variations. Politics is a struggle for power among groups. It is a problem of collective action among rational agents. It is a transaction between leaders and followers. It is an expression of cultural norms structured by institutions. Other perspectives could be added, and each has its own particular merits and blind spots.

Too often we fail to raise our sights and see that there is a larger arc of movement encompassing all these perspectives. When politics is happening there is teaching and learning going on. This learning process occurs at individual and societal levels. It occurs via the struggles for power, rational calculations, leader/follower transactions, and all the other things that make up political life. Politics schools people in ways of understanding their world, its problems, and possible ways forward. In one sense, seeing politics as a form of social teaching and learning is as old as Aristotle and the wisdom literature of the ancient world. In another sense it is as recent as the neglected insights of Karl Deutsch, Ed Lindblom and current advocates of the "deliberative" turn in democratic theory.

To view politics as learning is not to assume anyone is getting smarter. What is being learned may make us or the institutional systems we inhabit more stupid. To render a reasonable judgment on that score, political scientists need to ask, not just who has the power, but who is teaching and learning what? That is on the essentially descriptive, empirical side of political analysis. There is also the question of how truthful, realistic, and thus sustainable are the things being taught and learned through political processes? That is on the evaluative and ultimately practical side of political analysis. The stakes vary widely—from the effectiveness of particular public policies to the fate of entire human societies.

Of possible related interest: Chapters 4, 24, 27, 34.

28

12

ROUNDING UP THE ACTIVISTS

M. Kent Jennings
University of California, Santa Barbara

Despite the recent gains in our understanding of political participation, large areas remain understudied. One such area is that of issue activists. People often become involved in politics because they care about some issue. Oddly enough, however, issues usually do not receive much attention in treatments of participation. If issues are motivators, we should be paying more attention to what kinds of issues stimulate what kinds of people. Yet there are very few sizeable studies of domain-specific issue activists, their composition, how they are recruited, their motives, and what they actually do.

A particularly difficult topic for investigation is that of issue migration, of how and why activists move (or do not move) from one issue arena to another. Admittedly, studying issue migration poses a strong challenge in research design. One solution would be to capture a set of issue activists in various domains at an early stage in their activist careers, and then follow them over an extended period of time. Alternatively, one could canvass current activists in a number of issues at a given point in time and develop activist life histories based on careful retrospective accounts. A modification of that design would be an accumulation of independent studies of single issue activists, again relying on detailed retrospective accounts to chart issue migration.

The access and logistical difficulties inherent in these designs are formidable but not impossible to overcome. Local rather than national settings are probably the most feasible sites for such research.

Of possible related interest: Chapters 3, 10, 72, 83.

Suggested additional reading

Brady, Henry. "Political Participation." In *Measures of Political Attitudes,* edited by John P. Robinson, Phillip R. Shaver, and Lawrence W. Wrightsman. San Diego: Academic Press, 1999.

Carroll, William K., and R.S. Ratner. "Master Framing and Cross-Movement Networking in Contemporary Social Movements." *Sociological Quarterly* 37 (1996): 601–625.

McAdam, Doug. "'Initiator' and 'Spin-off' Movements: Diffusion Processes in Protest Cycles." In *Repertoires and Cycles of Collective Action,* edited by Mark Traugott. Durham, NC: Duke University Press, 1995.

13

THE TROUBLING
PERSISTENCE OF INJUSTICE

Michael L. Frazer
Harvard University

Over the past 35 years, normative political theorists and political philosophers have gone from forming small, outcast minorities in their respective
fields to being at the forefront of research in both philosophy and political
science. Philosophers have come to realize that their contribution to ethical
and political discourse can involve much more than the mere analysis of
moral language, while political scientists have largely abandoned their
insistence on a wholly value-neutral social science in favor of fruitful
collaboration with the normative theorists in their midst. The result has
been a far richer understanding of the ideals of justice which ought to
govern our democratic society.

Strangely, however, our democratic society has remained stubbornly
unjust.

Normative political theorists and empirical political scientists alike have
had remarkably little to say about the troubling persistence of injustice,
perhaps because the subject falls through a gap between their respective
subfields. Addressing the persistence of injustice seems to involve examining how and why reality systematically falls short of our ideals, and hence
cannot be a matter of either empirical description or normative evaluation
alone.

Yet this account of injustice as the failure of the world to live up to our
moral demands oversimplifies the question at hand. In *The Faces of Injustice*,
Judith Shklar argues that we must not take it for granted that "injustice is
simply the absence of justice, and that once we know what is just, we will
know all we need to know" (p. 15). Although Shklar has many provocative
suggestions about how injustice may be more than just a privative
phenomenon—about how a sense of injustice or unfairness may be more
basic to human experience than a sense of justice or fairness—her work has
yet to inspire the sort of further research which the subject so richly
deserves. Until we have a fuller theory of injustice as something more than

the mere absence of justice, we cannot even begin the joint empirical–theoretical project of examining why injustice is so obstinately persistent.

Although I can hardly begin to explain the persistence of injustice here, I do think I can conclude by ruling out one popular hypothesis. Philosophers since Socrates have always been tempted to explain injustice as a form of ignorance. If only we all had a full understanding of what justice requires—if only, that is, political philosophy had achieved its primary goal, and if only no one were left unaware of this glorious intellectual victory—then injustice would immediately whither away in the overpowering light of truth. It is understandable that philosophers would be drawn to this conception of injustice as ignorance, for it would make our work as teachers and researchers the key to ending injustice once and for all.

Of course, simply because a theory can be interpreted as a rationalization for one's own self-importance does not, in and of itself, prove that this theory is false. Experience, however, provides ample evidence that knowledge alone cannot bring injustice to its knees. To cite just one obvious example, the remarkable advances in social justice achieved in the U.S. in the middle of the last century were grinding to a halt at precisely the same time that normative political theory was beginning to pick up steam. Here is further support (as if any were still needed) for Hegel's famous dictum that the owl of Minerva flies only at dusk.

Of possible related interest: Chapters 50, **82**, *83, 95*.

Suggested additional reading

Shklar, Judith N. *The Faces of Injustice.* New Haven, CT: Yale University Press, 1992.

14

MAKING A NAME FOR ONESELF

Harvey Mansfield
Harvard University

I have a finding and an inquiry together. The finding is something perfectly obvious, but then science, and especially political science, often consists in reexamining something obvious that we have overlooked. The finding is that people and the societies in which they live have proper names.

What is the significance of that fact? Names mark off the differences between individuals and societies or other groups, and they do so because the differences are important to us. But science, or natural science, with its universality and its objectivity, is indifferent to proper names, and confines itself to common nouns. Even political science, with its sensitivity to importance, to the importance of importance, aims to abstract from individual data with names to arrive at universal propositions. Survey research is an example of this.

Yet human beings and their associations always have names; this is how they maintain their individuality. You can think your way to an abstract individual or society without a name, but you cannot live there. All human life takes place in an atmosphere of proper nouns. To make a name for yourself is to become important. To lose your name, to suffer a stain on your name, your reputation, is to live thinking less well of yourself, or among others who think less well of you. Does this matter? It appears that human beings like to think they are important. Perhaps they have to think so if they want to live responsibly. But how important are they, really—individually and collectively?

Science abstracts from the sense of one's importance, for that is precisely what would give a bias to the scientist. Political science can hardly do this, however. Politics, I venture to say, is more about human self-importance than the desire for power. You want power in order to make yourself important. Or you may consider yourself too important to want power. Harold Lasswell said, implied, that politics is about who gets what, when, how. Political scientists today talk about getting, and about what, when, how—but not enough about the who. How can political science acquire sensitivity to human importance? I answer, by making friends with literature, which is always about individuals with names. Of course, the individuals represent types: Achilles, Mr Darcy, Mrs Malaprop (who is named for a typical error). But they still have names. The literature in which they appear is not just a set of case studies, because an individual is not just a case, one substitutable for another.

Literature, which features human importance, also features style in what it conveys. Those two qualities of literature are connected, for style is needed to entertain and address readers who have opinions of their own and may resist the truths one may have come upon or found.

I leave this problem as an inquiry in the name of those political scientists, who by virtue of their stylish writing show how well they appreciate literature and who thereby show their concern for the special place of political science within science.

Of possible related interest: Chapters 3, 6, 13, 38.

Suggested additional reading

Aristotle. *Politics*. Indianapolis, IN: Hackett Pub., 1998.

Lasswell, Harold. *Politics: Who Gets What, When, How.* New York: P. Smith, 1936.

Plato. *Republic* (Books 3 and 4 on *thumos*). New York: Oxford University Press, 1994.

15

POLITICAL VARIATION
ACROSS CONTEXTS

Michael Jones-Correa
Cornell University

Social scientists, with ever-greater sources of survey and other data, and using the tools of multivariate analysis, have become adept at thinking of social phenomena as having multiple contributing factors, and at weighing the relative contributions of each factor to given outcomes. An upside of these approaches is a greater appreciation for the complexity of the social claims on individual attachments—through gender, for example, as well as race, and race as well as education. This appreciation, however, still tends to overlook the importance of variation across contexts.

By "change across contexts" I mean the ways in which similar indicators vary quite substantially by political actors' locations. These locations can be measured geographically—by census bloc or tract, by neighborhood, by city, by county, by state, by country, etc.—but these measures of geography are essentially proxies for the social networks or institutions in which individuals are embedded. An actor's geographical location simply becomes a way to link information on their attitudes, opinions, and behaviors with information about geographically specific social networks and institutions.

The insight that contexts shed light on what we know about political actors is not new: the American National Election Surveys, for example, have collected limited contextual data (respondents' congressional districts, etc.). And the institutional turn in political science also placed greater emphasis on actors' institutional contexts. But this additional attention in political science to context has only begun to take advantage of the changes in the forms and availability of social and political data; changes that will greatly facilitate the study of behavior and attitudes in the context of social networks, institutions, and location.

Many of these changes are due simply to the ubiquity of data in computer-readable form, but also, more importantly, to the tagging of these data with a geographic locator—often using U.S. Census FIPS codes. Once a piece of data has a geographic identifier, it can be matched with data linked to the same geography. For example, if we know a respondent's location by Census tract, then other information collected at the Census tract level can be appended to the respondent data. The analysis of geographically linked pieces of data has been driven by work in urban planning, geography, and biology, but has increasingly migrated over to the social sciences, and to a lesser extent, political science.

Again, the study of politics across contexts—the *raison d'être* for comparative politics—is not new. However, both the scope and level of detail possible in comparative research—not just across nation-states, but within them to the sub-national level—are greatly expanded by the geo-coded data available. In fields like migration studies, which have a strong geographical underpinning to them in any case, the use of geo-coded data changes the way that the demographics of immigration and its political consequences can be analyzed and understood.

In the U.S., for instance, one major change over the last 15 years has been the dispersal of immigration to areas that had received very little immigration for 100 years or more. Immigrants from Latin America, who make up the largest migrant stream to the U.S., while still concentrated in a handful of states (California, Texas, Florida, New York, Illinois) are now also a *national* presence, present in significant numbers in every region of the country. In 1990, U.S. residents of Latin American origin—Latinos—were the largest minority ethnic group in only 16 of the 50 states, and their share of the population exceeded 5 percent in only 15 states. In 2000, Latinos outnumbered all other racial and ethnic minorities in 23 states, and their population exceeded 5 percent in the same number of states. Because of this geographic dispersion, there is every reason to expect, say, that the experiences of Latinos vary widely across political and institutional contexts, with Latinos living in areas with comparatively small Latino populations likely to have significantly different social experiences than those living in high-density Latino areas.

For example, because levels of school funding, teachers' salaries, quality of infrastructure, test scores, and numerous other indicators correlate with a variety of social indicators as well as measures of second-generation immigrant assimilation such as English language use, geo-coded data can be used to view survey responses of immigrants' views of schools, and their children's educational outcomes, in the context of data on the schools their children actually attend. Since residential concentration is thought to be related to individuals' attitudes toward other racial/ethnic groups, as well as policy preferences toward those groups, survey data on immigrants' evaluations of race and ethnic relations can be enhanced by specific knowledge of the racial/ethnic composition of the neighborhoods in which they live. Likewise, because political scientists posit positive effects and externalities for minorities who are represented by co-ethnics holding political office, responses to questions about political efficacy can take into consideration whether respondents actually have co-ethnic political representation, and at which level—city, state, or Congress. In each of these cases, geo-coded data allow prevailing hypotheses to be examined more closely.

The linking of geographic data to other data generally expands the possibilities for comparison, the examination of variation, and the testing of hypotheses. Recent ventures in the study of American politics like the 2001 Social Capital Community Benchmark Survey, or the 2006 Latino National Survey take advantage of these features, and with the availability of data, and the awareness of the importance of politically relevant differences across contexts, these kinds of studies will become more common in political science. Along with new findings, these approaches will bring with them new questions and challenges: as with recent approaches to marketing and political campaigning, the sheer amount of information that can be accumulated about any individual or about individuals and their contexts, will raise serious issues about respondent confidentiality and privacy. The need to protect these will mean thinking about new ways to shield individuals while still allowing access to data. There is a great deal of promise inherent in thinking seriously about the role of context in politics, and some worries as well.

Of possible related interest: Chapters 30, **38**, 58, 71.

Suggested additional reading

Agnew, John. "Mapping Politics: How Context Counts in Electoral Geography." *Political Geography* 15 (1996): 129–146.

Huckfeldt, Robert, and John Sprague. "Citizens, Contexts, and Politics." In *Political Science: The State of the Discipline II*, edited by Ada Finifter, 281–303. Washington, DC: American Political Science Association, 1993.

Jones-Correa, Michael. "Institutional and Contextual Factors in Immigrant Citizenship and Voting." *Citizenship Studies* 5 (2001): 41–56.

16

HOMO POLITICUS IS NOT AN ISLAND

Claudine Gay
Harvard University

For scholars of public opinion and mass behavior, the archetypal citizen is often conceptualized as an unmoored social isolate—an individual without a home, wrestling alone with the predispositions in her head and with a cascade of messages from the media and political elites. Yet the reality is quite different: citizens exist and make decisions "in place"—in neighborhoods, in schools, on the job. Such sites are defined, among other things, by the resources and opportunities they provide, the burdens they impose or relieve, and the social observations and interactions they facilitate. What citizens infer, learn, and experience in their physical environments may have consequences for their decision-making about politics. Surely, it is unrealistic to assume that these experiences have absolutely no bearing on politics; this is precisely the assumption implicit in too many studies of political behavior. We know relatively little about how the contexts in which individuals are situated shape politically relevant beliefs and opinions and, subsequently, behavior: What features of contexts matter? What are the mechanisms of contextual influence? What is the range of behaviors and attitudes affected? A full and compelling account of the political life of the mass public is impossible without greater attention to these questions.

The atomistic view of citizens is no doubt part of the legacy of the behavioral revolution and, in particular, its signature data collection mechanism: the sample survey. A technology that depends on the random selection of unrelated individuals from unknown geographic locations is not particularly well suited to the study of context. But "citizen-as-social-isolate" also reflects a concession to the substantial methodological challenges facing any scholar who aspires to take context seriously. How does one begin to identify the effects of place when individuals are free to roam and to select environments—whether residential, occupational, or educational—that are consistent with their existing orientations and predispositions? The specter of selection bias has cast an inescapable shadow over this line of research, calling into question the validity of existing studies and discouraging further investigation. Thus it is not enough for scholars to take context into account when theorizing about mass behavior; we must also develop the methodological tools that will permit direct empirical tests of contextual hypotheses. Fortunately, political scientists are not alone in facing these challenges. There is a rich literature examining context effects in other social science disciplines, including sociology and economics. The substantive insights and the statistical innovations from this literature can and should be leveraged. Our approach to the study of mass behavior must recognize that *homo politicus* is not an island.

Of possible related interest: Chapters **15**, **17**, *19*, 37.

Suggested additional reading

Sampson, Robert, Doug McAdam, Heather MacIndoe, and Simon Weffer-Elizondo. "Civil Society Reconsidered: The Durable Nature and Community Structure of Collective Civic Action." *American Journal of Sociology* 111 (2005): 673–715.

17

THE SOCIOLOGICAL BASES OF POLITICAL PREFERENCES AND BEHAVIOR

Casey A. Klofstad
University of Miami

Most research in political science focuses on individual-level attributes, such as partisan identification, to explain citizens' preferences and how they express those preferences to the government. Far less attention is paid to sociological determinants of these phenomena, such as the nature of the individual's social environment.

There are two reasons why sociological variables are discounted in our field. First, this line of research was developed and is maintained by our reliance on large-scale social surveys like the American National Election Studies (ANES). The ANES and other such studies are invaluable repositories of information about political preference and behavior. However, the vast majority of these studies are focused on collecting information on individual-level characteristics. Far less space in these questionnaires is dedicated to the collection of data on social-level variables. Consequently, we spend far less time examining sociological explanations of individual preferences and behavior.

Second, analytical biases make it difficult to show the causal effect of social-level variables. For example, an argument made in the extant literature on civic participation is that discussing politics within his or her social network of peers causes a person to become more active in politics. However, this finding has been heavily criticized because it could be a case of reciprocal causation; individuals who are active in civic activities may just talk more about politics than their less active counterparts. This and other related analytical biases make social-level factors more difficult to study than individual-level factors.

These two issues are not trivial. However, political scientists can and should do more to study the sociological bases of political preferences and behavior. Making use of new and innovative methods of data collection

40

and analysis is a necessary step in this process. For example, a growing number of political scientists are using experiments (both in the field and in the laboratory), focus groups, participant observation, agent-based modeling, and other research methods that are tailored to studying the complex causal relationships that are generated by social-level variables. Other scholars use methods of data preprocessing, such as "matching," to make analyses of sociological phenomena less biased. Traditional research methods can also be adapted to more effectively address sociological hypotheses. The 2007–2008 ANES panel study is a prime example of how a traditional form of data collection can be adapted to study how changes in an individual's environment shape his or her preferences and behaviors over time.

Of possible related interest: Chapters **15**, **29**, **38**, 7 /.

Suggested additional reading

Ho, Daniel, Kosuke Imai, Gary King, and Elizabeth Stuart. "Matching as Nonparametric Preprocessing for Reducing Model Dependence in Parametric Causal Inference." *Political Analysis* 15 (2007): 199–236.

Klofstad, Casey A. "Talk Leads to Recruitment: How Discussions about Politics and Current Events Increase Civic Participation." *Political Research Quarterly* 60 (2007): 180–191.

Zuckerman, Alan S., ed. *The Social Logic of Politics: Personal Networks as Contexts for Political Behavior.* Philadelphia, PA: Temple, 2005.

18

COMMUNITY SOCIAL CAPITAL

Kristi Andersen
Syracuse University

Social capital may be hard (or contentious) to define, but I know it when I see it. Or, more precisely, I know it when I experience it, currently as an elected official in what I am confident is a community particularly rich in social capital. This recent experience has sharpened my existing intellectual interest in the contextual sources of civic and political engagement. Social or political capital, which I define broadly as interpersonal and inter-institutional connections which provide resources to accomplish collective civic and political goals, cannot—in my opinion—be reduced to attributes of individuals. So despite the many pieces of useful survey-based research which help us understand, for example, how membership in particular kinds of organizations develops particular kinds of civic skills, this kind of individual-level research can only get us part of the way towards under-standing the community dynamics that create varying levels of engagement (and political effectiveness) among citizens. The Social Capital Benchmark surveys have allowed interesting analysis of various sorts of intra-individual connections, but these connections are studied, for the most part, as individual attributes (whether considered as dependent or as independent variables).

What I would like to see is research which considers social capital to characterize *communities* and to be located *not* primarily within individuals. I realize that what constitutes a "community" could itself be a subject of research and theorizing, and in fact my personal experience suggests that politico-geographical boundedness and overlapping municipal jurisdictions may be important considerations in shaping the levels, contours, and targets of local political participation. This research would develop ways to measure such things as organizational capacity; organizational networks; connections between governmental agencies and bodies and community associations; the amount and character of publicly available information in the community pertaining to collective problems and issues; and even the way that the physical design of a community might work to unify or separate its members. I believe that this sort of research program would have the potential to sharpen current theories of social capital, which are often criticized as insufficiently political, and to begin to understand the mechanisms by which community dynamics shape social and political outcomes.

Of possible related interest: Chapters 17, 19, 83, 84.

Suggested additional reading

Freie, John F. *Counterfeit Community: The Exploitation of Our Longings for Connectedness.* Lanham, MD: Rowman & Littlefield, 1998.
Putnam, Robert D. *Bowling Alone.* New York: Simon and Schuster, 2000.
Verba, Sidney, Kay Lehman Schlozman, and Henry E. Brady. *Voice and Equality: Civic Voluntarism in American Politics.* Cambridge, MA: Harvard University Press, 1995.

19

TUNED IN, BUT
DROPPED OUT

Carole Jean Uhlaner
University of California, Irvine

Face-to-face contact is important, and political life would benefit if political actors and commentators paid more attention to this fact. We know that people are more likely to participate in politics when they are asked (recruited or mobilized). Thanks to field experiments, we know that asking via robo-call or email does little. In fact, the closer the request gets to a personalized request from a real human being, the more effective it is, and even more so if the human being is known. Why this is so is less clear, but theory suggests that a human desire for sociability and instinct for identity may drive the effect. The social capital literature tells us that face-to-face contact builds the network of norms and trust that constitute high social capital. Known opinion leaders help others process information. Political actors who understand the importance of face-to-face interaction, and do the best job of approximating (or even creating) it, will do well. Commentators will better understand political dynamics if they keep its importance in mind.

At the same time, however, our political life is becoming more electronically mediated into fragments. Even our social life has become plugged-in. People, especially younger people, walk around connected by ear-buds to music players while talking into video-playing, email-connected cell phones and ignoring the other people physically around them. Information comes from self-selected pieces of the internet instead of an edited newspaper or even narrow-cast television channels, let alone networks. The result is a reduction in shared experience and an even more dramatic reduction in face-to-face shared experience. We really do not know what politics will look like in this new world. Previous research suggests a decline in participation, in involvement, and in social capital, but perhaps the opposite will take place, especially among newer generations who grow up accustomed to interaction via screen and electrons. If so, how will electronic interaction manage to replace the face to face, and will the shift alter the shape of political interconnection?

Of possible related interest: Chapters 16, **18**, 32, 63.

Suggested additional reading

Green, Donald P. and Alan S. Gerber. *Get Out the Vote: How to Increase Voter Turnout*. 2nd ed. Washington, D.C.: Brookings Institution Press, 2008.
Uhlaner, Carole Jean. "'Relational Goods' and Participation: Incorporating Sociability into a Theory of Rational Action." *Public Choice* 62 (1989): 253–285.

20

COGNITION, EMOTION, AND SELECTIVITY IN POLITICAL COMMUNICATION IN A MULTI-FACETED WORLD

Rational Choice and Political Culture

Robert H. Bates
Harvard University

In this field, breakthroughs come from eliding seemingly incompatible approaches. One example might be the late-century fusion of Marxism and rational choice. Another, and the one that interests me, is the possibility of integrating cultural and rational choice theory.

Everyone knows that culture is powerful. Many who study the politics of culture feel that its power requires no explanation. Better, perhaps, to address the problem from a rational choice perspective, where the sources of its influence become problematic.

Viewed from that perspective, it seems strange that scholars with political agendas write about the past, when it is the future that they hope to shape. It is puzzling that people attend to debate, knowing that orators have agendas and that their appeals are self-interested. It seems odd that we know that preachers can act strategically and yet they are held in reverence: televangelists hold large audiences in their thrall, as they invoke the deity in support of their political agendas. The theater and dramaturgy of politics is powerful: it makes possible the photo-op and the sound-bite. But from what does that power derive?

Of possible related interest: Chapters 11, 27, 32, **51**.

Suggested additional reading

Goffman, Erving. *The Presentation of Self in Everyday Life*. New York: Bantam Books, 1959.

21

WHO WANTS WAR?

Anne Sartori
Northwestern University

Why do democracies go to war? Since democratic leaders are accountable to their peoples, one might expect that when a democracy goes to war, it is the case that a majority or a politically powerful minority wants war. Who are the winners within a democracy who motivate their country to fight, and who are the losers? Are the gains that motivate democracies to fight primarily material—territory or wealth—or are they intangible, psychological benefits such as pride, envy, revenge, or altruism?

Kant's well-known argument is that citizens, the likely soldiers, are the losers when a democracy goes to war. Yet ordinary people also may receive a greater share of the benefits of war if they live in a democracy. Moreover, as Jonathan D. Caverley argues in his dissertation, *Death and Taxes: Sources of Democratic Military Aggression*, citizens of some modern democracies can shift their countries to capital intensive (high-tech) war-fighting, thus reducing their share of the burden of war. Thus, it probably is not correct to consider citizens as a whole to be the losers from war, particularly not in democracies that have, or have the ability to acquire, advanced military technologies.

If some citizens are the winners and some are the losers in the event of war, can we say anything about who are which? Segments of the American public often are quite bellicose. Do support for and opposition to war correlate with the net benefits particular citizens or groups receive? For example, do conservatives and men, both of whom, on average, voice opinions that are more bellicose than average, receive greater-than-average net benefits from war? Do their opinions lead democracies into "extra" wars that the median voter does not want, given that both of these groups tend to have greater-than-average financial resources at their disposal?

Or are particular economic or political interest groups the winners in the event of war, and do the particular winners vary with the war in question? While the popular press tends to blame the military-industrial complex, Peter D. Feaver and Christopher Gelpi show in *Choosing Your Battles: American Civil-Military Relations and the Use of Force* that it is the civilians in government who are more likely to press for war. This trend may not be surprising given that military leaders are closer to the soldiers who die. But what motivates the civilians who favor war—economic interests, or psychological benefits?

Material benefits may be the primary reason why democracies fight; after all, when they do, they disproportionately win, as Dan Reiter and Allan C. Stam show in *Democracies at War*. However, the material explanation for the gender differences is questionable. Men may receive more loot than women, but in most democracies, they are much more likely to be the soldiers. (Of course, in countries without the draft, few men or women actually are at personal risk, unless war comes to their homeland.) Perhaps the aversion to loss of life is more altruism than self-preservation; after all, men are more likely to lose their lives in war, but women probably still are, on average, the more-involved parents of the young men who form the bulk of the cannon fodder in many countries. Does altruism motivate those who favor war as well, influencing, for example, the U.S. decision to intervene in Kosovo?

Some wars involving democracies are difficult to explain on material grounds. The British fought the Falklands War over a small, rocky territory far from their homeland with a population of less than 2000 and an economy in decline. Did they accrue indirect material benefits, or were they motivated by intangible factors such as pride or loyalty? Are the motives for war that many Americans call "ideological" (e.g., preserving democracy) primarily economic or psychological?

Of possible related interest: Chapters 20, 23, 55, 100.

Suggested additional reading

Caverley, Jonathan D. *Death and Taxes: Sources of Democratic Military Aggression*. PhD dissertation. University of Chicago, in progress.

Feaver, Peter D., and Christopher Gelpi. *Choosing Your Battles: American Civil-Military Relations and the Use of Force*. Princeton, NJ: Princeton University Press, 2005.

Reiter, Dan, and Allan C. Stam. *Democracies at War*. Princeton, NJ: Princeton University Press, 2002.

22

THE THREAT TO DEMOCRACY

Lawrence R. Jacobs
University of Minnesota

Democratic theorists and researchers have long feared that democracy and in particular the policy preferences of majorities threaten liberty. The Constitutional Convention in 1787 focused on tamping down the intense, participatory democratic life in the separate states where citizens were treating their representatives as delegates to follow their instructions. Rebellions of landless farmers intensified the fears of the Constitution's framers regarding the threats to individual liberty and, especially, private property.

The U.S. Constitution, as *Federalist* No. 10 explained, rejected a pure form of democracy in favor of a republic built on the "scheme of representation" that would "refine and enlarge" the policy preferences of ordinary citizens and deter the formation of majoritarian movements. The Framers attempted to prevent a programmatically oriented majority from wielding concentrated government authority by dispersing it into separate, competing components. They further diminished the majoritarian threat by empowering independent assemblies of electors with the selection of presidents.

In addition to institutional arrangements that channeled and tamped down majoritarianism, governing elites promoted norms that negatively stereotyped responsiveness to public opinion. From the authors of the Federalist Papers to Walter Lippmann and contemporary commentators like the *Washington Post*'s David Broder, scorn has been heaped on government officials who followed the majority's policy preferences. Indeed, the very term "pandering" was lifted by the Nixon administration from its original meaning—the procuring of prostitutes—to denigrate members of Congress who responded to majority opinion opposing the Vietnam War.

There have been two primary challenges to the anti-democratic tilt of American-governing institutions and norms. The first discounts the threat from below. Research by Sidney Verba, Kay Schlozman, and Henry

Brady demonstrates that the affluent and better educated (not majorities of the less advantaged) are disproportionately active in all forms of political participation—from voting to protesting, volunteering, and donating.

The second challenge arises from research demonstrating that government policies are often biased in favor of narrow groups of organized interests and the better off. Case studies over the past four decades show that pressure groups successfully fashion discrete economic and trade policies to serve their interests; aggregate studies using public opinion surveys by Larry Bartels, Martin Gilens, Benjamin Page, and myself, link government policies with the views of the affluent and organized.

There is a third, paradoxical, challenge to the Framers' fear of majorities that deserves closer attention by scholars and probing journalists—namely, the development and deployment of government institutional capacity (especially by modern presidents) to track public opinion in order to manage and shape it.

Although it is typically assumed that presidents poll in order to follow the public's policy preferences and therefore "pander" by responding to majority opinion, the White House's polling apparatus has evolved for the opposite purpose—to move public opinion to support the White House's policy proposals (as I have argued with Bob Shapiro in *Politicians Don't Pander*). Indeed, research in presidential archives reveals that polling on policy attitudes peaked under Johnson and then sharply declined under Nixon and Reagan.

According to research I have done with James Druckman, White Houses are less interested in tracking the public's policy preferences in part because they are using private polling for "message development", that is, to test market words, arguments, and symbols to publicly present already decided policy in alluring terms. Beginning in earnest under Richard Nixon and Ronald Reagan, presidents have also used their polls to attempt to shift the representative relationship from policy to nonpolicy considerations—namely, personal image and visceral emotional appeals. Success in shifting public evaluations away from policy-based evaluations expands the White House's discretion for making policy that follows the policy preferences of the president and his supporters and contributors.

The government's enormous institutional capacity to shape public thinking and evaluations poses a troubling normative test for the populist notion of democracy that Verba defined in his American Political Science Association's presidential address in 1996—namely, "responsiveness by governing elites to the needs and preferences of the citizenry." Government may respond to a "public opinion" that has been primed, framed, and managed to support proposals that majorities of Americans would not otherwise have favored.

Efforts at government opinion management challenge journalists to scrutinize the all-too common presumption that polling by politicians reflects a predisposition to follow public opinion. In challenging this presumption, it is important not to slip into an equally one-sided assumption—namely, that presidents and other authoritative government actually succeed in using in opinion management to produce the desired impact. Opinion-management efforts by rival politicians and well-funded interest groups, critical media coverage, and real world events may offset even determined efforts by presidents to move public opinion.

The triple barriers to the overbearing majorities feared by the Constitution's Framers return us to the normative question woven into Verba's writings: Is the "nightmare" facing American governance that the policy preferences of majorities will shape government decisions or, as David Easton warned half a century ago, that "power [will] concentrate in the hands of a minority"?

Of possible related interest: Chapters 34, 68, 89, 93.

23

NATIONALIST MISSIONS AND THE DEMOCRATIC CITIZEN

Katherine Tate
University of California, Irvine

My work resides in the field of public opinion and voting behavior. Many questions in this field are pursued using survey research methodologies and pertain to the interest and will of people to take part in politics. The field of public opinion and voting behavior has still unplowed areas, largely because of the growing complexities of human and group psychology as well as because of human diversity and human capital in a global world. Fields of inquiry extend out to the horizon, in fact.

The post-World War II questions others have pondered regarding how information can be monopolized by the government are relevant to scholars of public opinion once more. Scholars studying democratic states having democratic citizens need to recapture the concerns of America's founding fathers regarding how this new democratic flower that they grew in the New World can be hurt if voting citizens are swayed by demagoguery. The questions are no longer as simple as an examination of political tolerance and intolerance, based chiefly on a person's underlying psychology or group attributes. Here, I would suggest the relationship of citizens to the state and identification with its political and nationalist missions might be important components of their political attitudes and behavior regarding basic civil liberties and public policies as they respond to political leadership in challenging times. Basic civil liberties can be suspended in a state of war, and thus, survey researchers should examine how opinion is formed regarding the suspension of democratic rights as well as public policies targeting groups whose members reside racially or socially below a majority of citizens. The normative problem rests with the possibility of a democratic state whose interests might lie outside of the collective will and interests of its citizens.

Of possible related interest: Chapters 15, 39, 57, 90.

52

Suggested additional reading

Page, Benjamin, and Robert Shapiro. *The Rational Public*. Chicago: University of Chicago Press, 1992.

24

SOMETHING'S GOING ON HERE, BUT WE DON'T KNOW WHAT IT IS

Measuring Citizens' Exposure to Politically Relevant Information in the New Media Environment

Michael X. Delli Carpini
University of Pennsylvania

To say that today's information environment is radically different from that of even a decade ago may be stating the obvious, but in many ways the full range of the changes that have occurred are not fully appreciated and are even less well understood. The average U.S. household now receives over 100 television stations. According to a recent survey released by the Pew Internet and American Life Project, three-quarters of American adults have cell phones and use the internet, 4 in 10 have broadband connections and send and receive text messages on their cell phones, and 1 in 5 have created media content themselves, which they have then shared with others through the internet. According to this survey, almost one-third of Americans could be classified as heavy and frequent users of the new information technologies. At the same time, structural and content changes in both old and new media have all but obliterated traditional distinctions between news or public affairs genres, on the one hand, and entertainment and cultural genres, on the other. As mind-boggling as theses changes have been, they continue at a breakneck pace—for example, YouTube did not even exist in 2004.

These changes have profound implications for a wide range of topics of interest to political scientists. This is especially true for those of us concerned—both normatively and empirically—with the equitable, informed, and democratic engagement of citizens. To begin to study these important implications, however, we must first grapple with a seemingly mundane but ultimately crucial measurement problem: exposure. Put simply, we cannot gauge the positive or negative consequences of the new information environment on citizens' attitudes and actions without first being able to accurately gauge what information (in the broad sense of the word) people encounter. Exposure is the starting point for any theory that posits a link between the mediated world of politics and the behavior of citizens.

The sad fact is that even in the bygone era of many fewer media outlets and clearer (though always still somewhat ambiguous) lines between politically relevant and irrelevant genres, we have never been great at measuring individuals' exposure to information. And in the current, more complex, user-controlled environment, we are largely at sea on this topic. This is true whether we are attempting to measure overall media use (e.g., how often someone goes on-line), media use for the purposes of general political information (e.g., how often someone watches the national news or *The Daily Show*), and, especially, exposure to information about a particular topic (e.g., the numerous places one has been exposed to information about some particular aspect of the war in Iraq).

Developing new and innovative ways to measure politically relevant information exposure is a must if we are to test the continued efficacy of existing theories and findings related to agenda-setting; framing and priming; learning; attitude and opinion formation, reinforcement, and change; and political behaviors. It is also a must if we are to develop and test new theories about the impact of information in the new environment in which we live. At a minimum, we need to do enough in this area to reassure ourselves that extant measures, or slight variations on them, do well enough that we can maintain some degree of confidence in their reliability and validity.

Improving measures of information exposure may seem a rather narrow, even boring agenda, given all the exciting possibilities and unsettling concerns raised by the new world of mediated politics we now inhabit. But unless we can say with confidence what information has reached the eyes and ears of citizens, we will never be able to ascertain how this information affects those citizens, and thus never be able to maximize the new information environment's democratic potential or limit its more undemocratic tendencies.

Of possible related interest: Chapters 19, 38, 63, 69.

Suggested additional reading

Fishbein, Martin, and Robert Hornik, eds. "Measuring Exposure: Papers from the Annenberg Media Exposure Workshop." Special Issue of *Communication Methods and Measures* 2 (2008): 1–166.

25

WHAT WE STILL NEED
TO KNOW

Why and How People Become
Committed Democrats

Philip Oxhorn
McGill University

For almost half a century, large-scale survey research has played an increasingly prominent role in political science. Its origins date back to landmark studies of political culture that were often groundbreaking in their cross-regional and multi-disciplinary research designs, ultimately spawning a virtual subfield in comparative politics. Since then, numerous studies have attempted to track and understand political culture in a variety of contexts, building on advances in available methodologies and contributing to an important accumulation of knowledge regarding the beliefs and forms of political participation of the average citizen. Today, significant resources are now being devoted to conducting regional public opinion polls annually, including the *Eurobarometer*, the *Latinobarometro* and, most recently, the *Afrobarometer*, in order to accumulate an unprecedented amount of data addressing many of the same issues raised over 40 years ago by the original pioneering studies.

Ironically, however, just as the urgency of the question has perhaps never been as great, in many ways we are much farther than we were in the early 1960s from understanding the challenges of cross-regional, much less cross-cultural, patterns of political participation in order to help us comprehend processes of democratic cultural diffusion in ways that might constructively contribute to the emergence of a more democratic world. Despite the tremendous advances in survey research methodologies in recent decades and a substantial amount of survey data from around the world, advances have generally failed to keep pace with the growing complexity of the world in which we live.

When the original cross-regional public opinion surveys of political beliefs and culture were conducted in the late 1950s and early 1960s, the

world was increasingly polarized along an East–West axis based on ideology. Democracy's post-World War II "second wave" was in full swing, and
Italy and Mexico were considered examples of developing countries only
beginning to experiment with institutions of democratic governance.
Ironically, these pioneering studies of political culture took place during
the height of the Cold War, when (fairly or not) they were inevitably framed
in terms of the two superpowers' competition for dominance. At best,
political culture was seen as irrelevant given the dominance of ideology. At
worst, it became an *ex ante* justification for legitimizing whatever regime
was favored by either superpower.

To say that the world has changed considerably since then would be an
understatement. Italy is now a highly developed industrial democracy and
Mexico experienced a very different type of transition with the 2000
election of an opposition candidate to the presidency. Democracy's "third
wave" crested several years ago and we have now entered into a new period
that Freedom House describes as "freedom stagnation." And with the end
of the Cold War, ideology, not culture, is often seen as irrelevant. Instead,
the world is increasingly polarized along a new East–West axis defined
culturally according to Judeo–Christian or Islamic values, particularly after
the 9/11 attacks in New York and Washington, DC.

Yet while our research methodologies have in many respects become far
more refined compared to the early 1960s and the amount of survey data
that has been collected offers a treasure trove of insights that could hardly
have been imagined 40 years ago, we still do not really understand why
democracy's appeal seems to flourish in some societies, yet ebb and flow in
others, or seems unable to even penetrate whole regions. Part of the reason
for this is that we may have become prisoners of our own methodologies.
As our statistical skills and access to quantifiable data have increased, we
seem to have lost the boldness that characterized much earlier attempts to
test a new and untried methodology—survey research—not only on a
relatively large scale, but also on a scale that transcended "developing" and
"developed" countries, not to mention significant cultural and linguistic
barriers. While more-or-less parallel surveys are now carried out in much
of the world, their analysis often remains confined to single regions; the
systematic effort pioneered by the first studies that tried to engage in
genuine cross-regional research seems to have fallen by the wayside. In part,
this may also reflect a more pronounced tendency today to focus on complex
problems through the lenses of single disciplines or even methodologies,
sacrificing the multi-disciplinarity that defined the first cross-regional
large-scale public opinion surveys.

This is not to suggest that we have learned little about political attitudes
and participation over the past four decades. On the contrary, we now know
quite a lot about individual motivations and attitudes, particularly within
stable political systems like that of the U.S. A growing number of political

scientists have continued to contribute in important ways to our understanding of these fundamental political processes at the micro-level, and these insights frequently offer important perspectives on macro-level processes as well. Rather, it is to suggest that we need to rethink how we seek to understand these processes in order to go beyond both what we now know and what we thought we knew decades earlier. It's a challenge to think not only outside the box, but to draw bigger, more complex boxes that incorporate multiple dimensions, motivations, and methodologies to tackle some of the fundamental questions about politics and society that have been with us at least since the time of Plato and Aristotle. This is what was most audacious about the first large-scale public opinion surveys and it is this kind of audacity that we need when attempting to understand the potential for the spread of democratic practices today. While it might be tempting, from the vantage point of the tremendous advances we have made in statistical analysis, data management, and survey techniques, to dismiss such "audacity" as nothing more than the naiveté of smart people experimenting with new and untested methodologies, that would be a mistake. For while the questions themselves are quite old, there is a renewed urgency in finding positive answers to them in today's post-9/11 world.

Of possible related interest: Chapters **38**, 52, **57**, 84.

Suggested additional reading

Brady, Henry E., and David Collier. *Rethinking Social Inquiry: Diverse Tools, Shared Standards*. Lanham, MD: Rowman & Littlefield, 2004.

Katznelson, Ira, and Helen V. Milner, eds. *Political Science: State of the Discipline*. New York: W.W. Norton, 2002.

King, Gary, Robert O. Keohane, and Sidney Verba. *Designing Social Inquiry: Scientific Inference in Qualitative Research*. Princeton, NJ: Princeton University Press, 1994.

26

WHEN WE COULD DO SO MUCH BETTER

Democratic Commitment and Empirical Political Psychology

Virginia Sapiro
Boston University

For years, after describing myself as a political psychologist and receiving a quizzical look, I elaborate this way: As a political psychologist I try to understand why people say and do the things in politics they say and do, especially where they could say and do things that are so much better. In the case of gender and politics, why have the citizens and leaders of self-proclaimed democracies been so content to explain away the domination of the political system and decision-making within it by a group comprising less than half the population? Why, in apparently democratic political systems, are women so underrepresented within the ranks of the leadership, such that when a woman achieves a notable high office, it is still remarkable? Even though a woman has now made a serious run at the presidential nomination of her party, the situation has not been completely altered.

One of the toughest questions in this larger problem is why people who value equality and justice may nevertheless replicate older patterns of gender or race domination in the choices they make when they are in a position to empower other people. Results of research from the variety of disciplines that make up the interdisciplinary field of political psychology make it clear that "bad attitudes" (women should not hold positions of power) or crude nasty stereotypes (women cannot be competent to hold power) do not fully account for the political glass ceiling—the limitations on women's empowerment and political presence, even in democratic societies. Rather the differences derive from the differential resources and opportunities men and women have in their social and economic lives, the networks in which they are embedded, and stereotypes and expectations that shape perception and cognition, that lead people to see different qualities in people depending on whether they happen to be looking at a man or woman and depending on the context in which people are making judgments about other people's suitability for particular leadership positions.

But it is not enough to say that the problem of political domination is complicated, and individuals cannot make choices that lead to more democratic solutions. Indeed, research suggests that building systems of accountability into organizations makes a difference in whether change can happen, and when people are held and hold themselves accountable for the outcomes of their choices, they are likely to make less discriminatory choices.

Gender inequality—and other forms of group-based inequalities and power-laden inter-group dynamics in politics—is only one example of the important role of research in political psychology in furthering our understanding of the potential of democratic politics. But this linkage between empirical political psychology and democratic commitment raises interesting questions in the context of a discipline that has so long been marked by an undercurrent of debate and disagreement about the relationship of normative commitments to social science research. Whatever charges and counter-charges have been leveled in debates over social science methodology and the arts of social science research, much of the best, most instructive, most inspiring, and most rigorous political science research has been offered by scholars who begin with questions driven by commitment to a democratic society, and follow through with skilled use of research practices that allow us to listen to and really hear the subjects of our research systematically, giving us the opportunity to learn something we might not have expected to find in the first place.

Of possible related interest: Chapters *10*, 25, **61**, **62**.

27

POLITICAL SCIENCE
AND THE FUTURE

James Q. Wilson
Harvard University and University of California, Los Angeles

Political science is, I believe, the most important way to study organized human behavior because since the time of Aristotle it has taken the broadest possible view of group life, emphasizing as it does both formal and informal understandings, the characteristics of alternative forms of political rule, and the interaction between the economy and the polity and foreign as well as domestic affairs.

Other parts of social science have made important contributions to politics. We all are aware, of course, of the value that economics has brought to politics. Much good (and some harm) has come from this embrace. Parts of political science are amenable to economic analysis because they involve rational people choosing on the basis of fixed preferences among measurable alternatives, but much of politics is not about rational conduct, involves changing and not fixed preferences, and must grapple with variables that cannot be measured.

But there is another part of social science that has had very little impact on political knowledge, an omission that, I believe, ought to be remedied. Psychology and criminology have learned that it must grasp the link between learned behavior and biologic predispositions. Indeed, a growing feature of the study of evolution has been the rise of evolutionary psychology.

Some may suppose that I am raising once again the ancient debate between nature and nurture. But in fact there is no such debate because it is very difficult to think of any important part of human behavior that is not the joint product of biology and learning. There is probably no biologic basis for preferring the Red Sox to the Yankees, but there is such a basis for understanding whether people are or are not religious, conservative, criminal, moral, intelligent, energetic, or extroverted. These links and many others can be easily shown, as has been done by comparing identical twins raised apart. There is, of course, no gene for religion, morality, conservatism, or criminality, but the behavior of identical twins raised by different families (and sometimes even on different continents) suggests quite powerfully that some pattern of genes makes people more or less susceptible to the social processes that help produce these traits.

Consider political participation. As countless scholars have shown, it increases with the level of education people have. But we do not know that it is education that produces this link; having a college education may simply reflect having a higher IQ or being more disposed to link up with social currents. New research by James H. Fowler, Laura A. Baker, and Christopher T. Dawes indicates that genetic factors influence the decision to vote.

Or consider party affiliation. There is no good reason to assume that all of this is learned. Conservative or liberal parents tend to have conservative or liberal children, but is this connection the result of what the children learned at the dinner table or what they inherited from their parents or (more likely than either) the joint effect of biology and learning? "Conservatism" or "liberalism" are not inherited from some Republican or Democratic gene but they may be the result of a genetic predisposition to favor order and hierarchy as opposed to self-expression and autonomy. John R. Alford, Carolyn L. Funk and John R. Hibbing showed that genes strongly affect political ideology.

What kinds of people became Reagan Democrats or Howard Dean Liberals? There is no easy answer to these questions, but it is wise to indulge the suspicion that the former were not entirely motivated by the fact that they wore hard hats and the latter not wholly guided by what they learned in graduate school.

The difficulty with combining biology and political science is that studying the former requires one to find distinctive measures of the attitude and compare its frequency among parents and siblings, with special attention to those cases where one person has an identical twin or lives with an adopted sibling with whom he or she shares no biological identity.

And when we learn these things, we learn about the differences among populations of people, not differences that we can easily ascribe to particular individuals. But political science is, in part, a study of populations.

All of this is hard work, but work that can complete our understanding of politics. It was James Madison, after all, who wrote that "the latent causes of faction are thus sown in the nature of man."

Of possible related interest: Chapters 11, 17, **29**, 39.

Suggested additional reading

Alford, John R., Carolyn L. Funk, and John R. Hibbing. "Are Political Orientations Genetically Transmitted?" *American Political Science Review* 99 (2005): 153–167.

Fowler, James H., Laura A. Baker, and Christopher T. Dawes. "Genetic Variation in the Decision to Vote." *American Political Science Review* 102 (2008): 233–248.

Thomas J. Bouchard, Jr. "Genetic Influence on Human Psychological Traits: A Survey." *Current Directions in Psychological Science* 13 (2004): 148–151.

28

FAMILY MATTERS

David E. Campbell
University of Notre Dame

There is a daunting list of factors which affect civic engagement. Education, skills, efficacy, norms, mobilization, and trust are only a few of the most commonly cited; myriad others have been explored as well. One such theme which has, intermittently, guided the study of civic engagement is political socialization—which after a long hiatus has re-emerged on the contemporary research agenda. Within this boomlet of scholarship on socialization, the emphasis has largely been on schools, the media, and the electoral environment. For the most part, the family's influence has been ignored. As a consequence, we know little about how experiences at home affect us when we leave home. Given that the home is where most people spend the bulk of their formative years, it is unfortunate that we do not know more about how the family does, and does not, set us on a trajectory toward a lifetime of civic involvement.

Why would the family matter? Going back decades, a lot of work on civic engagement makes the case that the attitudes formed and skills developed in nonpolitical venues transfer to the political realm. Consequently, researchers have focused a lot of attention on the political consequences of ostensibly nonpolitical institutions, such as voluntary associations, churches, and the workplace. If we are willing to believe that experiences in these settings have implications for political involvement, then should we not also think it plausible that experiences in our most intimate social relationships (the family) during the most formative period of life (childhood and adolescence) also matter?

It would be an exaggeration to say that we know nothing about the family's influence on civic development, for in mining the literature one digs up nuggets of insight. For example, there is some evidence that learning democratic skills at home compensates for limited opportunities at school, and that children who talk about politics with their parents end up as adults who engage in political activity.

Such findings are important, but have only served to whet the appetite for further research. However, conducting such research is, if you will pardon the pun, not child's play. Studying the family's influence entails significant challenges. To see why, consider that our current—albeit limited—base of knowledge comes from two sources: cross-sectional surveys in which adults reflect back on their experiences while growing up, and panel studies in which the same people are interviewed at multiple points in time. Both have their strengths and their weaknesses. Researchers designing cross-sectional surveys today can craft whatever retrospective questions they feel are most appropriate, but will always have the nagging problem of respondents' faulty memories. Panel studies do not rely on respondents' memories, but are logistically difficult (not to mention expensive) to execute and are plagued with the problem of finding and reinterviewing the same respondents.

The solution is not to throw our hands up in despair, but rather to employ different methodologies to tackle different dimensions of the subject. Such problems are hardly unique to studying the family, as equally daunting challenges confront the study of almost any factor influencing civic engagement. Rather than shy away from such thorny issues, our best scholars should seek to solve them.

While understanding more about the family's influence on civic engagement would be worthwhile in any era, it is especially compelling now. We are living through a period of rapid, and tumultuous, change in the nature of family relationships and parenting philosophy. Perhaps not coincidentally, we are also living through a period characterized by two important trends. First, all young people have increasingly turned away from politics. In the midst of this decline, though, we see that adolescent girls are more likely than boys to indicate their intention to be civically involved as adults. Could changes in the home be associated with such changes in civil society? Do single-parent homes have a different democratic culture than two-parent homes? As women have increasingly worked outside the home, has this had any consequences for the political socialization of today's youth—either girls or boys, or both?

Consider also changes in parenting, exemplified by the very fact that "parent" has become a verb. Many children and adolescents today lead highly organized lives, where autonomy has been traded for structure. How have such changes affected the outlook young people have on civic and political involvement? In other words, many basic questions remain about how the family leaves an imprint on the nation's civic landscape, and how changes in the American family have, like plate tectonics, shifted the contours of that landscape.

In sum, political science awaits a comprehensive study of how the changing American family has affected civic engagement—of how, when, why, and for whom the family matters.

Of possible related interest: Chapters 17, 27, **29**, 53.

Suggested additional reading

Almond, Gabriel A., and Sidney Verba. 1989 (1963). *The Civic Culture: Political Attitudes and Democracy in Five Nations*. Newbury Park, CA: SAGE Publications, 1989. First published 1963 by Princeton University Press.

Burns, Nancy, Kay Lehman Schlozman, and Sidney Verba. *The Private Roots of Public Action*. Cambridge, MA: Harvard University Press, 2001.

Jennings, M. Kent, and Richard G. Niemi. *Generations and Politics: A Panel Study of Young Adults and Their Parents*. Princeton, NJ: Princeton University Press, 1981.

29

WHERE DO THE PREMISES OF POLITICAL CHOICE COME FROM?

Daniel Carpenter
Harvard University

I have made a career out of thinking about government bureaucracies and the way they function, but the questions that fascinate me most these days relate to the origins of attitudes, preferences, and ideologies—the premises of political choice, if you will. These are not questions that I am accustomed to studying, but they're sufficiently fascinating that I'm tempted to get a second PhD in Government, enlist Sid Verba as my advisor (including any and all necessary bribery to make that happen), and start cracking at new queries.

I have two cousins who grew up in Grand Rapids, Michigan. One ("Ann") is now a fundamentalist Christian, and almost certainly leans Republican in her voting habits, though I don't know for sure. Her younger brother ("Paul") is a choreographer for a major dance company in Chicago, is openly gay, and almost certainly leans Democratic, though again I don't know for sure.* Their parents—my uncle and aunt—were not very politically involved, and neither was a fundamentalist Christian or a left-wing radical when I knew them growing up. I've always wondered why my two cousins took such divergent social and political paths in their lives when they were raised just a few years apart, under the same household, in the same town, went to the same schools, and (from what I can tell) both had stellar grades, played musical instruments with skill, and largely stayed out of trouble.

---

*My attribution of political identities to Ann and Paul comes from conversations I have had with them and the judgments of others who know them. They may well be erroneous. Perhaps Ann is a passionate admirer of Hugo Chavez. Perhaps Paul wants to grow up and be Karl Rove. I'm betting against it.

I would wager that the divergent paths of Ann and Paul comprise something of a quasi-experiment that has been played out millions of times in the U.S. and other countries over the past half-century. Why do some people—from the same family origins—end up more "conservative" and embedded in religiously conservative cultures while others take a more "liberal" path?

There is more to the story of Ann and Paul than just the story of two individuals who have similarity on a number of attributional features (kinship, wealth, education, region, genes, and others) but who lead quite different lives today. In other words, when Ann and Paul become "data" for political scientists to think about, we shouldn't think of them as "independent and identically distributed observations." In two compelling ways, I suspect there is a deep dependency among their identities, first a dependency between the two of them and second a dependency among the different facets of their identities.

The plausible dependency between them is that Ann and Paul's lives seem to contrast so much that it is doubtfully coincidental. Perhaps part of Paul's identity consists of a negation of the world in which Ann has become ensconced (and which is well established in the Calvinist and conservative region of southwest lower Michigan). Or perhaps Paul's gay identification (and perhaps his "coming out" experience) reinforced Ann's commitment to more conservative social values. As in many families, I suspect (but do not know) that Ann and Paul may have consciously and unconsciously reinforced each others' adult life courses.

The other dependency is that I do not think that Ann's attraction to the Republican Party is simply epiphenomenal to her fundamentalist beliefs. They are part of the same conceptual and symbolic framework; they are for many people bundled together. Nor am I sure that Paul was "gay first, then liberal later." In the political environment of our times—and even among those whose levels of observable "participation" is low in the sense that they rarely vote—I would hazard that political meaning figures heavily in religious identity and even sexual orientation.

The notion of different facets of identity (or preferences) as bundled— such that it is woefully inaccurate and misleading to say that one is "causing" the other—does not mean that the bundles are so fixed and categorical as to defy imagination. There are gay conservatives and there are left-wing evangelical Christians. Yet these "exceptions" imply something about the stability of the "normal categories," and about the way that facets of individuals' lives travel together or associate.

This sort of inquiry does, moreover, leave us with questions that I think modern social scientists are ill-equipped to address, about as ill-equipped as I am to answer the question of Ann and Paul. Consider first questions related to religious faith. Why did the evangelical Christian movement attract certain individuals and not others? Why have Pentecostal movements surged in some Latin American countries rather than others in the last two decades, and why didn't this version of Protestantism appeal more to Latin Americans in the early twentieth century? What if we had compelling micro-level data on why some members of the same evangelical church are drawn into formal political participation while others seek other avenues of expression? Or why, among members of the same family, do some take up fundamentalist expressions of faith while others do not?

At some level, I would think that political scientists need to peer into family and kinship structures, to study preference and network formation. How do children, adolescents, teenagers, and young adults sort themselves into available identity bundles? What if we tracked the individual-level (or family-level) evolution of political preferences in the same way that the National Longitudinal Study of Youth tracked individual employment and educational experiences over time? How do young persons' perceptions of FDR, Eisenhower, JFK, Ronald Reagan, Bill Clinton, and George W. Bush influence their near-term and long-term political preferences and voting behavior?

Finally, a question that relates to data I am examining now and over the coming years. In the antebellum U.S., vast evangelical movements associated with the Second Great Awakening swept through the northern states and pulled many into deeper religious fervor. At the same time, a burgeoning anti-slavery movement was asking people to take sides on the most disturbing and pressing issue of the time. I have collected data from about 4000 of these petitions and I hope to collect much more. At the micro-level, these petitions offer us a window into lives that contain at least as much puzzling variation as the question of Ann and Paul. Within one family, why did one son sign an anti-slavery petition while another did not? Why did one resident of a street become engaged with broader anti-slavery activity while her nextdoor neighbor declined? Why did some families have their children sign the petition with them, while other heads of household (often mothers) refused to let their children even see the petition?

I conclude with this example because it is far from clear to me that the best way to address these questions is through experimentation (laboratory or "field"). And in the use of observational data I am generally of the opinion that no such thing as a "natural experiment" exists. The historical study of family politics, church and synagogue politics, school politics, and neighborhood politics offers rich opportunities for analysis. Along with methods of political psychology, and the analysis of networks and ethnography, the historical study of preference formation seems ripe for addressing and opening questions that sorely need rigorous asking.

Of possible related interest: Chapters **17**, **27**, **28**, 54.

30

IMMIGRATION, PARTISANSHIP, AND ELECTORAL CHANGE

Norman H. Nie
Stanford University

Since parents serve as their children's most important source of partisan cues, the large wave of recent immigrants and their offspring who are without relevant partisan attachments, represents a vast reservoir of un-committed and low-turnout voters. These voters could have a profound impact on the shape of the electorate, depending on when and how they are fully mobilized into the partisan and participant electorate. Since the 1965 Immigration Act more than 26 million legal immigrants have entered the U.S. Some have become citizens, others have not, but few came with germane partisan cues or guides for themselves or, perhaps more importantly, for their more than 30 million children who are born in the U.S. and thus are automatically American citizens. Add to this the 12 to 20 million undocumented, mostly Hispanic/Latino immigrants who have high birth rates and about 25 million American-born children who similarly lack partisan guides. What, if anything, will bring these 50 million naturalized Americans or American citizens with foreign-born parents into the active electorate? And what factors will determine the direction of their partisan attachments?

Previous studies suggest that many groups who fail to acquire familial partisanship may remain on the political sidelines until some new com-pelling issue or cluster of issues with high emotional salience "jolts" them into the active electorate. Historically, these "jolts" and their causes have been discovered using the National Election Study (NES) survey data, which have been collected bi-annually since 1952. One of the early and critical findings to come from the NES was the recognition that major segments of the electorate maintained a long-term standing psychological attachment to one or another of the political parties, which the Michigan group termed "partisan identity."

70

From then until now, the NES and its panel studies, as well as numerous matching parent–child surveys, have shown that partisan identity appears to be not only parentally inherited, but also a highly stable and long-term commitment when compared to all other political and social attitudes, issue positions, candidate evaluations, and other predictors of the vote. When measured for the same respondents across elections separated by four or more years, partisan identity displays three times the stability of any other type of politically relevant attitude or belief—save religious affiliation, which appears to be akin to partisanship in important ways. For example, research has shown that partisanship tends to be acquired relatively early in life and, like religion, is strongly influenced by parental preferences. Further, as Jennings and Stoker demonstrate, the clearer, more consistent, and more frequent parental partisan messages are, the more likely the parental position will be adopted by the offspring, and the longer it is likely to endure through the child's life.

However, in periodic historical circumstances, the configuration of these standing commitments in the electorate appears to change in fundamental ways. It usually, but not necessarily, happens over a series of adjacent elections when voters respond to new highly salient issues with patterns of cleavage that are not well aligned with existing party divisions. These transformations are often due to some mix of "conversion" of existing voters' party allegiances, new voters moving into the electorate and old ones dying out. There are good reasons to believe that in some transformational periods, intergenerational partisan transmissions decline drastically, as young adults may enter the electorate with different highly emotional issue concerns and social values from their parents. This, in turn, may lead offspring to break the normal generational transmission linkages. This appears to be what happened in the mid-1960s through the early 1970s, melting away the "New Deal" alignment of the 1930s.

At other historical moments, the most important factor in an electoral transformation appears to be the rapid entrance into the active electorate of previously nonvoting eligible voters. In the case of the New Deal realignment, these were largely naturalized immigrants and, in even greater numbers, their children, who were born here but given few relevant partisan cues. Many grew up speaking the language of their parents and were imbued with little relevant political content. As they grew into adulthood after World War I, they seemed to sit outside of electoral politics. As the *Changing American Voter* and Kristi Andersen's *The Making of a Democratic Majority* clearly demonstrate, when the sons and daughters of immigrants found themselves in grave economic circumstances during the Great Depression, it is little wonder they rushed toward the hope offered by Roosevelt's New Deal policy. They, and those who mobilized against them, became the stuff of American party cleavages that lasted until the mid-1960s.

In the pattern uncovered in the *Changing American Voter*, the New Deal "dealignment" of the partisan landscape in the late-1960s and 1970s changed due to the other variation of the partisanship transmission phenomenon—the sons and daughters of adherents of both parties, but most particularly Democrats, failed to follow their parents' partisan attachments, with many choosing to call themselves Independents. In general, from the mid-1960s through the 1980s, partisanship became much weaker in terms of the percent who called themselves strong partisans and as a guide to electoral choice. However, partisanship came bouncing back in all dimensions with a furious intensity in the mid-1990s. Yet, at the same time we have seen an atypical substantial build-up of citizens who claim to be independent, or apolitical with no partisan attachments. A substantial segment of these are the Hispanics we discussed above.

Naturalized immigrants and their children from southern and eastern Europe played a critical role in the New Deal realignment of the 1930s. There is no doubt that there is a parallel, and perhaps even larger, pool of similarly "nonimmunized" Hispanic voters today, yet well into the 2008 campaign there seems to be neither the cluster of issues nor the party mobilization that is likely to change relatively low rates of Hispanic turnout as of now. When and if critical new issues emerge, however, Hispanics have the ability through the weight of their numbers to transform the American electorate for a generation to come.

Of possible related interest: Chapters 28, 34, 58, 68.

Suggested additional reading

Andersen, Kristi. *The Creation of a Democratic Majority, 1928–1936.* Chicago: University of Chicago Press, 1979.

Converse, Philip E. "Researching Electoral Politics." *American Political Science Review* 100 (2006): 605–612.

Nie, Norman H., Sidney Verba, and John R. Petrocik. *The Changing American Voter.* Cambridge, MA: Harvard University Press, 1976.

31

DECISIONS PEOPLE MAKE IN SMALL GROUPS

John Aldrich
Duke University

A great many of our political decisions are made within small groups. Sidney Verba's first book, *Small Groups and Political Behavior* (1961), marks something close to the end of major efforts in several disciplines to take these small, informal groups seriously as loci of decision-making. This is evidently true of this discipline, but it is also true, with the major exception of families, in sociology. In psychology, the study of social settings has, at least in the American academy, gravitated toward the study of how an individual views some social context, rather than the study of social interactions. In economics, the Marshallian view was to make households a single person-like entity and to privilege individual choice. In our discipline, we are terrific at understanding individual choice, the role of organizations and large groups such as reference groups and others that shape our identity and beliefs and thus our choices, and of the influence of institutions in inducing political preferences and in constraining and channeling choice. But we rarely consider the immediate and direct interaction in which a great deal of political consideration, judgment, and choice is made. This lacuna is to our detriment, leaving us adrift in answering a large range of questions, such as the following. Is Antonin Scalia an articulate conservative ideologue on the Supreme Court or is he also able to persuade and thus build coalitions? Does he shape Clarence Thomas' views, as some allege, or is Thomas an equally independent decision-maker? Campaigns use focus groups extensively. Does a group of six or so offer keen insight to the public's mind, akin to application of Condorcet's Jury Theorem, in which the group is better than any one of its members in discerning the truth, or is it more like Janis' *Group Think* in which we observe the convergence of opinion not around what it "truly" is in each individual's mind (if that is even meaningful) but what is collectively the most persuasive voice in that particular group at that particular moment? Would it have been better (from his perspective) for Colin Powell to have resigned earlier and gone public with his views, or was he correct in staying in office and trying to work to balance the perspectives offered by Dick Cheney and Donald Rumsfeld? Do happily married couples make similar political choices because they share common experiences or because their interactions create common understandings of those experiences? While these are hardly the only valuable questions to ask, they are important and, as of now, too little studied.

Of possible related interest: Chapters 16, **29**, *40, 54.*

Suggested additional reading

Verba, Sidney. *Small Groups and Political Behavior.* Princeton, NJ: Princeton University Press, 1961.

32

WHY DO (SOME) PEOPLE ACQUIRE COSTLY POLITICAL KNOWLEDGE?

Torben Iversen
Harvard University

Almost all work in political science and political economy assumes that people have certain basic desires—for power, money, and so on—and that these desires translate into policy preferences. Yet, a very fundamental result in rational choice theory, first stated by Downs, is that people are rationally ignorant about politics. And many undoubtedly are. Larry Bartels, for example, reports that a solid majority of Americans favored Bush's proposal to repeal the federal estate tax, even though the tax affects only the wealthiest one or two percent of Americans, and even though the same majority believes that the government can and should reduce inequality.

Such confusion is likely to have significant consequences for public policies. As Bartels' results make clear, those with a lot of political information also tend to express policy preferences that are better aligned with what can reasonably be assumed to be in their economic interest than those with little information. Since those with higher incomes and education also tend to be better informed, public policies are likely to reinforce existing inequalities. This is one likely reason that democracy does not lead to as much redistribution in inegalitarian societies as standard political economy models imply (what Peter Lindert has called the "Robin Hood paradox").

Yet political knowledge, like voter turnout, is not simply a function of people's socioeconomic position. High-status individuals also have an incentive to be rationally ignorant, and we know that socioeconomic status is only a weak predictor of voter turnout. If we want to understand why democratic governments are more responsive to some people's interests than to others, and how governments shape and reshape inequality as a consequence, we therefore cannot simply fall back on standard class analysis. We need a micro-level theory of preferences that explains why some people choose to acquire political knowledge while others do not—and who falls into which group.

In recent papers with Sam Abrams and David Soskice we inquire into this question. Unlike standard rational choice models, we assume that people are social beings who care a great deal about what others think about them. The desire to earn the respect and esteem of those around us can be a powerful individual incentive to act in ways that at first blush appear unselfish, even irrational—such as voting or being informed about public affairs. Informed voters may be good for democracy, but few people learn about politics because they worry about the survival of democracy. More likely they do so because they want to maintain or improve their standing in groups where politics is a key matter for discussion. Who wants to be the dud who never knows what is happening in the world? When political knowledge becomes a marker for group standing, the desire for approval can turn into a powerful engine of political knowledge acquisition.

Verba, Nie, and Kim long ago observed that individual resources will be harnessed for political purposes primarily when people with such resources come into contact with others who are politically active, and they specifically pointed to political discussion as a catalyst for activism. It is not hard to spot the individual incentive to acquire political knowledge in these settings. The exact same logic would apply if the informal groups and networks to which people belong are focused on baseball, movies, or what have you. In all cases, most people will develop an interest in, and knowledge about, the relevant topic for the sole purpose of being able to contribute productively to the discussions of the groups to which they belong. We may call it the water cooler theory of political knowledge.

The ramifications of the logic extend far beyond the water cooler. First, the extent and nature of social interaction varies across socio-economic groups. Discussion of politics is more likely to emerge in settings with recurrent social interaction between individuals who can be assumed to have well-aligned interests. Relatively older, well-educated, and high income people tend to be in such stable networks more often than younger, low-educated, and low-income people (who move around a lot and spend more free time in front of the TV than in social groups). Second, because political elites understand the water cooler logic, they will use their local presence to try to shape the agenda in informal groups via affiliated "opinion leaders" who are eager to initiate political discussion. The intensity of such behavior will increase around elections, but it is also likely to vary systematically with the design of political institutions. It is well known, for example, that parties in proportional representation (PR) systems have a stronger incentive than parties in majoritarian systems to mobilize voters outside the middle classes, and to the extent such mobilization occurs via agenda-setters with close party connections, a likely by-product will be greater dispersion of political knowledge. The distribution of political knowledge, and thus the effective representation of different interests, will also vary with the importance of unions, churches, and other organizations in the daily lives of people. Insofar as these organizations make politics a subject of recurrent discussion, political knowledge becomes a marker for social standing and people will go to considerable length acquiring such knowledge.

Because the distribution of political knowledge is so critical for who gets what from democratic politics, coming up with answers to the question of why some people acquire political knowledge promises to open a new foray into the causes of redistributive politics.

Of possible related interest: Chapters 22, **42**, **49**, *100*.

Suggested additional reading

Abrams, Samuel, Torben Iversen, and David Soskice. "Rational Voting with Socially Embedded Individuals." Available at: http://www.people.fas.harvard.edu/~iversen/PDFfiles/AbramsIversenSoskice2008.pdf

Iversen, Torben, and David Soskice, "A Water Cooler Theory of Political Knowledge and Voting." Paper presented at the Annual Meeting of the American Political Science Association, Boston 2008.

33

A POLITICAL VIEW OF POLITICAL IDEOLOGY

John Zaller
University of California, Los Angeles

Left–right ideology is the most under-researched of the major forces in American politics. It pervades law-making, judicial decision-making, party politics, and most other elite politics. Ideology is a less profound force in mass politics, but still significant. Even when innocent of ideology themselves, voters still choose between ideological agendas.

Philip Converse's "The Nature of Belief Systems in Mass Public" is our best study of ideology, but leaves much of its argument only sketched. Converse maintained that ideology originates among creative elites, but named no names. He recognized that ideology and party both organize politics, but does not discuss how they relate to one another. And he overlooked the substantive content of ideology, that is, the values and interests it presumably organizes. In this contribution, I try to stir interest in these still under-studied matters. In contrast to much theorizing about ideology, I rely on political rather than psychological categories of analysis.

Elite sources of ideology

An ideology is commonly defined as a set of preferences organized by some value or values. The organizing values may be anything people consider important—freedom, tradition, national greatness, or interest. Because values are statements of ends rather than means, an ideology based on fixed values may favor different means in different times. For example, an ideology devoted to national greatness may favor tariffs at one point but not another. All ideologies, even classic ones like Marxism, exhibit this changeability.

Ideologic change must therefore have a central place in the study of ideology. To explain it, I posit a social process in which ideological leaders continuously update the application of core values to new conditions. These leaders are not, for the most part, great theorists. They are a mix of merely prominent intellectuals, group leaders, scientists, and wonks. Their role is that of secular moralist—figuring out what is right for society, given their values and the situation society faces. An example may clarify their role.

In the 1990s, a group of defense experts known for generally conservative views argued for a more assertive U.S. foreign policy, including pre-emptive war against Iraq. Not all conservative experts shared the view of these "Neo-conservatives," but the conservative president elected in 2000 appointed Neo-conservatives to high positions. Thus buttressed by political authority, their precepts drew support from other conservative leaders and became, for a time, part of conservative ideology.

One can identify ideological leaders on opposing sides of nearly every controversy. Although leaders invoke expertise, many issues are at most only partly technical. Hence, ideological leaders end up making policy prescriptions on the basis of informed, value-driven judgment.

I suggest that ideology may be viewed as a collection of the prescriptions of these specialists, each working on a different problem but sharing common values. What binds the prescriptions into an ideology is not intellectual synthesis, but the deference of individuals, at both the mass and elite level, to specialists who share their values. An ideology is more like a coalition of independent actors than a coherent system of ideas. For example, consumer advocates, feminists, and civil rights leaders, none of whom knows much about global warming, may defer to environmental specialists who seem to be like-valued; in this way, concern about global warming becomes part of liberal ideology.

Party and ideology

In bundling policy prescriptions into competing agendas, ideologies organize political conflict. Political parties, by drawing groups into competing electoral alliances, also organize conflict. How are these two forms of organization related? Hans Noel of Georgetown University has shown that ideological innovations emerge in political discourse as much as 20 years before they appear in party voting. More specifically, ideologically identifiable writers raise a new policy demand, thereby associating it with a larger ideological agenda. The new agenda diffuses (as described by Converse) from these ideological writers to politically attentive citizens, who turn to parties to implement it. By Noel's plausible account, ideologies organize political conflict for parties rather than vice versa.

Values and ideology

A major problem in the study of ideology is that its constant change makes it hard to pin down. Liberalism, for example, was internationalist in the 1930s and isolationist in the 1970s; conservatism made a parallel shift in the other direction. Does ideology, then, really stand for anything at all as regards foreign policy? Yet the names of America's left–right ideologies reveal enduring values. Conservatives want to conserve something; liberals want to liberate people from something. What exactly?

Conservatives want to conserve traditional morality and practice, most obviously as regards sex, family, religion, and responsibility for economic welfare; liberals want to liberate people from elements of this same tradition. As Herbert McClosky shows in his posthumous *Ideologies in Conflict*, two centuries of conservative writers have wanted a society in which everyone, high and low, leads virtuous lives based on traditional rules; liberals want a society in which individuals achieve happiness through personal freedom from many of these same rules. Liberals are especially opposed to traditions that undermine equality.

These enduring commitments are consistent with short-term change; indeed, they necessitate them. Thomas Jefferson, usually regarded as a liberal despite ownership of slaves, favored small government because he believed big government would invariably be dominated by the well-off and used to perpetuate inequality; a century later, liberals began to favor big government because they believed, in a more democratic age, that the popular classes could control it for egalitarian purposes.

In summary

Conservative slogans in past wars include "America First," "My Country Right or Wrong," and, most recently, "God Bless America," which indicate commitment to America above other nations. A liberal bumper sticker from the current war captures its more egalitarian perspective, "Bless Us All." Conservatives dislike the United Nations (UN), in which the U.S. is one nation among many, whereas liberals like the UN and the idea of "One World" in which their own nation is not dominant. Changing postures on international engagement in response to changing conditions are not inconsistent with these enduring values and may, from each ideology's perspective, serve them.

A friend who studies ideology in Congress told me that, for his purposes, "Ideology is what ADA scores measure." Political science should aim higher. I suggest that ideologies are collections of policy prescriptions advocated by specialists having similar values concerning order, tradition, freedom from constraint, and equality. Members of the public internalize the agenda that suits their own values and seek to implement it through parties and other means.

Of possible related interest: Chapters 12, **27**, **47**, 50.

Suggested additional reading

Constantini, Edmond, and Kenneth H. Craik. "Personality and Politicians: California Party Leaders, 1960-1976." *Journal of Personality and Social Psychology* 38 (1980): 641–661.
Noel, Hans. "The Coalition Merchants: How Ideologues Shape Parties in American Politics." PhD dissertation, UCLA, 2006.

34

GUESS WHAT?
VOTERS ARE SMART

Gerald M. Pomper
Rutgers University

For the past 40 years, political science research has demonstrated the basic political competence of American voters. Without the necessity of footnotes, any specialist in voting behavior—and most of their colleagues— could reel off a roster of all-stars (may I give a hint with the name of V.O. Key?) who provided excellent studies to support this fundamental conclusion.

This general judgment follows from more and many detailed findings:

- Voters respond to changing perceptions of the achievements and record of candidates.
- Party loyalty is based on a reasonable combination of retrospective judgments and evaluations of future outcomes.
- Party loyalty is primarily based on cognitive evaluations of candidates and parties rather than inherited identifications.
- Voters recognize, and vote upon, differences in party programs, and cast their ballots essentially in accord with their own policy preferences.
- Demographic characteristics have less influence on the vote than political evaluations.
- Purely personal characteristics of candidates are far less important than voter evaluations of such relevant political characteristics as competence, experience, integrity, and compassion.
- Despite limits on their time and knowledge, voters find sufficient low-information political guides to vote in accord with their own preferences and interests.

As one major author put it, the voter seems to be "a reasonably rational fellow." But you would not believe that if you accepted the view of the electorate typically presented by the media, political consultants, public officials in unguarded moments, and even voters when they discuss other voters. Rather, in this more negative portrait, the electorate is seen as uninterested, uninformed, and unable to link its policy preferences and interests to its ballots.

This dim view comes partially from the limited knowledge of the alleged pundits themselves. If they have studied political science at all, it was probably many years ago, when our discipline was prone to denigrate the voters' abilities. For example, the original Michigan studies, grounded in data of the 1950s and considerably outdated today, are still cited by columnists writing in the twenty-first century.

More basically, there is self-interest involved. If voters are dumb, then the pundits are relatively smart. If voters are clueless, then they need the guidance of their betters. Syndicated columns, television analyses, and internet blogs follow, providing large incomes for the "necessary" guiders of the deficient democracy of the U.S. If voters are prone to manipulation, then there also is a hugely profitable market for the manipulation skills of advertisers, pollsters, and campaign consultants. If campaigns are no more than presentations of self, then the important skills are the petty knacks of barbers, cosmetologists, and pretentious linguists.

A low estimate of voters also provides an easy excuse for losing candidates. Their defeats can be explained away as due to the voters' dense or misguided minds, not their own lacks of character, achievement, or program. Republicans can console themselves that George Bush's low ratings are due to manipulation by the media; Democrats can take solace that John Kerry lost the 2004 election because of manipulation by advertisers.

Political science may also bear some responsibility for the lack of attention to its important findings on the reasonableness of the electorate. The discipline rewards esoteric and quantitative research, emphasizing the search for theoretical constructs and sophisticated methodology. These are worthy goals, but they create distance between the academy and popular understanding.

In the discipline, political relevance, engagement, even clear writing are denigrated. When the wisdom of research is presented in obscure scholastic terms, it becomes lost amid the simplicities of the conventional wisdom. The ivory tower is, too often, preferred over the public marketplace of ideas.

Voting studies now tell us that voters are basically smart, that a busy and nonacademic electorate can make sense of the confusions of politics. But we have not been smart in communicating that important set of findings. Inadvertently, we have become enablers for those politicians who would seek to manipulate the electorate to the nation's harm. We may have little opportunity left to revitalize American democracy. It is time to tell others what we know.

Of possible related interest: Chapters 11, 36, **68**, 72.

Suggested additional reading

McCarty, Nolan M., Kieth T. Poole, and Howard Rosenthal. *Polarized America: The Dance of Ideology and Unequal Riches.* Cambridge, MA: MIT Press, 2006.

Weiner, Marc D. "Political Parties: The Best Evidence of Genuine Popular Liberty". Ph.D. dissertation, Rutgers University, 2008. Forthcoming Transaction Press.

35

EXTRA! EXTRA! EXTRA INFO NEEDED WITH SURVEY REPORTING

Andrea Louise Campbell
Massachusetts Institute of Technology

I wish political scientists could impart to journalists, in particular, a bit of statistical theory and survey practice to inform their reporting of poll results. For the media, survey results can serve as filler on slow news days, can add color to otherwise prosaic stories, or indeed can even BE the story—as when presidential popularity falls to such a low point that the incumbent's very ability to govern is questioned. And some media reporting of surveys is of fairly high quality: often the media report on trends or on differences among subgroups, implicitly acknowledging that a given marginal doesn't tell us much about "what the people think," but that change over time or relative differences can be meaningful. They also now, after decades of reporting point estimates only, often give a "margin of error" with the results. On the other hand, media treatments rarely note that the margin of error is larger for subgroups, so that apparent differences between, say, black women and black men may really be indistinguishable from zero. Certainly there is little acknowledgment that factors such as question wording, item order, and differences in likely voter and other types of screens might influence survey responses (not to mention nonresponse bias and threats to random sampling, polling difficulties with which we political scientists are still grappling). As fascinating and informative as poll results can be, I would feel better if they came with more complete descriptions and cautions for readers among the public.

Of possible related interest: Chapters 12, **36**, **37**, **67**.

36

WHAT SHOULD JOURNALISTS AND POLITICIANS KNOW?

Beyond the Margin of Error

Morris P. Fiorina
Stanford University

For two generations students of mass behavior have known that representative samples were crucial to their ability to make valid inferences. In the past generation the more general notion of selection bias has become widely (although not yet universally) appreciated. Somewhat less widely recognized but becoming increasingly more so is the related, still more general concept of endogeneity.

While some basics of survey research such as sampling error and even measurement error arising from question wording by now have diffused into the more sophisticated stratum of the journalistic community, the concept of selection bias remains poorly appreciated in practice even if recognized at some abstract level. It is not just that Iowa caucus-goers are unrepresentative in the sense that Iowa is whiter and more rural than most of America; it is also that whatever factors motivate 10 percent (plus or minus) of Iowans to attend the caucuses make them different from other Iowans (not to mention most Americans). Ordinary people know less, care less, have different priorities and make decisions differently than those who constitute the highly politicized circles in which political journalists move. Journalists, in turn, confirm the inaccurate images carried by politicians who move in the same unrepresentative circles.

Endogeneity is even trickier. Too much political argument presumes one-way causation: x causes y. But more often than not, y also causes x, or y causes z which in turn causes x. Failure to see how variables are embedded in webs of mutual causation leads not merely to mistaken academic inferences, but to decisions that hurt the country. For example, in his recent book, *Building Red America,* journalist Thomas Edsall reports that pollster

Matthew Dowd convinced Republican chief strategist Karl Rove to abandon the "compassionate conservative" strategy that the Bush campaign followed in 2000 and concentrate instead on maximizing support from the evangelical base. Dowd's analyses reportedly showed that there were almost no swing voters left to persuade, only committed partisans. Surely, any political science student of elections would have cautioned these politicos that swing voters are made not born. Vote choices depend on the positions and actions of the candidates as well as the positions of the voters. A look at the historical record would have shown few swing voters in 1984 but lots of them in 1992 (Ross Perot got nearly 19 percent of the popular vote). And even in 2000, had high-level strategists looked down ballot to state level races, they would have seen far more partisan variability than they were seeing at the national level.

I take it as axiomatic that accurate information is important both to politicians who aspire to public office and to citizens who choose those who represent them. But failure to take account of selection bias and endogeneity means that interpretations of American politics advanced by journalists and politicians are inaccurate in major respects. Overlaid on long-standing news selection principles—conflict, negativity, deviance from the norm—that distort reality are claims that reflect journalists' interactions with self-selected elite actors who are unrepresentative of the larger constituencies they purport to represent. Interest group leaders boast of the length of their email lists, and all sides claim that public opinion is with them, but journalists and politicians seldom attempt to verify the competing claims—to ascertain whether the emperors have any clothes.

Of course, wishing that considerations like selection bias and endogeneity were more widely appreciated will not make it so. In the late twentieth century many members of our profession attached low priority to communicating with poorly informed journalists and confused members of the public, but that situation seems to be changing—a welcome development. If not us, who?

Of possible related interest: Chapters **35**, **67**, **68**, 96.

Suggested additional reading

King, Gary, Robert O. Keohane, and Sidney Verba. *Designing Social Inquiry*. Princeton, NJ: Princeton University Press, 1994.

37

THE NEED FOR SURVEY REPORTING STANDARDS IN POLITICAL SCIENCE

D. Sunshine Hillygus
Harvard University

There is widespread recognition that survey research today faces significant methodological challenges. People are harder to reach and, when reached, they are less willing to answer questions. Survey results will be biased if those who do not respond are systematically different from those who do. Bias can also be introduced when some members of a study population are excluded, either intentionally or unintentionally, such as the Random Digit Dial telephone surveys that exclude households without landline telephones (i.e., cell phone-only households). At the same time, new technologies have made it less expensive to conduct a survey—especially using opt-in internet samples—so we now find the academic landscape dotted with more original surveys than ever before. While this explosion of data sources offers exciting potential for new research, too often these surveys are marred by less rigorous and less transparent methodological standards that have the potential to undermine any substantive conclusions.

In a world with more surveys but also more threats to survey methods, it has become more difficult—but also more important—to evaluate survey quality. Yet, I often hear the opposing argument that because all surveys today are flawed, we might as well do cheaper, opt-in web polls. Those in the internet polling business often justify their work by saying that media, political, or advocacy polls need not be held to the same standards as academic research. While that might well be the case, the unfortunate reality is that there are few academic survey quality standards, either. Indeed, media organizations are more likely than academic journals to have written survey-quality standards. The Associated Press, The *New York Times*, and ABC News, among others, have developed internal standards for judging whether or not they should report a survey. In political science, by contrast, journal readers and reviewers (and the scholars themselves) have little guidance in gauging whether or not they should trust the results of a survey. The absence of quality standards jeopardizes our ability to accurately measure the wants and needs of the American public and threatens the credibility of the entire survey enterprise.

What should we do? First, and foremost, we must increase methodological transparency. Although we have come to expect scholars to report sampling error (e.g., margin of error, standard errors), there are many other sources of errors in surveys—measurement error, nonresponse error, and coverage error, to name a few. Over the last several decades, survey methodologists have had significant success developing methods for measuring, understanding, and adjusting for these different sources of error. Yet too little of this knowledge has filtered to political scientists, and descriptions of survey methods often neglect basic aspects of the design that are essential for the assessment of survey quality, much less replication of the results. At a minimum, readers should have enough information about the survey-design and data-collection procedures to scrutinize how both sampling and nonsampling errors might influence the reported results. Readers should be able to determine whether a survey's design and implementation were appropriate for the research question and whether the survey's knowledge claims were warranted given the methods used. Towards this aim, we should develop a set of minimum survey quality standards in political science.

Second, we must advocate for high-quality surveys. While no survey is perfect, increased transparency will make it clear that not all survey methods are equal. There is an inevitable tradeoff between cost and quality, and scholarly work should resist the temptation to compromise survey accuracy. It is possible to get a large number of interviews on the internet for very little money, but the use of nonprobability samples comes at a clear cost to quality. The scientific basis of surveys—the fundamental ability to generalize beyond just the pool of people who answered the questions—rests on statistical theory. Without an appropriately designed probability-based sample, there is no well-grounded theoretical basis for making claims about representativeness or generalizability. Increased transparency and scrutiny in publication standards should help incentivize researchers to conduct higher-quality survey projects. But scholars must also make the case to foundations and government agencies that it is worthwhile to fund more expensive research. Quality standards will help make clear exactly why it is necessary.

Finally, political science should take the lead in advancing survey quality. Surveys are more than just a research tool for the discipline; as one of the key means by which the public's preferences are communicated to elected officials, surveys are an integral part of the political dynamics that we seek to explain. The scientific study of public opinion has been historically built in political science, so it is especially fitting that we take the lead in shaping the future of survey research methods. Towards that goal, we should be conducting more original research on survey quality. Scholars could and should incorporate in the design of new surveys a plan for collecting benchmarks on survey quality. It should become routine in political science, as it is in so many other social sciences, for new theoretical concepts to incorporate sound empirical design principles, with survey questions and other measures undergoing cognitive testing and other validity and reliability checks. On the bright side, the methodological challenges facing survey research create the opportunity for innovation. But this will require the sharing of knowledge and expertise with survey scholars across academic disciplines—sociology, psychology, health policy, education, and so on. Moreover, the nature of survey research means that much of the knowledge remains clinical, coming from practitioners in the commercial, nonprofit, and government sectors. The future of survey research requires bringing together scholars who are focused on survey methods, practitioners who conduct surveys and the organizations, and individual users who benefit from the methods, best practices, and results. The very first step is to establish a baseline of minimum quality standards, against which we can measure our eventual improvement.

Of possible related interest: Chapters 25, **35**, **38**, **57**.

Suggested additional reading

Biemer, Paul, and Lars Lyberg. *Introduction to Survey Quality*. New York: Wiley, 2003.

Groves, R., F. Fowler, M. Couper, J. Lepkowski, E. Singer, and R. Tourangeau. *Survey Methodology*. New York: Wiley, 2004.

Weisberg, Herbert F. *The Total Survey Error Approach: A Guide to the New Science of Survey Research*. Chicago: University of Chicago Press, 2005.

38

THE CHANGING EVIDENCE BASE OF SOCIAL SCIENCE RESEARCH

Gary King
Harvard University

I believe the evidence base of political science and the related social sciences are beginning an underappreciated but historic change. As a result, our knowledge of and practical solutions for problems of government and politics will begin to grow at an enormous rate—if we are ready.

For the last half-century, we have learned about human populations primarily through sample surveys taken every few years, end-of-period government statistics, and in-depth studies of particular places, people, or events. These sources of information have served us well but, as is widely known, are limited: Survey research produces occasional snapshots of random selections of isolated individuals from unknown geographic locations, and the increases in cell phone use and growing levels of nonresponse are crumbling its scientific foundation. Aggregate government statistics are valuable, but in many countries are of dubious validity and are reported only with intentionally limited resolution or after obscuring valuable information. One-off, in-depth studies are highly informative but for the most part do not scale, are not representative, and do not measure long-term change.

In the next half-century, these existing data collection mechanisms will surely continue to be used and improved—such as with inexpensive web surveys, if the problems with their representativeness can be addressed—but they will be supplemented by the profusion of massive databases already becoming available in many areas. Some produce extensive or continuous time information on individual political behavior and its causes, such as based on text sources (via automated information extraction from blogs, emails, speeches, government reports, and other web sources), electoral activity (via ballot images, precinct-level results, and individual-level registration, primary participation, and campaign contribution data), commercial activity (through every credit card and real estate transaction and via product radio-frequency identification), geographic location (by carrying cell phones or passing through toll booths with Fastlane or EZPass transponders), health information (through digital medical records, hospital admittances, and accelerometers and other devices being included in cell phones), and others. Parts of the biologic sciences are now effectively becoming social sciences, as developments in genomics, proteomics, metabolomics, and brain imaging produce huge numbers of person-level variables. Satellite imagery is increasing in scope, resolution, and availability. The internet is spawning numerous ways for individuals to interact, such as through social networking sites, social bookmarking, comments on blogs, participating in product reviews, and entering virtual worlds, all of which are possibilities for observation and experimentation. (Ensuring privacy and protection of personal information during the analyses to be conducted with this information will require considerable effort, care, and new work in research ethics, but should not be markedly more difficult than the now routine medical research involving experiments on human subjects with drugs and surgical procedures of unknown safety and efficacy.)

The analogue-to-digital transformation of numerous devices people own makes them work better, faster, and less expensively, but also enables each one to produce data in domains not previously accessible via systematic analysis. This includes everything from real-time changes in the web of contacts among people in society (the Bluetooth in your cell phone knows whether other people are nearby!) to records kept of individuals' web clicking, searches, and advertising clickthroughs. Partly as a result of new technology, governmental bureaucracies are improving their record keeping by moving from paper to electronic databases, many of which are increasingly available to researchers. Some governmental policies are furthering these changes by requiring more data collection, such as the "No Child Left Behind Act" in education and via the proliferation of randomized policy experiments. All these changes are being supplemented by the replication movement in academia that encourages or requires social scientists to share data we have created with other researchers.

These data put numerous advances within our reach for the first time. Instead of trying to extract information from a few thousand activists' opinions about politics every two years, in the necessarily artificial conversation initiated by a survey interview, we can use new methods to mine the tens of millions of political opinions expressed daily in published blogs. Instead of studying the effects of context and interactions among people by asking respondents to recall their frequency and nature of social contacts, we now have the ability to obtain a continuous record of all phone calls, emails, text messages, and in-person contacts among a much larger group. In place of dubious or nonexistent governmental statistics to study economic development or population spread in Africa, we can use satellite pictures of human-generated light at night or networks of roads and other infrastructure measured from space during the day. The number, extent, and variety of questions we can address are considerable and increasing fast. Hundreds of years from now, social science today will look like it did when they first handed out telescopes to astronomers.

If we can tackle the substantial privacy issues, build more powerful and more widely applicable theories with observable implications in these new forms of data, help create informatics techniques to ensure that the data are accessible and preserved, and develop new statistical methods adapted to the new types of data, political science can make more dramatic progress than ever before. The challenge before us as a profession, before each of us as researchers, and before the broader community of social scientists, is to prepare for the collection and analysis of these new data sources, to unlock the secrets they hold, and to use this new information to better understand and ameliorate the major problems that affect society and the well-being of human populations.

Of possible related interest: Chapters **15**, 24, 39, **52**.

39

FMRI AND PUBLIC OPINION RESEARCH

Ikuo Kabashima
University of Tokyo

Researchers of public opinion continue to grapple with ever-present problems. Among these are the classic debates over how to interpret both response instability and the apparent lack of constraint governing attitudes; the ever-increasing rates of nonresponse to public opinion surveys; and the difficulties associated with obtaining responses on sensitive issues, particularly those on which the demand characteristics are high. Crucial questions remain about citizens' political sophistication and decision-making capacities, questions that lie at the heart of the democratic experience.

To overcome these difficulties, some researchers have turned to increasingly complex statistical methods. Methods that have grown so complicated that they are not universally or easily understood.

An alternative approach to dealing with these issues—and one that presents political science with a prime opportunity to be scientific—is to utilize Functional Magnetic Resonance Imaging (FMRI). While neural scientists and cognitive psychologists routinely use FMRI, political science has yet to embrace its full potential, perhaps put off by the cost and the difficulty of analyzing the results that necessitate collaboration with neuroscientists. Yet the potential benefits by far outweigh the negative aspects.

The basic idea behind using FMRI in social scientific research is to expose participants to two or more types of experimental stimulus and to then compare how the different stimuli are processed in which parts of the brain. This is achieved by comparing the blood oxygen-level dependent (BOLD) signal time induced by the different stimuli. Changes in blood flow and blood oxygenation in the brain (collectively known as hemodynamics) are closely linked to neural activity; changes in blood oxygenation lag neuronal activity by a couple of seconds. The brain is "mapped" by setting magnetic resonance imaging (MRI) scanners to show up the increased blood flow to the activated areas of the brain on functional MRI scans, in essence, successively scanning "slices" of the brain for BOLD signals.

The BOLD response patterns indicate which areas of the brain participants use in responding to the stimuli: whether participants are using areas of the brain associated with affective phenomena, emotional learning and processing, or areas associated with "higher" order functions such as reasoning or information processing.

At the University of Tokyo, we are beginning a project using FMRI. We believe this research allows us to probe further issues that have a direct impact on the quality of democracy such as how citizens reason about political choice; more specifically, we seek to understand the mechanisms and circumstances in which citizens are tolerant.

Of possible related interest: Chapters 27, 38, 72, 91.

40

SPECIAL INTEREST POLITICS

Jeffry A. Frieden
Harvard University

Interest groups are crucial building blocks of politics. Modern political economists have made substantial advances in understanding how and why special interest groups organize, and how they affect politics and policies.

Many political scientists downplay serious analysis of interest groups. Special interests are often invoked as a backdrop to the evolution of both the political process generally and particular policies, typically as a foil to the broad public interest. But an explicit focus on particularistic groups is often regarded as mundane, conspiratorial, or deterministic. As a result, few political scientists pay systematic attention to the specific organization, preferences, and impact of interest groups. This is in contrast to the detailed and compelling analyses of political institutions common throughout the profession.

Political scientists have been very successful at clarifying and explaining the structure and function of parties, legislatures, executives, bureaucracies, and other political institutions at both the domestic and international level. However, it is hard to imagine that we could reach a full understanding of the impact of political institutions without knowing a great deal about the interests that are transmitted through these institutions to public policy. This would be like focusing solely on the sausage machine that is the political process, while ignoring the nature and quality of the meat (and filler) that is fed into the sausage machine.

In fact, modern approaches to special interests have gone far beyond the simple observation that they are active, and important, in politics. Thirty years ago, the Stigler–Peltzman model of regulation clarified the tradeoff between special and general (public) interests. It suggested important avenues by which features of economic activity (such as barriers to entry, and supply and demand elasticities) might affect group interests, and group policy preferences. Among the subsequent developments and extensions that have informed the analysis of interest-group politics are:

- group organization, particularly in light of well-known problems of collective action;

- the character of affected assets, especially how easy it is for firms and individuals to redeploy among uses or places;
- features of the national economy, and how firms and individuals are affected by their position within this endowment space (of land, labor, capital, and other resources);
- labor skills and wage structure, and how they affect preferences over social insurance and redistributive policies;
- natural or potentially constructed barriers to entry, and how they affect policy preferences;
- interest groups' incentives to make or keep redistributive policies more or less efficient.

In all of these instances, scholars have developed logically rigorous arguments about what various groups are expected to prefer, in such a way as to allow serious empirical work to assess the relative importance of interests, institutions, ideology, and other factors in the political process. Perhaps the best-developed literature along these lines is in trade policy, where the importance of special interests is obvious and has been subjected to systematic analysis for many decades. The high level of development of theoretical and empirical studies of trade-policy interests has indeed allowed scholars to build up an impressive series of institutional arguments about how everything from legislative–executive interactions to partisan politics affects trade policy. But there are also important contributions in issue areas ranging from financial regulation to international debt, from farm policy to the political economy of development.

All studies of politics—including those concerned primarily with electoral politics, or bureaucratic delegation, or legislative structure— would benefit from more explicit attention to the interests of powerful and concentrated social groups. These groups are central to the policymaking process in almost every arena. Rather than simply nodding in their direction, social scientists would gain by taking advantage of the current state of the art in the study of special interests.

Of possible related interest: Chapters **41**, 42, 81, 100.

Suggested additional reading

Mitchell, William, and Michael Munger. "Economic Models of Interest Groups: An Introductory Survey." *American Journal of Political Science* 35 (1991): 512–546.

Rogowski, Ronald. *Commerce and Coalitions.* Princeton, NJ: Princeton University Press, 1989.

41

AN EVER FAINTER VOICE

Jeffrey M. Berry
Tufts University

We're not very good at connecting the dots.

By "we" I'm referring to those of us who study interest groups. One of the central research problems we face is determining how the mobilization of interests into organizations translates into public policy outcomes. What levels of mobilization, what types of organizations, and what tactics of advocacy lead to what kinds of government responses? These are the most basic of interest group questions but our progress in answering them is modest.

We assume that the level and quantity of representation makes quite a bit of difference. Isn't it obvious? Those who are better represented in the political system certainly seem to have been rewarded with benefits like tax breaks and regulatory advantages. In contrast even those toward the bottom of the income spectrum who work full-time may lack the basics of a safety net, such as health insurance.

Yet recent research demonstrates that the level of interest group resources is statistically unrelated to policy outcomes or political effectiveness. Similarly, research on political action committees has not revealed a consistent relationship between campaign donations and floor votes. One explanation, of course, is that it is often the case that policymaking pits one side with significant resources against another side with significant resources.

Despite many years of study the pathways of influence remain unclear. Our tools of measurement may be getting ever-sharper but the policy-making process remains stubbornly complex. And much remains beyond measurement. A particularly difficult problem is understanding the impact of the *lack* of representation. It is here that the dot-connecting problem is especially challenging. For both the poor, the near poor, and lower middle class, advocacy on their behalf by organizations directly representing their interests is not completely absent. Moreover, very expensive social programs that benefit such constituencies have endured over a long period of time.

What is notable, though, is that the face of representation for these constituencies has changed significantly. The base of advocacy comes, of

98

course, not from groups but from the Democratic Party. Space does not allow for an adequate analysis of how the Party has been transformed, but it is evident that even as conservatives have abandoned the Democrats, it has not become a more forceful and committed advocate for the lower range of the economic continuum. While organized labor remains a vital force in the Party and even though minorities have become a much larger proportion of all Democratic loyalists, it is also true that the Party depends on a white suburban base that has become more important over the years. It's easy to think of the Democrats as a liberal party but hard to think of it as a working class party.

Changes in the interest group world have been even more dramatic. Unfortunately, there's no clear baseline as to how many of the poor, near poor, and working class were represented by various interest groups during the heyday of the New Deal. What we do know, however, is that organized labor encompasses a far smaller percentage of the workforce today.

At the same time labor was declining, liberal citizen groups were ascending. National organizations representing consumer, environmental, and good government interests have flourished. Environmental groups in particular have built enormous memberships and appear to be highly successful lobbies in Washington and around the country. But these kinds of citizen groups represent the haves, not the have-nots or the have-a-littles. As they've become a vital intellectual voice that defines the ongoing mission of the Democratic Party, they crowd the voices of traditional liberalism.

The exploding numbers of nonprofits are one source of real growth in organizations that are partial to the interests of the poor and disadvantaged. As the American welfare state has moved decisively away from income maintenance and toward social services, nonprofits have increasingly become the administrative arm of government. Yet the nonprofit sector remains weak. A primary reason is that these organizations have an exaggerated fear of the Internal Revenue Service (IRS) and its ambiguous limits on lobbying by organizations allowed to offer tax deductions for donations. A nonprofit providing job training, for example, has a clear interest in representing its clientele as broader government support for such programs benefits both the organization and those who need workforce training. Yet the nonprofit is likely to hold back or not lobby at all because it fears that overt lobbying might lead to a revocation of its advantageous tax status.

Taking all these sources of potential representation into account, how do we explain what appears to be a deteriorating political condition for the have-nots and have-a-littles? As Jacob Hacker has persuasively documented, policy outcomes are becoming more and more adverse to even those who work but are not wealthy. Health insurance and employer-based retirement plans have become increasingly elusive.

To put this in the rawest of terms, think of an adult, working full-time at Wal-Mart making say, $8.50 an hour ($17,680 a year). In political terms, who speaks for the working class individual making $8.50? Leaving the parties aside, which interest groups? That's not easy to establish. Indirectly, organized labor provides some general advocacy before government, though Wal-Mart and most other employers are not unionized. Citizen groups have other priorities and while nonprofits may provide these workers services in the local community, they provide little political representation for the working class in general.

The answer, of course, is that at best the $8.50 Wal-Mart employee has marginal representation in our interest group system. And those who aren't in the workforce are even worse off in terms of representation. Government continues to support some programs that benefit this worker (Social Security, Medicare) but we live in an era where public policy seems increasingly unsympathetic to such working class individuals. We know the relative lack of interest group representation has some impact on relevant policy but we only know so in general.

Of possible related interest: Chapters 6, 8, 12, 42.

Suggested additional reading

Berry, Jeffrey M., with David F. Arons. *A Voice for Nonprofits*. Washington, DC: Brookings, 2003.

Hacker, Jacob S. *The Great Risk Shift*. New York: Oxford University Press, 2006.

Schlozman, Kay Lehman, Benjamin I. Page, Sidney Verba, and Morris P. Fiorina. "Inequalities of Political Voice." In *Inequality and American Democracy*, edited by Lawrence R. Jacobs and Theda Skocpol, 19–87. New York: Russell Sage Foundation, 2005.

42

EXPLORING POLITICAL INEQUALITY

Benjamin I. Page
Northwestern University

During early struggles to extend the right to vote, some affluent Americans feared that newly empowered lower-income majorities would seize and redistribute their wealth. Despite periodic alarms, no such wholesale redistribution has occurred. In fact there is little sign of class-based politics or of highly egalitarian social welfare policies in the U.S. It's a puzzle. Why don't the poorest 50 percent + 1 of Americans band together and outvote the affluent minority?

Possible solutions to this puzzle fall into two general groups: hypotheses about *political inequality*, which assert that—despite formal equality—lower-income majorities do not actually have the power to get their way; and hypotheses about *acquiescence*, which assert that most Americans go along with a high degree of economic inequality and do not in fact favor extensive redistribution. Sidney Verba and his colleagues have made important contributions related to both sets of hypotheses. These contributions lay the groundwork for what I consider to be a broad and compelling agenda for future research.

Verba, Schlozman, and Brady's *Voice and Equality* stands as the most important piece of work concerning exactly how, to what extent, and why U.S. citizens do not all have an equal voice in mass politics. When it comes to who votes, who gives money to politicians or works in campaigns, and who contacts public officials, lower-income Americans are markedly underrepresented. This kind of political inequality is solidly documented and analyzed.

Yet questions remain. Is this in fact the major source of political inequality in the U.S.? The class bias in turnout, while understandably alarming to democrats, is probably too small to account for the extremely nonegalitarian shape of U.S. public policy, especially since it is not clear that nonvoters actually tend to favor much different policies than voters do. The evidence that even the small-time campaign money givers who show up in national samples are relatively quite affluent, and have objective interests quite different from those of most Americans, points in a some-what different direction. Perhaps something big is happening outside the survey data, among major money givers and organized interests.

To me, a striking shortfall in studies of American politics to date has been the general failure to test (or to integrate into mainstream political science) the hypothesis that political inequality proceeds chiefly from the political power of corporations, wealthy individuals, and organized interests. This is not easy to investigate; crucial data on money givers' interactions with politicians are carefully kept secret, and quantitative analysis (e.g., of the possible gate-keeping role of big money for election to Congress or the presidency) is difficult. It may be that the best way to get relevant evidence is to conduct archival research on historical cases.

Work on the New Deal by Ferguson, Swenson, Domhoff, and others suggests that our main social programs may have been enacted only because of cooperation from important factions of business. This may help explain the skimpy nature of such programs. We need to know much more about what U.S. corporations want from politics, what they get, and how they get it. Is it true, for example, that the policy right turn of the Reagan years, which lingers with us still, resulted mainly from a turn against social welfare programs by corporations that had once been relatively progressive? If so, exactly how and why?

Similar questions can be asked about the core activists of the Republican and Democratic parties. In a two-party system with substantial partisan control over nominations, the activists of both parties together may—despite their ideological differences—exercise a measure of duopoly power on behalf of the affluent. If they do, how, why, and to what extent do they do so?

A related set of research questions concerns possible structural sources of political inequality. For example, has global economic competition put tight constraints on redistributive policies, making them very costly or altogether infeasible? Comparative research suggests not: the U.S. is an outlier. Why? Has globalization empowered business and defanged labor more in the U.S. than elsewhere? If so, how and why?

The acquiescence hypotheses have a long history in work by Hartz, Lane, Lipset, Hochschild, McClosky and Zaller, and others. Perhaps Americans don't seek extensive redistributive programs because they are content with the American dream that hard work will bring economic success. Or because they believe that material inequality is necessary for incentives to work and invest. Or because they think government programs are inherently ineffective, inefficient, or destructive of freedom. Or because they feel alienated and powerless. Much is known about what views the average American holds on such matters. But surprisingly little is known about exactly how those views relate to one another in belief systems, or how much each contributes to attitudes about redistribution.

102

Schlozman and Verba's *Injury to Insult* made important progress on such questions in the context of unemployment. Why, they asked, do unemployed Americans not rebel against their fate and insist on redress from government? The answers appear to lie in specific sorts of acquiescence. We would do well to extend similar analyses to citizens' preferences concerning redistribution in general and specific public policies, from progressive taxes to programs concerning jobs and wages, healthcare, and retirement pensions.

To the extent that authentic beliefs and preferences produce acquiescence to inequality, U.S. politics may be more truly democratic than some observers have inferred from our inegalitarian policies. On the other hand, to the extent that relevant beliefs and preferences are based on false or misleading information, further research questions concern possible manipulation of opinion, false consciousness, or hegemony. Such phenomena could constitute another face of power and be a major source of political inequality. Research into such matters is notoriously difficult but badly needed.

Of possible related interest: Chapters **43**, **48**, *61*, 82.

Suggested additional reading

Page, Benjamin I., and Lawrence R. Jacobs. *Class War? Economic Inequality and the American Dream*. Chicago: University of Chicago Press, 2009.

43

VOICE, AND THEN WHAT?

Larry M. Bartels
Princeton University

Political scientists have done a great deal to document and account for disparities in political participation in the U.S. and other contemporary democracies. The next order of business is to trace the implications of those disparities for democratic policymaking.

In *Voice and Equality*, Sidney Verba, Kay Schlozman, and Henry Brady argued that "inequalities in activity are likely to be associated with inequalities in governmental responsiveness." Similar arguments appear frequently as motivating assumptions in the literature on political participation. It is striking, though, how little political scientists have done to test the assumption that inequalities in participation are politically consequential. For the most part, scholars of participation have treated actual patterns of governmental responsiveness as someone else's problem.

The extent to which scholarly attention has focused on disparities in political participation probably reflects, in part, the simple fact that those disparities are (relatively!) easy to measure. As Verba and Gary Orren put it in *Equality in America*:

> Political equality cannot be gauged in the same way as economic inequality. There is no metric such as money, no statistic such as the Gini index, and no body of data comparing countries. There are, however, relevant data on political participation (p. 15).

Now, more than 20 years later, we have even more and better data on political participation. But how much closer are we to being able to gauge the reality of democratic equality in the terms proposed by Robert Dahl on the first page of *Polyarchy*: "the continued responsiveness of the government to the preferences of its citizens, considered as political equals"?

Recent work by Martin Gilens and by Lawrence Jacobs and Benjamin Page, among others, has made some significant headway on this research agenda. Jacobs and Page found that the foreign policy views of ordinary citizens had little apparent impact on the views of government officials. Business leaders and experts were much more influential. Gilens found that the policy preferences of middle-class and poor people on a wide range of issues were virtually unrelated to subsequent policy changes, except insofar as they happened to coincide with the policy preferences of rich people. My own analysis of roll call votes cast by U.S. senators provided equally stark evidence of disparities in responsiveness to the views of rich and poor constituents.

To what extent, if any, do these disparities in political influence stem from disparities in political participation? Here the available evidence is a good deal thinner. I found that the views of citizens who reported contacting public officials received extra weight in the policymaking process, providing some support for the notion that "inequalities in activity are likely to be associated with inequalities in governmental responsiveness." However, the differences in responsiveness associated with contacting were modest in magnitude, and sometimes entirely absent. (For example, I found no effect of contacting on senators' responsiveness to constituents' views regarding the specific issue of abortion.) And I found even less evidence of differential responsiveness to the views of voters by comparison with nonvoters.

If our evidence for the impact of political participation on policymaking is sparse—and decidedly mixed—we know even less about how that impact varies with the characteristics of the people doing the participating. Robert Weissberg has argued that political activism "does perform as advertised, but only *sometimes*, and even then usually for those who already enjoy many advantages." In particular, Weissberg suggests that "shouting louder ('voice') is likely to be futile . . . for those mired in poverty." If that is true, equalizing voice may do little to equalize political influence—sobering and important news for many democratic activists. Unfortunately, as with so much else about the political significance of participation, we simply don't know.

Of possible related interest: Chapters 22, **42**, **45**, **82**.

Suggested additional reading

Bartels, Larry M. *Unequal Democracy: The Political Economy of the New Gilded Age.* New York and Princeton, NJ: Russell Sage Foundation and Princeton University Press, 2008, chap. 9.

Gilens, Martin. "Inequality and Democratic Responsiveness." *Public Opinion Quarterly* 69 (2005): 778–796.

Jacobs, Lawrence R., and Benjamin I. Page. "Who Influences U.S. Foreign Policy?" *American Political Science Review* 99 (2005): 107–124.

44

THE IMPACT OF UNEQUAL POLITICAL PARTICIPATION ON POLICY OUTCOMES

Eric Schickler
University of California, Berkeley

Over the past several decades, students of political participation have provided a wealth of evidence that inequalities in resources translate into unequal participation in the political process. But with a few noteworthy exceptions, American politics scholars have not taken the next step of demonstrating the conditions under which such inequalities in participation affect policy outcomes. While scattered work suggests that the potential impact is substantial—such as Larry Bartels' research demonstrating that senators are much more responsive to high-income constituents than to low-income constituents—legislative scholars have not, as a whole, taken up the challenge of assessing how inequalities in turnout, campaign contributions, and other forms of activism affect the laws produced by Congress. One reason is that studies of mass behavior and legislative politics have for the most part been treated as entirely separate fiefdoms in American politics. Partly as a result, the leading models that we use to understand lawmaking say remarkably little about the mass "input" side, beyond the information that can be summarized in the location of the median voter in the electorate and perhaps the median voter in the majority party. This is not a call for attempting to demonstrate that policies are consistently distorted by income inequalities. After all, on many issues, income is uncorrelated with mass opinion. Nonetheless, better integrating mass behavior into the study of legislative politics will enrich out understanding of core features of democratic accountability in the United States.

Of possible related interest: Chapters 32, **42**, **43**, *49*.

Suggested additional reading

Bartels, Larry M. *Unequal Democracy: The Political Economy of the New Gilded Age.* New York and Princeton, NJ: Russell Sage Foundation and Princeton University Press, 2008.

Gilens, Martin. "Inequality and Democratic Responsiveness." *Public Opinion Quarterly* 69 (2005): 778–796.

45

PARTICIPATION MATTERS

Jan Leighley
University of Arizona

One of the things that participation scholars know is that participation matters, for citizens, for elected officials and other elites, and more generally for political systems. The normative arguments are plentiful, and intuitively it makes sense. We also have a fair amount of empirical evidence on this point. We know that participants are different from nonparticipants with respect to social class and material needs, and sometimes with respect to ideological orientation and policy preferences. Most directly, we also know that elites reward—through the provision of favorable public policies—those who participate.

This last point highlights the fact that elected officials appreciate the reality of participation as a democratic linkage between citizens and elites. That they often oppose proposals to make voting "easier" or other forms of participation more accessible, then, is perhaps not surprising.

Yet what citizens likely most appreciate is only that "money matters," as distinct from other types of political engagement. Perhaps they are right to suggest that money is (most) critical in these matters of political influence. But they are certainly wrong to think that it is the only way in which elected officials are held accountable. If they knew this, they might consider participating in new or different ways.

And that would make for a very different politics *and* political science: whether as citizens or scholars, we would have a lot more fun, and perhaps even be a little more confident in this democracy that is ours.

Of possible related interest: Chapters 5, **42**, **43**, 85.

Suggested additional reading

Griffin, John D., and Brian Newman. "Are Voters Better Represented?" *Journal of Politics* 67 (2005): 1206–1227.

Hill, Kim Quaile, and Jan E. Leighley. "The Policy Consequences of Class Bias in American State Electorates." *American Journal of Political Science* 36 (1992): 351–365.

Martin, Paul S. "Voting's Rewards: Voter Turnout, Attentive Publics, and Congressional Allocation of Federal Money." *American Journal of Political Science* 47 (2003): 110–127.

46

PARTICIPATORY DISTORTION ($$) TAKES OFF!!

Philip E. Converse
University of Michigan

In *Voice and Equality*, Sid, Kay, and Henry note that participatory distortion is "more pronounced" for making financial contributions than for other kinds of political activity (p. 517). Truer words were never spake. On the other hand, this judgment was based on data collected about 1990. In the interim, there has been a lot of action in this department, none of which could be taken as upsetting this generalization. But it does suggest that however pronounced the distortion may have been in 1990, several secular trends in the interim may have increased the distortion in striking degree.

For openers on the supply side, the "dot.com boom" of the 1990s saw chief executive officers appropriate a lion's share of new productivity profits, such that the ratio of their "normally expected" pay to the average pay of their underlings advanced from something like 40 times greater to something like 400 times greater. This trend has already been picked up in Gini Coefficients on the distribution of income in the U.S., such that we have left the general moderate neighborhood of our industrialized European peers and are moving upward toward now-industrializing China, with Mexico and Brazil within increasing reach.

More recently we can add the very outsized lagniappe donated by the George W. Bush Administration to the very wealthy in major cuts in the progressivity of income tax schedules. This is only beginning to register in further summations of the distribution of income, and the more interesting data in any event involve the distribution of accumulated wealth, which for obvious reasons registers at a slower pace. These tax reductions have been put in place despite the fact that the electorate as a whole feels strongly that the rich do not pay their proper share of taxes. Indeed, even the wealthiest fifth of the U.S. electorate (best data I can find) show a small majority of the same mind.

In short, there are mountains of newly accumulated wealth available for investment in tighter plutocratic control of our democratic process. And it seems that this process is more than ready to soak them up.

The evidence here lies in major developments since 1990 on the demand side, where political contributions are concerned. One hopeful counter-step in the campaign finance area, due to Senators McCain and Feingold, seems to have been largely emasculated through erosions I cannot entirely understand. Far more powerful has been the trend noted in *V&E* toward increasing professionalization of many "political services," from lobbying to large-scale campaign organizing. We are treated in the spring of 2007 to another large leap forward in demand, thanks to a presidential campaign season which has been already tiresome at 10 months or so in duration, to something more like 20 months. Some countries formally limit the duration of political campaigns, and in modest degree succeed, and it is not to my mind an anti-democratic maneuver. The growing supply of wealthy dollars to subsidize such a new campaign duration is underscored by the likely fact that all of the front-runners will sidestep their share of public campaign dollars because they can do better in the private economy.

The array of multifarious topics that deserve study under this rubric may seem to belie the "single question/finding" emphasis of our prompt for this exercise. On the other hand, it is the felicitous nature of the whole concept of "participatory distortion" that all sorts of more specific topics and venues can be factored into a single variable to express the degree to which activities like financial contributions can be summed relative to the one person, one vote, base for democratic voting.

If a sea change in the role of money in democratic politics is upon us, further study is in order. Some such is emergent: I have recently been able to examine an excellent book manuscript by Larry Bartels entitled *Unequal Democracy: The Political Economy of the New Gilded Age*. It covers a good deal of what has happened since 1990, including some counter-intuitive findings that public fervor for a more progressive tax structure stops abruptly short of wanting to see the estate tax saved, even among voters who are aware that they will never be eligible for such a tax. But this is just a strong beginning for a wider front of research needed.

Of possible related interest: Chapters 32, **42**, **47**, **48**.

Suggested additional reading

Bartels, Larry M. *Unequal Democracy: The Political Economy of the New Gilded Age*. New York and Princeton, NJ: Russell Sage Foundation and Princeton University Press, 2008.

47

THE RASHOMON WORLD OF MONEY AND POLITICS

Thomas E. Mann
The Brookings Institution

Among the many pearls of wisdom to emanate from the lips of Daniel Patrick Moynihan during his long and illustrious career in academia and public life was this favorite of mine: "Everyone is entitled to his own opinion. He is not entitled to his own facts." If only it were so. In today's world of ideologically polarized parties, the partisan and ideological lenses through which citizens view politicians and issues also refract what ought to be less subjective indicators of the world as it is—that is, facts. There are distinct Democratic and Republican views of the state of the economy, progress in the war in Iraq, and many other matters on which people with different values and policy preferences ought to be able to agree.

The demise of broadly accepted facts is especially evident in national policymaking circles, where in recent years competing teams of politicians largely talk past one another in highly stylized debates with facts and evidence marshaled in a transparently selective fashion to buttress pre-existing positions deduced from ideological frames. The lack of honest and serious policy talk in Congress has been all too apparent in recent years. The centralization of power and the marginalization of committees within Congress and an ideologically driven advocacy culture outside have contributed to a decline of deliberation in American public life.

The dominance of competing world views has characterized the public debate about the efficacy and desirability of campaign finance reform in general and the impact of the Bipartisan Campaign Reform Act of 2002 (BCRA, also known as the McCain–Feingold bill) in particular. That public debate has generated more heat than light on central questions about the role of money in politics. A deep philosophical divide between proponents and opponents of campaign finance regulation produces Rashomon-like divergences in describing, explaining, and evaluating campaign finance practices and reforms. Adversaries often see a different set of facts and almost always interpret those facts in fundamentally different ways.

Sounds like an ideal situation for political scientists to come to the rescue. If they (the press, politicians, and public) knew what we know, the ideological blinders might come off and a more informed and constructive deliberation on the admittedly difficult issues of money and politics might ensue. Of course, that assumes we political scientists are not subject to the same philosophical or ideological blinders as those active in the public arena. For many decades we political scientists working on campaign finance fancied ourselves an intellectual truth squad, endowed by our training and research to cut through the cant in the public debate, exposing specious claims and ill-advised reform proposals. We felt most comfortable challenging the accuracy of factual assertions of reformers, questioning the efficacy of negative regulation, warning of the risks associated with the law of unintended consequences, and emphasizing the values of free speech, increased campaign communication, strong parties, a pluralistic interest group environment, and vigorous electoral competition.

What began as an empirically based enterprise over time developed a world view of its own—call it professional skepticism—one that shaped the questions posed, evidence marshaled, and conclusions reached. A more protean discussion among students of money and politics in the wake of significant changes in the political world in the 1980s and 1990s led some to question their prior positions and opened within the discipline a chasm not so different from that evident in the public arena. This philosophical divide was evident in the constitutional challenge/defense of McCain–Feingold and in evaluations of its impact on the 2004 and 2006 elections. Scholarly supporters of the law saw its modest goals (the elimination of party soft money and the regulation of electioneering communications in order to enforce longstanding prohibitions on corporate and union treasury spending in federal elections) as largely realized. Scholarly critics viewed the law as more ambitious and more constraining on legitimate campaign activity. And they concluded that it failed to realize its objectives but produced harmful side effects.

Political scientists in both camps run the risk of framing and interpreting their analyses in ways that too easily reinforce their preexisting views. If you are convinced philosophically that campaign finance regulation cannot work, then you are likely to see it not working; if you judge any regulation of political communication a restraint on free speech, then you will see such speech diminished; if you believe any campaign law written by incumbents will advantage incumbents, then all campaign law will advantage incumbents; if you believe denying a political party an existing revenue source inevitably weakens that party, then McCain–Feingold must have weakened the parties. The same points can be framed as a critique of those defending the law.

Between these warring political science camps, however, exist a number of political scientists less invested in the public debate and more likely to produce reliable and useful empirical assessments of the limits and possibilities of campaign finance regulation. I hope they increase in number and public visibility and have their voices leaven the public debate on campaign finance reform.

Of possible related interest: Chapters 33, 49, 51, 66.

Suggested additional reading

Mann, Thomas E. "Linking Knowledge and Action: Political Science and Campaign Finance Reform." *Perspectives on Politics* 1 (2003): 69–83.

48

DOES RISING ECONOMIC INEQUALITY MATTER?

Christopher Jencks
Harvard University

Over the past generation the richest one percent of American families has almost doubled its share of after-tax income (from 7.5 percent in 1979 to 15.6 percent in 2005). We know remarkably little about how this change has affected American politics, or how parallel changes in other rich English-speaking countries have affected their political institutions and policies.

Ask a political scientist whether income inequality matters and their answer is almost always, "Of course." At least since Harold Gosnell's 1927 book, *Getting Out the Vote,* political scientists have known that more educated Americans are more likely to vote. After World War II the same pattern showed up in the National Election Study when scholars compared the voting rates of different income groups.

Voting is not, of course, the only way citizens influence politicians' behavior. Working in political campaigns, giving money to political candidates, contacting government officials, and taking part in community affairs also matter. Indeed, they usually matter a lot more than just going to the polls, both because fewer people engage in these activities and because those who do engage in them are more valuable to candidates seeking election or reelection.

In 1972 Sid Verba and Norman Nie's magisterial *Participation in America* showed that these activities were even more dominated by the affluent and well educated than polling booths were. Six years later, working with Jae-On Kim, Verba and Nie reported that the same pattern held in Austria, India, Japan, the Netherlands, Nigeria, and Yugoslavia. Today socioeconomic disparities in both voting and other forms of political participation are one of the best documented and least controversial findings of political science.

Recent work has also shown that politicians are more attentive to the views of their most affluent constituents. When Larry Bartels examined roll-call votes in the U.S. Senate, he found that senators' voting records matched the views of their most affluent constituents far more closely than the views of the less affluent. Indeed, senators appeared to put no weight at all on their poorest constituents' views. Martin Gilens found the same pattern when he looked at the relationship between rich and poor respondents' policy preferences and subsequent changes in national policy.

All this evidence certainly shows that well-educated and affluent citizens exert a disproportionate influence on American politics. But it does not tell us whether the post-1980 rise in the share of income going to the rich (or the decline in their share between 1929 and 1949) affected rich Americans' ability to determine the course of national politics.

Many voters assume that politicians pay more attention to the views of the rich because these are the people who provide most of the campaign money. If that is the explanation of politicians' behavior, greater income inequality will almost certainly enhance the influence of the rich, because their role in funding campaigns will grow.

But politicians might also pay more attention to the views of their affluent and well-educated constituents because such people are more likely to know what their representative is doing and more likely to vote based on such knowledge in future elections. Alternatively, politicians may vote the way their affluent constituents want them to vote because most politicians are themselves fairly affluent, and they also tend to have affluent friends. If these are the main reasons why politicians cater to the affluent, changes in economic inequality may not change politicians' behavior much.

The repeal of the inheritance tax and the skew of the tax cuts during George W. Bush's presidency were vivid symbols of growing deference to the concerns of the very rich. The median voter hypothesis predicts, of course, that such policies will provoke a backlash, in which less affluent voters rediscover the advantages of financing government by taxing people richer than themselves. Until November 2006, however, it looked as if American politics were being shaped by the source of the median campaign dollar, not the median vote. If the median campaign dollar rules, one would expect the influence of the rich to rise and fall in tandem with their share of total income. One would also expect that when the political influence of the rich rises, legislators should support policies that make the distribution of income even more unequal. In principle, such a spiral could continue until some exogenous cataclysm—think global warming, nuclear terrorism, or another Great Depression—transformed the political landscape.

Since November 2006 that landscape has looked a bit different, but no one knows whether this change is a short-term backlash against an incompetent president and an unpopular war or an early sign that American voters now want fundamentally different distributional policies. We badly need a longer-term perspective on how massive changes in the distribution of income have affected politics in both the U.S. and other democracies, and how politics in turn have affected the distribution of income.

Fortunately, we now have annual tax data from a large number of rich democracies on the share of national income going to households near the top of the economic ladder. In some cases these data go back to the 1930s or even earlier. We now need to investigate the mechanisms by which changes in the fortunes of the rich affect their ability both to shape public opinion and to influence politicians' behavior independent of public opinion.

Of possible related interest: Chapters **42**, **44**, **46**, **49**.

Suggested additional reading

Bartels, Larry M. *Unequal Democracy: The Political Economy of the New Gilded Age.* New York and Princeton, NJ: Russell Sage Foundation and Princeton University Press, 2008.

Gilens, Martin. "Inequality and Democratic Responsiveness." *Public Opinion Quarterly* 69 (2005): 778–796.

Verba, Sidney, Kay Lehman Schlozman, and Henry Brady. *Voice and Equality: Civic Voluntarism in American Politics.* Cambridge, MA: Harvard University Press, 1995.

49

REDISTRIBUTION WITHOUT REPRESENTATION AND REPRESENTATION WITHOUT REDISTRIBUTION

James E. Alt
Harvard University

For something as central to political life as taxation, and despite dramatic changes in tax policies in recent decades, it is surprising how little systematic theoretical and empirical research there is on the political economy of tax policy. We have seen:

- most of the advanced world flee from high marginal income tax rates, often substituting fees and indirect taxation;
- inequality increase in many countries;
- voter support for redistribution apparently remain strong;
- political parties generally swing to the right on tax policy, but sometimes converge and sometimes polarize.

There is no obvious party-political pattern, so we do not know how to connect these dots. Count me among those who not only think this is a pity, but wonder how it happened, and would also like to see much more effort go in this direction.

Of course, I can speculate. About a quarter of a century ago, Allan Meltzer and Scott Richard published a seductively simple model. It focused on a single dimension: tax conflict between citizens due to the fact that they have different incomes. Citizens have different views about taxation based on their position in the income distribution: richer (poorer) citizens favor lower (higher) taxation. The tax system was also a single dimension, the rate of income tax, with the proceeds of taxation transferred uniformly to citizens. With appropriately "single-peaked" preferences a referendum (or competition by two parties each of which cares only about winning) will result in the voter with median income choosing the level of taxation. Leaving aside issues of perceptual bias as well as inequality in participation, this happens in a way that reflects inequality as well as how far increases in taxation reduce pre-tax labor earnings.

Despite the fact that the model does not describe any real tax system, it has implications to tempt comparative empirical work. One is that "middle" classes should have disproportionate influence in determining tax policy outcomes. Another is that competing parties will offer the same tax policies. Many quote its central empirical prediction that more pre-tax inequality should go hand in hand with more income-targeted redistribution. And yet, in study after study this central empirical prediction *fails*. This happens, moreover, even though the last quarter-century seemed made for the model: as tax rates on top incomes dropped in most advanced industrial countries, policy (in the sense of the promised tax rate of the party for whom the median voter voted) moved steadily to the right.

Innovations were proposed to resolve this puzzle. Making the goal of policy be to provide insurance rather than redistribution was one. Others sought to consider contrary effects of social divisions including religion, moral values, race, and employment. Adding the politics of proportional representation and legislative bargaining also changed the picture. But the prominence of the U.S. and UK in inspiring flight from high top marginal income tax rates means we ought to be able to say more about tax policy in systems where competition is broadly between two main parties with usually loyal core supporters and more persuadable "swing voters" who vote for whichever party has a better policy stance on issues they view as salient. These "decisive" voters choose between alternatives proposed by the competing parties, which may or may not converge. We need to figure out when they do, and with what consequences.

In their recent book *Polarized America*, Nolan McCarty, Keith Poole, and Howard Rosenthal provide a minimal, straightforward, tractable model in which the income distribution is just like Meltzer-Richard, but parties make tax pledges and redistribution generates some deadweight loss from taxation. The welfare of any voter is simply her post-tax income, as affected by the deadweight loss factor. As before, the median voter always wants some redistribution, but here the desired tax rate falls as the deadweight loss increases (government efficiency falls). So there is a tradeoff between the desire for redistribution and voter "trust," or willingness to have the government act as their agent with more of their money.

The model lets us also track the effects of parties polarizing separately from the effects of inequality. If parties are polarized, voters have to choose between party promises, and indeed the median voter's wishes may not be decisive. This makes a representative voter choose, based on her relative income position, the gap between parties, the size of government, and the deadweight loss factor. Part of the choice is familiar: favoring the Right more because they tax less (the more so the better off one is) and, as long as deadweight loss and/or scale of government is not too large, favoring the Left because they redistribute more. With a little algebra we can see that:

- inequality changes how much relative income matters, and how inequality affects the party advantage depends on whether income is above or below average;
- if the parties polarize more, the choice between parties is starker, and other things equal, there are clear conditions under which polarization favors the Right;
- if the deadweight loss (or the scale of government) increases, the extra burden or waste (we can't separate them in this model) always favors the Right.

But crucially now the net "voter demand for redistribution" here is conditional. It depends not only on the first of these effects, but how that stacks up against the other two.

This model offers many exciting avenues for investigating the political economy of tax policy. How often does the median voter vote for a party with a nonmedian promise? This view of the world has other related implications. Even if voters do not polarize, elites (parties) can, with partisan advantages. Can transparency and information, especially targeted information, have a role in polarizing parties? Do parties with large advantages over others for nontax reasons find it less necessary to make tax promises designed to appeal to politically decisive voters? These are just some of the lines that open up.

Of possible related interest: Chapters 32, 44, **48**, 50.

Suggested additional reading

Bartels, Larry M. *Unequal Democracy: The Political Economy of the New Gilded Age.* New York and Princeton, NJ: Russell Sage Foundation and Princeton University Press, 2008.

Graetz, Michael J., and Ian Shapiro. *Death by a Thousand Cuts.* Princeton, NJ: Princeton University Press, 2005.

50

THE IDEOLOGICAL ORIGINS
OF REDISTRIBUTION

Eric Nelson
Harvard University

The issue of economic inequality has been a perennial focus of political science, and a great deal of recent work in the field has prompted us to scrutinize the range of responses to this problem available to the modern, liberal democratic state. Among these responses, by far the most frequently employed is redistribution: the use of the coercive power of the state to transfer wealth from the comparatively well-off to the comparatively disadvantaged (either in the form of direct payments or in the guise of social programs). Yet one of the most obvious stories one could tell about the course of post-war political theory in the Anglophone tradition would center on its failure (despite numerous attempts) to reconcile the practice of redistribution with the fundamental, normative commitments of liberalism. The problem is straightforward. Liberal political theory envisions a right-bearing citizen who is to be treated as an end, rather than a means, and who is to be left alone to follow the dictates of his own conscience unless his actions threaten the similar rights of others. But redistribution seems to assume a rather different sort of citizen: one whose assets are to be regarded as presumptive community property, to be disposed of (with or without his consent) according to the wishes of society as a whole (as determined by the majority of citizens, or their representatives). Here the citizen is regarded as a means, not an end. Liberalism and redistribution, in short, seem to rely on incompatible visions of the relationship between states and persons. Theorists have, accordingly, encountered great difficulty when trying to combine them in a single framework.

Given the centrality of this problem to contemporary political theory—and given the coincident burgeoning of the historical study of political thought beginning in the 1960s—it is somewhat surprising that scholars have generally neglected to ask how redistribution came to occupy its dominant place in modern political thought and practice. Reflection on this question reveals that redistribution has a decidedly illiberal pedigree. Its first post-classical champions in Europe were seventeenth-century Protestant exegetes who regarded God as the ultimate owner of all men and all property, and who accordingly believed that the Biblical land laws should govern the distribution of wealth. Its banner was then taken up by political disciples of the ancient Greek philosophers, who believed that nature had designed a small number of men to rule over others—and who were prepared to enforce economic equality in order to insure that these few natural aristocrats, rather than the corrupt rich, would be given the reins of government. What these two world-views have in common is the belief that human beings should be required to conform their behavior to an external and objective standard of the good life (hierarchical nature, as interpreted by Plato; or the word of God, as revealed in Scripture), and that there is, accordingly, no "right" to live in contravention of this standard. Redistribution, in short, did not grow up as part of liberalism, but rather as the brainchild of its antagonists. Those of us living in modern liberal democracies are therefore bound to ask whether we can have our rights and our redistribution too.

Of possible related interest: Chapters **33**, 49, 82, 91.

Suggested additional reading

Nelson, Eric. *The Greek Tradition in Republican Thought*. Cambridge: Cambridge University Press, 2004.

Nozick, Robert. *Anarchy, State, and Utopia*. New York: Basic Books, 1974.

Sandel, Michael. *Liberalism and the Limits of Justice*. Cambridge: Cambridge University Press, 1982.

51

REUNITING INTERESTS
AND VALUES

David C. Leege
University of Notre Dame

In recent decades, political scientists have taught approaches based on rational choice and cultural politics as alternate lenses for perceiving and interpreting political phenomena. In reality, the two operate simultaneously. Interests and values/ideas are often inseparable and serve one another.

In a book that explores paradoxes in party loyalty and turnout, Leege and associates have developed a theory of cultural campaigning. The work examined presidential campaigns from 1952 to 2000, attempting to understand why Republicans fairly regularly won the White House despite Democratic majorities or pluralities in party identification, and turnout declined despite increasing magnitudes on predictor variables for participation. Drawing from Swidler's classic exploration of the concept "culture," the authors assumed that cultural identities, norms, and boundaries, far from being fixed and universal for a national society, constituted a "tool kit" for elites to utilize in pursuing their aspirations. Further, some elements of culture are often competitive and decentralized by constituent groups in society.

When political parties take the shape of coalitions composed of groups with competing values and interests, through time some coalition members are overlooked, taken for granted, or consciously jettisoned. These processes create vulnerable targets for the rival party to neutralize or attract in elections.

Currently there is a range of advanced tools for the conduct of campaigns—demographic data, past voting records, and credit card and website consumer patterns arranged by zip codes; current and past polling data; both mass and narrow cast media; direct mailings; the ubiquity of presentational forms offering powerful symbols of attraction and revulsion; and the ever-present electoral college, reducing campaigns to solid bases and contested states. Given these tools, modern campaigners have found it efficient to deploy cultural wedge issues to shape the size and composition of the electorate. Campaigners decide what topics and modes of cultural discourse will mobilize the faithful, demobilize sectors of the opposition altogether, or stimulate some vulnerable sectors to the opposition to defect. Simultaneously, then, rational choice axioms and propositions work collaboratively with cultural politics axioms and propositions.

Since the campaign is permanent and politicians like to stay in office as much as gaining office in the first place, policy options and legislative procedures are often manipulated in the same manner as election agendas and discourse. All this is well illuminated by the theory. What is not so clear are the explanations for electoral or policy failures, and they present an agenda for future research:

- Is there a value hierarchy constructed such that broadly consensual values set boundaries on the deployment of cultural threats to a target group's values? For example, the 1988 Willie Horton advertisements, in their various racially strident iterations, were withdrawn by the Republican candidate. Was this because of tolerance and egalitarian values that the country now embraced, or because the candidate felt his interests in reelection were threatened by his campaign's manipulation of values now outside the mainstream? Or, given the nature of micro-targeting, had the goal with the target groups already been achieved with the first advertisements?
- When do politicians miscalculate the depth of cultural commitment? For example, sensing widespread disapproval of continued troop deployment in Iraq expressed through the 2006 elections, Democrats initially chose budgetary strategies for starving the war effort. In showdowns between the President and the Congress on national defense issues, however, would the President usually have the upper hand because of constitutional norms that Americans accept? Or, is this issue framed through both patriotic and primary group symbols (the troops are from our families) that have precedence over all else? To use another illustration, in the wake of the Supreme Court's ruling on late-term abortion (2007), will the framing of life and personhood trump the framing of a woman's right to choose, and will a successful life/personhood framing result in declining support for politicians who rally round the individual rights framing?
- Why do values/ideas (ideology) obsess politicians to the point where it endangers their tenure in office and their ability to govern? Does placing ideas over interests reflect respect for an external authority which rationalizes/sanctifies the idea? For example, many modern-day conservatives place deep faith in an acquisitive view of human nature most forcefully propounded by Milton Friedman. Public policy and party discipline must flow from this assumption. Yet, when the public

does not share this pristine teleology, why would elected politicians not moderate their policy actions?

Of possible related interest: Chapters 20, 38, 47, 68.

Suggested additional reading

Green, Donald, Bradley Palmquist, and Eric Schickler. *Partisan Hearts and Minds: Political Parties and the Social Identities of Voters.* New Haven, CT: Yale University Press, 2002.

Leege, David C., Kenneth D. Wald, Brian S. Krueger, and Paul D. Mueller. *The Politics of Cultural Differences: Social Change and Voter Mobilization Strategies in the Post-New Deal.* Princeton, NJ: Princeton University Press, 2002.

Swidler, Ann. "Culture in Action: Symbols and Strategy." *American Sociological Review* 51 (1986): 273–286.

52

USING RESEARCH TO FOSTER DEMOCRACY

Kenneth Stehlik-Barry
SPSS, Inc.

Political science needs to institute an ongoing, coordinated study of tolerance and link the research results to real world solutions that policy-makers can draw upon to craft strategies for mitigating conflicts among groups. Since the turn of the millennium, a number of factors have emerged that represent challenges to the growth of political tolerance in democratic societies. The events of September 11, 2001, clearly changed the landscape in terms of weighing the relative importance of security and civil liberties. The murder of Dutch filmmaker Theo van Gogh and the Madrid train bombing in 2004, the London Tube bombings in 2005, and the riots outside Paris that same year are other examples of events that create a climate less conducive to political tolerance. Views on Islam and ethnic groups with ties to Islamic countries were also influenced by the events of that now infamous day. Immigrant groups have become a concern in many democratic societies for a variety of reasons. In Europe, immigrants are often from Islamic countries with very different traditions regarding a wide range of social customs (e.g., the role of women), and their very presence in growing numbers challenges the relative homogeneity of many nations (e.g., France). In other countries, most notably the U.S., immigration both legal and illegal has become a more contentious issue in recent years. The increasing percentage of Hispanics in the population is a regular topic of discussion along with the related concerns regarding border control, English as the only language, and rights for the children of illegal immigrants. With the aging of the post-World War II generation and the generally higher birth rates of immigrant groups, these issues will become more prominent in the coming decade.

In addition to the tolerance issues related to the civil liberties of ethnic and religious subgroups within democratic societies, there are issue-based divisions that, in the absence of a strong norm of tolerance, have the potential to create divisions deep enough to threaten regime stability. The

126

environment, abortion, gun control, same-sex marriage and a host of other issues can divide communities, large and small, to the point the underlying social cohesion necessary for a democratic society to function effectively dissolves. Growing disparity in economic status within societies likewise has the potential to bifurcate societies into haves and have-nots. There is also the prospect that the economic hegemony the U.S. has enjoyed for decades may be coming to an end as the economies of India and China shift the focus more to Asia. Even beyond the direct economic impact of such a change, the psychological impact on Americans who have not had to share the economic spotlight with other societies could be substantial in terms of creating a more xenophobic and less tolerant view of other groups both within and outside the country. Other nations may experience similar strains as their economic status relative to other countries declines. In the past, situations such as these have led to the search for scapegoats to blame for the declining economic prospects people experience, and minorities have typically been singled out as targets. To predict what is likely to happen during periods of extended economic stress, it is necessary to understand how changes in the economic fortunes of individuals influence their level of tolerance.

A comprehensive understanding of these shifting and emerging aspects of political tolerance can only be achieved by a concerted research effort similar in approach to the American National Election Study but on a global scale. Cross-sectional surveys and the monitoring of print and electronic media (including blogs) can provide a continuous flow of data. Secondary analysis of large-scale projects such as the Pew Global Attitudes Survey, the General Social Survey, and the World Values Survey has potential to extend our knowledge in this area. To accomplish the objective outlined here, however, a dedicated focus on tolerance needs to be integrated in all surveys in a more comprehensive manner.

It is also important to institute panel studies so that individual level change can be observed as well. This is a more expensive and methodologically challenging undertaking but the payoff in terms of deeper understanding of life cycle and short-term influences can be substantial. Finally, community-focused studies can prove to be extremely helpful in differentiating the circumstances under which tolerance triumphs. The examples of catastrophic failure (e.g., Darfur) are unfortunately not as rare as one would like but they are still too few in number to develop generalizations. By using individual communities throughout democratic societies as the unit of research, the N will be sufficiently large to observe a broad range of combinations in terms of the inputs used for modeling efforts. It will also be possible to test predictions by applying the models to evolving situations in various communities and comparing what happens to the prediction.

To provide a context for the survey results, data from a wide range of sources will need to be collected, and such key factors as the level of support

127

for tolerant responses to specific events, the framing of news coverage and commentary related to specific groups (ethnic and issue-based) will need to be quantified. Fortunately, developments such as the ability to acquire media and blog data via RSS feeds and increasingly robust techniques for working with unstructured data can simplify what would, until recently, have been a nearly impossible task. This makes it possible to track fluctuations in the "temperature" of the sentiment as well as the framing of the messages allowing for comparisons before and after specific events. By linking these environmental factors to levels of tolerance at the individual level, a much deeper understanding of tolerance can be achieved. With this knowledge in hand, it should be possible to identify in advance situations with a high risk of deteriorating into violence, and hopefully, the factors that must be altered to avert such an outcome.

Of possible related interest: Chapters **38**, 53, 71, 84.

Suggested additional reading

Chong, Dennis, and James N. Druckman. "Framing Public Opinion in Competitive Democracies." *American Political Science Review* 101 (2007): 637–655.
Elkins, Zachary, and John Sides. "Can Institutions Build Unity in Multiethnic States?" *American Political Science Review* 101 (2007): 693–708.

53

MORAL CONVICTIONS, RELIGION, AND DIVERSITY

Our Political Atmosphere

William C. McCready
Knowledge Networks, Inc.

Clifford Geertz described culture as "webs of significance which we ourselves have spun" and what we need to know is more about how those webs affect our choices and provide structures for our collective decisions. Religion (belief, faith, and practice), moral conviction, and cultural diversity are among the poor stepchildren in academic research, yet in most of the recent presidential elections they have provided swirling storms of controversy that have tossed about many an aspiring presidential vessel. Our socio-political context is like a micro-weather system with currents and pressures and constantly changing internal structures. The micro-weather system metaphor seems an apt one to describe the political and civic contexts in which we live out our lives. In order to better understand the ways that these forces affect the collective choices we make, we need to develop methodologies and structures of inquiry that enable us to analyze the complex interactions that produce our "socio-political weather."

We need to know:

- the role that strong moral convictions play in people's political behavior;
- the interaction between religious commitment, engagement, and strong moral convictions in determining electoral outcomes;
- the role that cultural diversity plays in attenuating and exacerbating these interactions;
- how changes in any of these factors and interactions affect the political process. (Think of the complex data-driven models for weather that we now have—only for politics instead.)

Working in the fields of sociology of religion, American ethnicity, and survey research since 1964, I've seen many attempts at analyzing the effects of one or more of these elements on electoral behavior. The problem is that scholars tend to chip away at reality from their own disciplinary points of view. We now have the ability to apply complex modeling methodologies to questions that require high levels of data integration, but we do not have the requisite frameworks for interdisciplinary scholarship to pursue these types of questions. We need new structures of inquiry—a scholarly network to integrate theories, experiments, and analyses that mirror the comprehensiveness of the simulation programs that are available to help us interpret these complex data.

My "weather model" analogy stems from the observation that meteorological science made a major leap forward when meteorologists came to realize that we exist at the bottom of an atmospheric ocean and that three-dimensional currents were the "stuff" of their predictive models and analyses. Politically, we live at the bottom of a three-dimensional socio-political-economic ocean and currents such as morality, religion, and culture produce an ever-changing environment that keeps surprising us and engulfing us from time to time. We need to know more about the nature and function of the organic and changing structure in which we live and we need a collaborative interdisciplinary intellectual method to accomplish this.

What we require is an ongoing scholarly dialogue that involves researchers from various disciplines who can put aside their discipline-specific perspectives and listen to one another and help one another understand the social facts before them. The scientists and engineers working at Los Alamos and the University of Chicago and Berkeley accomplished in concert what they could never have accomplished working independently. Regardless of one's perspective on the history of nuclear weapons, the Manhattan Project was, in the words of Fermi, "superb science." Who would have thought in 1942 that we could come to understand the nature of the atom and split it, yielding vast amounts of energy, within two years? The effort required that scientists and engineers collaborate in a unique manner. Not each working in their own habitat, but all working together to allow the synergies of their perspectives to focus on the problem before them. This is an excellent historic model for us to follow. These days we don't even have to move everyone to a "Los Alamos" research community—a virtual community would do just fine.

To learn what we need to know about the ways that the complex mix of religion, moral conviction, and cultural diversity affect us, we need a social science "Manhattan Project" that will focus our scholarship on producing models that better describe the currents within which we now live. For example, the work of social psychologists that examines the nature of moral conviction and its connection to political engagement has clear application to our understanding of political behavior, but even more it represents a research venue that begs for the collaboration of social psychologists with political scientists and economists and sociologists and historians to develop a comprehensive model of how moral convictions operate within the realm of personal political decisions. The same opportunities exist with regard to examining the interactive roles of culture and religion on civic engagement and political behaviors.

The key to understanding how religion, moral conviction, and cultural diversity operate within our social system is in knowing how people "belong" to the society and how they identify as part of groups within society. Belonging to a group provides a sense of security but it can also exacerbate intolerance of those outside the group. "Becoming an American" is much easier than belonging to more homogenous societies; you just agree to live by the rules set forth in the Constitution. (It's much more difficult to "become French" for example.) This feature of U.S. society is a combination of strength and weakness. Our diversity, a historic strength, requires that our civic discourse be a civil one, but that same diversity makes it difficult to engage in civil civic discourse amidst the storms produced by religious, moral, and cultural currents swirling throughout our social atmosphere.

What we need to know requires the "mapping" of those currents and their interactions and it requires a collaborative effort between social scientists of many stripes. Determining what we need to know is one thing; creating the intellectual environment within which we can learn it is quite another. While the effort is considerable, the outcome seems one that is worth pursuing in the light of an urgent need to better understand our civic interactions.

Of possible related interest: Chapters 33, 54, 57, **75**.

Suggested additional reading

Burger, Peter, and Thomas Luckman. *The Social Construction of Reality: A Treatise in the Sociology of Knowledge.* Garden City, NY: Doubleday, 1966.

Haidt, J. "The Emotional Dog and its Rational Tail: A Social Intuitionist Approach to Moral Judgment." *Psychological Review* 108 (2001): 814–834.

Skitka, L.J., and C.W. Bauman. "Moral Conviction and Political Engagement." *Political Psychology* 29 (2008): 29–54.

131

54

EQUALITY AND INCLUSIVENESS, DIVERSITY AND CONFLICT

John R. Petrocik
University of Missouri, Columbia

Equality and inclusiveness are defining properties of the contemporary democratic order. We usually do not ask "Who is eligible?" but it is a hard fact that societies do not easily include everybody (or "*just anybody*") among those eligible for equal treatment, even when the rhetoric and the public ethos—especially in the United States—condemn distinctions when they are group-based. The U.S. has always struggled with group-based divisions, and religious, ethnic, racial, and linguistic (hereafter termed "communal") divisions have trumped most other types (including gender barriers). We excluded slaves (later freed African-Americans) and the Native Americans who met the European settlers when the latter arrived in North America. Eligibility questions were raised about immigrants from Ireland, Scandinavia, Germany, Eastern Europe and Russia, and southern Europe. Protestant America questioned the American credentials of Catholics and, perhaps a bit more closely, Jews, when they arrived in large numbers (a great read here is Samuel Freedman's *The Inheritance: How Three Families and America Moved from Roosevelt to Reagan and Beyond*). Asians, Hispanics, and the other "new" immigrants have only made the inclusion questions more vexing.

The first solution for including strangers was assimilation into the English Protestant culture (a disputed course of action even then) and we are now *unsettled* on diversity (Milton Gordon offers a great history of this in his *Assimilation in American Life*).

The U.S. may manage the diversity-equality-inclusiveness dilemma better than most nations. But success notwithstanding, the very fact of our social diversity and the corresponding need to decide whether the newest "strangers" fit in have made equality and inclusiveness constant political issues for the American democratic order. Perspective is hard to achieve, and

132

academics have not managed to communicate a useful conceptual or empirical perspective.

What scholars need to study and report

Social diversity is a source of conflict. Social diversity places us within networks of common experiences that buttress a powerful tendency to create social identities. We look at the world through lenses shaped by these identities, others are inclined to see us in these terms, and the resulting categories influence our behavior toward each other. Not all identities are consequential and their salience is not constant. Those that shape our relationships can become insignificant; inconsequential differences can become important. But those that matter, when they matter, shape a relatively homogeneous milieu for similarly situated individuals who have similar experiences, leading in turn to an ever more distinctive group identity and group-based sets of beliefs.

Aggregated to the societal level, social identities create occasions for inter-group conflict because they provide an operating framework for political competition. Virtually all parties and candidates identify constituencies in social group terms, however much their rhetoric may lack group appeals. Political strategy and sincere commitments lead to political programs that promote group competition and group distinctions.

The challenge of explaining equality and inclusiveness

What needs better understanding in every democratic order is how salient communal identities are, how difficult it is to avoid them, how thoroughly they will dominate our relationships, and what institutions might moderate or exacerbate some of their consequences. The democratic political ethos of the twenty-first century views communal conflict as a breakdown, often promoted by self-interested political entrepreneurs. That is too simple, to the point of being simplistic. Social identities provide raw material for self-serving issue entrepreneurs, but communal conflict is a systematic manifestation of the tendency for individuals to form social identities around communal differences. A democratic order committed to equality and inclusiveness needs to manage social identities, not ignore or deny them.

In this "post-9/11 era" social identities may be more consequential than they were in the recent past. Traditionally, as Lijphart observed, "social homogeneity and political consensus are regarded as prerequisites for, or factors strongly conducive to, stable democracies." Horowitz's study of ethnic identity confirms Lijphart's assertion when he demonstrates how commonly the modern nation-state has been organized around a single social group. But the single-nation/single-state combination is rare in the current world, and migration has increased intra-nation diversity that often coincides with inter-nation conflicts. A better understanding of whether and how individuals manage ethnic loyalties while adopting or retaining the civic culture and common loyalty expected by the democratic order seems necessary for answering what are likely to be perpetual questions about who is eligible for inclusion and equal treatment.

Of possible related interest: Chapters **10**, *29, 31, 51, 52.*

Suggested additional reading

Gordon, Milton. *Assimilation in American Life: The Role of Race, Religion, and National Origins.* New York: Oxford University Press, 1964.

Freedman, Samuel G. *The Inheritance: How Three Families and America Moved from Roosevelt to Reagan and Beyond.* New York: Simon & Schuster, 1996.

Lijphart, Arend. *Democracy in Plural Societies: A Comparative Exploration.* New Haven, CT: Yale University Press, 1977.

Sidanius, J., and F. Pratto. *Social Dominance: An Intergroup Theory of Social Hierarchy and Oppression.* New York: Cambridge University Press, 1999.

55

THE END OF "THE PROTESTANT NATION"

Byron Shafer
University of Wisconsin

Political scientists argue about the shaping effect of religion on politics: does its influence come by way of theological positions, beliefs about social behavior, or organizational activities? Yet the argument is often vitiated by jumping between aspects of both religion and politics or, even worse, by just focusing on the latest incarnation of religious influence, whatever and wherever it is. In this regard, does anyone even remember that, within the adult life of Sid Verba, American politics has eradicated a major Protestant–Catholic division and seen the effective demise of Mainstream Protestantism? How did this happen?

America as the ultimate "Protestant Nation" is an eighteenth-century notion. The realization of Protestant (theological) themes in a new world—the possibility that things like personal responsibility, individual destination, or the priesthood of all believers, could be operationalized by way of a new national character—was present almost from the beginning. Subsequently, moral revivalist movements within Protestantism made major contributions to *political* upheavals, including both the Revolutionary War and the Civil War. The late nineteenth century then objectified all of this in a series of ongoing conflicts over how far Protestant themes could be driven into the specifics of governmental policy.

That story is familiar enough, as embodied in the ethnocultural interpretation of American political history. Yet the modern mythology is that these conflicts receded until, say, the 1980s, when the current evangelical renewal brought cultural issues, theologically tinged, back to center-stage. The point here is that this simply ignores the degree to which American politics at the end of World War II was structured essentially as Protestant–Catholic conflict. Rich Catholics *still* voted Democratic. Poor Protestants (outside the South) *still* voted Republican. The two branches of Protestantism may not have communed together, but they voted together. Catholics picked up the spare change, a scattering of "others" plus "none."

Flash forward to a world in which mainstream Protestants are politically indistinguishable from Catholics, a world in which religiosity itself, rather than denomination, increasingly structures politics. Simultaneously, there is promising new work about a growing (rather than declining!) role for the class cleavage in postwar American politics. Yet this does not appear to be the explanation for the decline of those religious cleavages, stretching all the way back to the founding, that gave definition to the notion of the "Protestant nation." They disappeared within the lifetime of almost everyone reading this volume. Why did they disappear (only) at this point? What did they morph into, or did they truly vanish? What else were the social forces that caused this transformation doing in American politics at the same time? Might we treat the entire story differently if we knew the answers?

Of possible related interest: Chapters **53**, 54, **63**, **75**.

Suggested additional reading

Kleppner, Paul. *The Cross of Culture: A Social Analysis of Midwestern Politics, 1850-1900*. New York: Free Press, 1970.

Layman, Geoffrey. *The Great Divide: Religious and Cultural Conflict in American Party Politics*. New York: Columbia University Press, 2001.

Shafer, Byron E. *The Two Majorities and the Puzzle of Modern American Politics*. Lawrence, KS: University Press of Kansas, 2003.

56

RELIGION AND POLITICS: A SOLEMN HIGH WARNING

The Political Force of Group Consciousness

Bill Schneider
CNN

In their 1972 book, *Participation in America: Political Democracy and Social Equality*, Sidney Verba and Norman H. Nie develop a "group consciousness model" of political participation as an alternative to the standard socioeconomic model: "It predicts that a sense of group consciousness leads citizens to participate well beyond what their socioeconomic status would predict" (p. 257). The model works particularly well for African-Americans whose participation rates matched or exceeded those of comparably educated whites.

Go back to 1987, when a Democratic-controlled Senate was voting on the confirmation of Robert H. Bork to the U.S. Supreme Court. Bork became a symbol of the most divisive issues in American politics, race, and religion. The most effective argument against Bork was that he wanted to upset the status quo on those issues. "The American people don't want to go backward on race, on privacy, on one-man one-vote, on free speech," Senator George J. Mitchell (D-ME) said in a radio address.

Southern Democrats held the key swing votes in the Senate. Their survival depended on holding together a fragile biracial coalition. Several southern Democratic senators got in touch with me to find out how their black constituents felt about the Bork nomination. I informed them that the polls showed very little support for Bork among black voters. The senators knew that, if they voted to confirm Bork, they would not only anger their black supporters but also risk re-opening racial wounds that had only just begun to heal.

On October 23, 1987, Bork was rejected by a vote of 58 to 42 in the Senate. Fifteen southern Democratic senators voted against his confirmation. Only two Democrats voted to confirm Bork (Ernest Hollings of South

Carolina and David Boren of Oklahoma). The overwhelming rejection of Bork by southern Democrats was clearly attributable to an energized black electorate, intensely conscious of its own interests.

Move forward to 1991, when the Democratic-controlled Senate was voting on the confirmation of Clarence Thomas to the Supreme Court. What started out as a confirmation hearing turned into a trial. Most speakers in the Senate debate focused on one issue: who was telling the truth, Thomas or his accuser, Anita Hill. Only a few senators bothered to address such issues as Thomas's constitutional philosophy, his judicial experience or his legal qualifications. Refusing to confirm Thomas became tantamount to declaring him guilty of sexual harassment. For most senators, it was a charge that could not be proved.

What clinched Thomas's victory was his decision to play the racial card. Thomas called the hearings "a high-tech lynching for uppity blacks" and accused his opponents of playing into "the most bigoted, racist stereotypes that any black man will face." Black support for Thomas shot up, from 54 percent favoring his confirmation before the hearings to 71 percent afterwards, according to a Gallup-CNN poll.

Southern Democratic senators were once again the key swing voters. Just like four years earlier, southern Democratic senators were eager to know how their black constituents felt about the Thomas nomination. I informed them that the polls showed strong support for Thomas among black voters (including black women).

Thomas was confirmed on October 15, 1991 by a vote of 52 to 48. Eight of the eleven Democrats who voted to confirm Thomas were southerners. When Thomas played the race card and won the sympathy of black voters, many southern Democratic senators came out for him and provided his crucial margin of confirmation. The fates of Robert Bork and Clarence Thomas were determined, more than anything else, by the response of black voters to their nominations.

At the same time, Anita Hill's testimony became a consciousness-raising event for women. Before her testimony, many men regarded sexual harassment as a joke. After her testimony, it was a crime. When Ronald Reagan moved the Republican Party to the right after 1980, a gender gap emerged in American politics. Women started voting more Democratic than men because they differed on issues like the use of force and the social safety net. The Anita Hill testimony added the element of group consciousness. 1992 became the Year of the Woman: voters elected 24 new women to the House of Representatives and five to the Senate.

The Thomas confirmation hearings became one of those rare occurrences—a true consciousness-raising event. Women were no longer just different, politically. They suddenly became conscious of their own distinctive needs and interests. It happened virtually overnight, as these events often do.

Having grown up in the South, I had witnessed a consciousness-raising event before. Prior to 1955, many southern whites allowed themselves to believe that segregation worked. When Rosa Parks refused to give up her seat to a white man on a Montgomery, Alabama, bus, it had a galvanizing impact on black consciousness. African-Americans gave voice to their rage and humiliation over being forced to live under segregation. Before 1955, blacks tended to vote Democratic because many of them were poor. After 1955, a new group consciousness emerged. They began to vote as blacks.

Group consciousness—often stimulated quite suddenly by sensational events—is a driving force in American politics. Verba and Nie discovered its power 25 years ago, when they wrote, "Group consciousness may substitute for the higher social status that impels citizens into political participation. It may represent an alternative mechanism for mobilizing citizens to political activity" (p. 151). That is precisely what we in the media have seen happen, again and again.

Of possible related interest: Chapters 10, 52, 57, **62**.

Suggested additional reading

Bishop, Bill. *The Big Sort: Why the Clustering of Like-Minded America is Tearing Us Apart*. Boston, MA: Houghton Mifflin, 2008.

Dionne, E.J., Jr. *Souled Out: Reclaiming Faith and Politics after the Religious Right*. Princeton, NJ: Princeton University Press, 2008.

57

GOING GLOBAL

New Challenges and Opportunities in Research on Democratic Participation and the Civic Culture

Pippa Norris

Harvard University

Over the past half-century since the Civic Culture study, the study of public opinion has gone global. What triggered these developments? And what are their implications for new research challenges in the study of political participation and cultural values?

Despite important transatlantic connections in the community of social scientists and market research organizations, the vast majority of political and social attitudinal surveys in the 1930s and 1940s were based on samples of the population in each nation. The use of dedicated cross-national surveys using a single common instrument or battery of questions—and thus the systematic analysis of cross-national public opinion—first arose with the 1948 study "How Nations See Each Other" by William Buchanan and Hadley Cantril, the USIA International Relations survey, the 1956 International Stratification survey by Harry B.G. Ganzeboom and Paul Nieuwbeerta, the 1957 Pattern of Human Concerns survey, also by Cantril, and above all the path-breaking and widely influential 1959 Civic Culture Study by Gabriel Almond and Sidney Verba.

This influential model triggered a quantum leap in the methods and concerns common in comparative political science. It was followed by a number of cross-national studies that investigated citizen participation as well as surveys, sometimes by multilateral organizations, that explored mass attitudes towards European integration and institutions and public commitments to materialist and post-materialist values. Reflecting the steadily expanding borders of the European Union, the Eurobarometer surveys, launched in 1974 and carried out every spring and fall since then, now cover 27 countries. The development of the Eurobarometer contributed directly towards the European Values Survey. Beginning in 1990 the survey was replicated as the World Values Study. This project has now carried out representative national surveys of the basic values and beliefs of the publics in more than 90 independent countries, containing over 88 percent of the world's population and covering all six inhabited continents.

During the half-century since the Civic Culture study, the availability of these and other cross-national datasets has revolutionized the study of public opinion. What facilitated these developments?

Many political and intellectual factors have contributed to the internationalization of attitudinal and behavioral surveys. For one thing, as the world has become more interconnected through globalization, the social sciences have been transformed by similar processes. The gradual expansion of the borders of the European Union has played a direct role, as the European Commission has monitored public opinion on a regular basis since the early 1970s through the Eurobarometer and related surveys of mass and elite opinion. In turn, the existence of the Eurobarometer, including the fieldwork organizations and collaborators, served as a model shaping many other initiatives, such as the 1979 European Elections Study and the 1981 European Values Study. Regional and international associations of political scientists have strengthened professional networks and institutional linkages, notably the International Political Science Association and the European Consortium of Political Research, with regular workshops and conferences that have bolstered intellectual and social networks among teams of collaborators.

Particular scholars in the field have had a decisive and enduring impact. Many colleagues have contributed to this process, in particular the early Civic Culture pioneers, Sidney Verba at Harvard University, and Gabriel Almond at Stanford. Other notable leaders include Jacques-Rene Rabier in the European Union, Ronald Inglehart at the University of Michigan, Jacques Thomassen at the University of Twente, and Roger Jowell at City University. All have served as intellectual leaders in the profession—initiating, managing, and sustaining major cross-national surveys that, in turn, have had multiplier effects through the funding of public opinion institutes and the training of the next generation of field-work staff and survey analysts.

The most recent spur has been the events of 9/11 and their aftermath in the Afghanistan and Iraq Wars, renewing American interest in public opinion in the rest of the world. In particular, this concern has stimulated new research in areas such as the Middle East where cross-national social science surveys have previously been nonexistent or scarce. These developments have gradually transformed the geographic scope of coverage, with an exponential surge in the available survey resources occurring during the last decade.

These resources provide new ways to globalize our understanding of comparative public opinion, allowing scholars to shift "from nations to categories," one of the key but elusive goals of comparative politics scholars. There are multiple methodological and technical challenges that continue to be raised by cross-national research into social and political attitudes—ranging from issues of conceptual equivalence to questions about the quality and standards used for questionnaire development and piloting, sampling, fieldwork, and analysis. Nevertheless, using these resources, the sub-discipline can build upon the insights of decades of studies to deepen insights into critical issues of democratic consolidation and cultural change.

Most importantly, the availability of many large-scale multi-national surveys covering many societies allows us to move from the analysis of countries to the study of public opinion under a wide variety of institutional and societal contexts, such as in developing and post-industrial economies, in predominately Muslim or Orthodox societies, in newer democracies in Mediterranean and Eastern Europe, or under democratic and autocratic regimes. Through this process, the sub-field is gradually moving from the comparison of individuals and groups within countries as the core unit of analysis towards the comparison of people living under different types of societies and regimes, a development that is capable of providing powerful new insights for the study of comparative politics. The study of global public opinion still needs to address fully the challenge of understanding cultural attitudes and values within a broader institutional context—such as how voting behavior is shaped by electoral systems, how attitudes towards democracy are influenced by regime performance, and how public participation responds to the legal context of civil liberties and political rights—but these sorts of issues represent an exciting and important new agenda for the next generation of researchers.

Of possible related interest: Chapters **25**, 37, **52**, **53**.

58

THE EFFECTS OF IMMIGRATION AND SENDING COUNTRIES' OUTREACH ON AMERICAN PUBLIC OPINION AND POLITICAL BEHAVIOR

Rodolfo O. de la Garza
Columbia University

The literature on public opinion and political behavior needs to be more attentive to the effects of migration. According to the International Organization for Migration, international migration has reached its highest level ever, and its growth is likely to continue. Social scientists and policymakers in the U.S. and immigrant-receiving countries therefore need to pay increased attention to immigration and its effects.

The significance of immigration for the industrialized states, especially in North America and Europe, is evident from the role they play as receiving countries: Of the 36 million who migrated between 1990 and 2005, 33 million wound up in industrialized countries, and 75 percent of all international migrants now live in only 28 countries. Migrants, in short, settle in a relatively small number of countries with one out of every four living in North America and one of every three in Europe

Although emigrants change the composition of constituencies in sending countries, the nonparticipatory character of many or most of those political systems suggests that even large outflows will not directly alter political processes in sending states. The democratic character of the major immigrant-receiving countries, by contrast, suggests that a large influx of immigrants has the potential to alter their political conditions substantially. Ongoing debates and events in countries such as the U.S., Holland, Germany, France, and Spain, to name a few, illustrate how increases in the number of immigrants can influence domestic politics. For these reasons it is imperative that studies of public opinion and political behavior do more than treat immigrants as minorities and develop approaches that not only analyze specific characteristics of these populations but go beyond that to measure the impact of home country political socialization on political outcomes in receiving states such as the U.S. Additionally, there is an increasing urgency to analyze the effect that increased home-county outreach initiatives have on immigrants. How many immigrants do they reach? Do they stimulate or impede political socialization into receiving countries? How do these interact with receiving country initiatives and institutions to affect the political incorporation of immigrants and national policy priorities? As immigration continues, such questions will only become more important to the understanding of electoral life in the U.S. and all immigrant-receiving states.

Of possible related interest: Chapters 30, 54, 73, 79.

Suggested additional reading

Zolberg, Aristide. *A Nation by Design: Immigration Policy in the Fashioning of America*. New York, and Cambridge, MA: Russell Sage Foundation and Harvard University Press, 2006.

59

EXORCISING
HUNTINGTONIAN SPECTERS

Ary Zolberg
New School for Social Research

Similarity between old and current unauthorized immigrants: We have good information regarding unauthorized immigrants legalized under the provisions of the 1986 Immigration and Reform Control Act (IRCA) thanks to two surveys conducted for the Department of Labor: the 1999 legalized population survey (LPS-1) conducted on a sample of 6193, and a 1992 follow-up (LPS-2) on a sample of about 4000 who had participated in the first survey.[*] About 70 percent came from Mexico; almost 80 percent of the men and 65 percent of the women reported finding a job within the first year. Many experienced initial downward mobility in comparison with their jobs in the country of origin but resumed their position after learning English and legalizing their status.

Although it is inherently difficult to obtain reliable information about undocumented aliens, researchers from the Migration Policy Institute have provided a persuasive 2004 estimate using the "residual method."[†] This estimates the unauthorized population as the total number of foreign-born counted in surveys and in the Census minus an estimate of the legally resident immigrant population based on birth, death, and legal immigration statistics. The resulting figures are then further adjusted for the likely under-enumeration of the unauthorized population in the database. In 2004, the foreign-born population of the U.S. reached 35.7 million

[*]The following is drawn from Mary G. Powers, Ellen Percy Kraly, and William Seltzer, "IRCA: Lessons of the Last U.S. Legalization Program," published in the Migration Policy Institute's (MPI) Migration Information Source, July 1, 2004. MPI is an independent research organization based in Washington, DC.
[†] Jennifer Van Hook, Frank D. Bean, and Jeffrey Passel, "Unauthorized Migrants Living in the United States: A Mid-Decade Portrait" published in the MPI's Migration Information Source, September 1, 2005.

persons, of whom approximately 10.3 million (29 percent of the foreign-born) were unauthorized. They had grown from about 3.5 million in 1990 to 8.5 million in 2000, that is, a net increase of about half a million per year during the 1990s, resulting from about 750,000 yearly arrivals and between 200,000 and 300,000 departures. A clear majority (57 percent) came from Mexico, another 24 percent from Central and South America; most of these entered by surreptitiously crossing the southern border; most of the remainder, 9 percent from Asia, 6 percent from Europe, and 4 percent from Africa, were "overstayers" who entered legally as visitors or students but remained beyond their authorized period. Today's unauthorized population is somewhat less concentrated than its predecessors. Young adults of working age are still clearly overrepresented (74 percent between 18 and 49) as against 46 percent of the native population. Their educational attainment tends to be lower than that of legal immigrants and natives. Contrary to common belief, they are only slightly more male (54 percent) than legal immigrants (48 percent) or natives (49 percent). They are no longer as concentrated in low-level agricultural jobs as commonly thought (in 2000, only 4.2 percent); the male level of participation in the labor force is similar to that of natives (85 percent versus 90 percent), but that of females is much lower (55 percent of women aged 25–44 versus 76 percent of natives). Accordingly, the poverty level among unauthorized is much higher than among natives or legal immigrants.

Of possible related interest: Chapters 30, 38, 54, 92.

60

ADDING IN SEX
DISCRIMINATION TO
LEGACIES OF WRONGDOING

Eileen McDonagh
Northeastern University

Most people, including political scientists, are well acquainted with the association of race discrimination with wrongdoing in the context of American political history. Too often, however, when we turn to gender, we find a narrative that ignores or detaches sex discrimination from stories about legal coercion or conflict, and in so doing, from the very development of the American state or analyses of contemporary American society. We can see the contrast by a comparison of the treatment of two egregious institutions present at the founding of the American state: chattel slavery and coverture marriage.

Yes, we know about slavery, and there are today concerted efforts to find ways to compensate for the way slavery robbed so many African-Americans of their social, economic, and political rights. In 2004, for example, eight descendants of slaves filed a $1 billion lawsuit against Lloyds of London, Fleet Boston, and R. J. Reynolds, on the grounds that these companies had profited as a result of supporting the institution of slavery. The plaintiffs were able to use DNA evidence to link themselves to African ancestors who had been victims of atrocities in the context of the slave trade. One of the plaintiffs, for example, Deadria Farmer-Paelmann, was able to make a direct connection between herself and the Mende tribe in Sierra Leone, a group of people who were routinely kidnapped, tortured, and shipped in chains to the U.S.

Similarly, Harvard law professor, Charles Ogletree, is among those planning a lawsuit to gain reparation compensation for African-American descendants of slaves. He notes the many precedents set by governments or companies that have offered apologies and monetary compensation for their roles in slavery or discrimination. A decade ago, for example, the U.S. paid $1.2 billion to Japanese-Americans to compensate in part for herding them into internment camps during World War II. Similarly, Germany and Austria paid hundreds of millions of dollars to Jewish victims of the Holocaust. The U.S. also has paid reparations to several American-Indian nations.

Institutionally, therefore, it is common to define the political history of the U.S. as one most marred by the presence, if not endorsement, at its Founding of the evil of slavery and, by extension, by the albatross of race discrimination that still follows. As Dinesh D'Souza emphasizes, even with the landmark civil rights legislation of the 1960s, race remains the most divisive social issue of our time.

Without in any way diminishing the significance of race in general or the legacy of slavery in particular as examples of wrongdoing in the development of the American state, it is also important to incorporate an understanding of the way gender in general and the institution of coverture marriage in particular historically limited women's full participation in American society, thereby constituting another legacy of wrongdoing whose effects are still felt today. At the Founding of the American state, for example, common law prevailed, which, according to the Blackstone Commentaries, defined marriage in terms of the husband and wife becoming one, where that one was the husband. Thus, married women until well into the nineteenth and even twentieth centuries were "civilly dead," and as such, could not in their own right sue or be sued, make contracts, draft wills, or buy or sell property, have the right to their own wages, have a right to participate in decisions about their children, or have the right to choose their domicile. In addition, wives did not even have civil rights in relation to their bodily integrity, since courts ruled that a husband had a right to discipline his wife by beating her, as long as the stick he used was no thicker than his thumb, from which the phrase, "rule of thumb," derives.

Redressing sex discrimination by means of legislation or court cases lags behind that of other subordinate groups in part, perhaps, because it is so difficult to see it as a "problem" in the first place. Consequently, men disadvantaged by class received the right to vote by means of state-level legislation in the early nineteenth century and African-American men by means of the Fifteenth Amendment in 1870. No women, however, had comparable voting rights until as late as 1920 with the addition of the Nineteenth Amendment to the Constitution. Similarly, in 1865, the Thirteenth Amendment was added to the Constitution to prohibit slavery, but it is not until as late as 1971, in *Reed v. Reed*, that the Supreme Court ruled that the principle underlying coverture marriage—the subordination of wives to their husbands—was unconstitutional. This, despite the fact that coverture marriage was an archetypical anti-liberal institution that deprived women of their civil rights. Equally significant, however, is the invisibility of the institutional history of coverture marriage and its discriminatory legacy. While most Americans accept slavery as the "original sin" marking the American state, they draw a blank if asked what they think about coverture marriage. Most are unfamiliar with the term, including the way it undermined women's chances for social, economic, or political equality.

Undoubtedly it is more difficult to identify coverture marriage as evil because women necessarily consented to the institution of marriage in contrast to slaves who by definition could not consent to the institution of slavery. However, therein lies a problem. As constitutional law scholar Reva Siegel notes, it is common to view women's experience of sex discrimination as a product of their own consent and/or public policies enacted to benefit and protect them. This rationale underlies widely diverse public policies from protective labor legislation for women in the early twentieth-century decades of the Progressive era, to today's coercively sex-segregated public restrooms and coercively sex-segregated sports teams, and to the 2008 Supreme Court decision in *Gonzales v. Carhart* that the prohibition of partial birth abortion rights is "good" for women, that is, that banning such procedures protects women from themselves by blocking their choice of such a procedure.

True, sex-segregated restrooms and sports teams may seem less significant than earlier forms of sex discrimination, such as the denial of voting rights, access to one's wages, or the right to serve on juries. However, let us not underestimate the social and political *meaning* of coercive sex segregation, whatever its form. The meaning underlying such policies is the assumption that women are inferior to men and, thus, need protection (such as protective labor regulations and "female-only" sports teams) or are only suited for traditional domestic roles as wives and mothers, and, thus, need to be separated from the public sphere of politics, such as voting arenas or jury duty. While the content of the public policy may vary in its centrality to participation in a democratic state, the real culprit in all coercive sex-segregated policies is their commonality of defining women as inferior in comparison to men and/or as only suited for one sphere of activity, the private sphere of the family, rather than both the private sphere and the public sphere of political governance. Such principles, whatever their policy content, undermine a view of women as equal to men, and, concomitantly, women's opportunities to participate equally with men in social, economic, and political environments.

There is a large and respectable body of scholarship in political science and related fields that challenges the idea that any form of *coercive* discrimination is beneficial to a subordinate group. I would like to see this perspective applied more consistently to all forms of coercive sex segregation. Doing so would provide an important supplement to the narrative of wrongdoing that focuses almost exclusively on race and slavery in the development of the American state to include recognition of the parallel legacy of sex discrimination. Adding in an understanding of the legacy of sex discrimination as a mode of wrongdoing expands our understanding of the historical and contemporary obstacles standing in the way of fulfilling the democratic promise of equality for all.

Of possible related interest: Chapters 25, 56, **62**, 94.

Suggested additional reading

Brown, Wendy. "Finding the Man in the State." *Feminist Studies* 18 (1992): 7–34.

Sapiro, Virginia. "Democracy Minus Women Is Not Democracy." In *Citizenship and Citizenship Education in a Changing World*, edited by Orit Ichilov. London: Woburn Press, 1998.

West, Robin. "Jurisprudence and Gender." *University of Chicago Law Review* 55 (1988): 1–72.

61

GENDER INEQUALITY

Nancy Burns
University of Michigan

Compared to many other inequalities, gender inequality is especially sneaky and resilient.

I think of it this way, first, because unlike some other inequalities, it is an inequality made among friends and family members and sometimes accommodated by women. Justified in the name of children, this inequality can seem powerfully functional. Historically, there would have been a serious layer of that kind of hostile sexism that sounds like racism. Not so much, now. Misogyny—like biologic racism—isn't said out-loud quite as much as it used to be.

When I say that it is different because it is made among friends and family, I mean that we act out this inequality on people we love, not just on strangers and acquaintances. We act it out on our children and partners. And, so, it can feel softer and more textured on the giving and receiving ends.

This family-centered aspect of gender inequality has two big parts. First, it is a way we organize our family life. It is a division of labor. And, as any family sociologist with systematic data will tell you, it takes pretty constant swimming upstream to keep traditional divisions of labor out of families, especially when those families have children in them.

I can imagine a world that is otherwise, that makes a division of labor around pregnancy, childbirth, and nursing temporary, not something that comes to shape lives together for the long run. Were that division of labor temporary, it would have much less chance of generating inequality.

The second part of family-centered roots of inequality is that we teach our daughters and sons what they are good at, where to find support for self-esteem. We often have gender-based expectations about abilities and interests. Scholars have demonstrated clearly the way sometimes tiny differences in parental and teacher expectations generate hierarchically different outcomes for daughters and sons, demonstrating with systematic data how self-fulfilling those expectations can be.

These family-centered inequalities could stop at the front door. But they don't. They feed into and provide rationales for inequalities in a host of

151

other social and political institutions. Other institutions organize them-selves around this family-centered inequality, making inequality cumulate in people's lives.

The second reason I find gender inequality sneaky and resilient is exactly that: that it often works subtly by cumulating across social spaces, across institutions. Partly this cumulation comes from the seeping out of division of labor at home. This seeping out helps ensure women access to worse jobs and lower incomes than men.

Sometimes institutions have narratives about why women should be discouraged from positions of power. Religious institutions come to mind. Sometimes the inequality is enacted without much of a narrative. The work-force is an obvious example here, with its connections to family work, with its assumptions about who should be telling whom what to do, with its assumptions about what women and men are good at, about what work they enjoy. Sometimes there is overt violence as well. But so much of the system that allots women and men jobs and prestige is not as blatant as that.

Almost all social situations and institutions make available the raw materials to make gender as hierarchy relevant. People use those materials. And so gender gets made and remade across resource-endowing institu-tions, not ever in a way that makes men less powerful than women, but also not always in a fully narrated way. It is sneakier than that. Gender inequality may be hard to eradicate because it is in most everything and, crucially, because its injustices often seem like small potatoes.

The small potatoes add up, though, to systematically lower levels of resources—resources like money, fancy jobs, and positions of leadership, resources that give people access to political power. They add up to lower levels of political action. Though it is a pretty messy counterfactual to contemplate because of the cumulation across so many social spaces within individuals' lives, I wonder what the political agenda would be like were it otherwise.

Of course, it is not otherwise.

And that brings me to my last point, the way politics itself could alter private inequalities. This third thing is that the inequality is not countered by powerful language offered up by social movements and political elites. This language could act as a repertoire to guide thought and action. I think of the language of the Civil Rights Movement this way, as a set of tools people can use, now, to analyze race in black and white.

When I think of the Women's Movement, I think its successes came more from calling into question essentialist accounts of gender than from putting wholly new accounts in place. I wonder whether part of the problem of generating such a new narrative comes from the small-potatoes way the inequality is often cumulated.

There is perhaps less cumulation of gender inequality now than there once was. One part of this is about narratives. Thanks to discourse entrepreneurs, we have more ways gender inequality is storied, now. Ordinary people have more tools to use to unthink gender hierarchy, to imagine a world without it.

In the end, I find gender inequality sneaky and resilient because:

- it is often privately, personally, lovingly, quietly enacted;
- it is linked to pregnancy, childbirth, and nursing, things that can make private inequality seem powerfully functional;
- it is made and remade across institutions;
- it often feels like small potatoes.

It is lacking many discursive entrepreneurs—activists who generate compelling words justifying equality, activists who give ordinary people a repertoire to use to think and act equally.

Of course, these characteristics have consequences for research. They mean that people may have a hard time finding the words to talk about gender inequality, that gender inequality may seem natural. They mean that researchers must often cumulate such inequalities—across time or across institutions—to see them. They mean that researchers interested in inequality have to look at, but also beyond, politics practiced in public to capture the way gender inequality is created and sustained. And they mean that it is illuminating to put gender inequality side by side with other inequalities, for the good comparative analysis can offer.

Of possible related interest: Chapters 10, 25, 62, 65.

Suggested additional reading

Burns, Nancy, Kay Lehman Schlozman, and Sidney Verba. *The Private Roots of Public Action: Gender, Equality, and Political Participation.* Cambridge, MA: Harvard University Press, 2001.

Goffman, Erving. "The Arrangement between the Sexes." *Theory and Society* 4 (1977): 301–333.

Jackman, Mary R. *The Velvet Glove: Paternalism and Conflict in Gender, Class, and Race Relations.* Berkeley, CA: University of California Press, 1994.

62

GENDER DIFFERENCES AS THE BASIS FOR A REFOUNDATION OF THE SOCIAL SCIENCES

The Political Integration of Women:
Explaining Women's Slow Advancement
into Political Office

Michele Swers
Georgetown University

The ascension of Nancy Pelosi to Speaker of the House marks a major milestone in the history of women's participation in American politics. However, the media attention lavished on Pelosi masks a more persistent trend in women's political participation, the slow pace of women's integration into political office. Indeed, in comparison to their numbers in the general population, women are greatly underrepresented at all levels of political office. For example, in the halls of Congress women constitute only 16 percent of the membership in the House and Senate. Furthermore, the political representation of women in the U.S. lags behind the advancement of women in other developed nations, particularly the Nordic countries where the proportion of women in the lower house of Parliament ranges from 37 percent in Denmark to 47 percent in Sweden.*

While scholars have spent years examining the institutional and sociological factors that contribute to women's underrepresentation in elective office, we have yet to develop a consensus around the primary factors that contribute to this imbalance in order to inform efforts at reform. With regard to institutions, scholars note that American women are disadvantaged by an electoral system that features weak parties, candidate-centered

*Interparliamentary Union 2007, http:// www.ipu.org/wmn-e/world.htm.

154

campaigns, a strong incumbency advantage, and single-member districts in which candidates need only win a plurality of votes rather than a system of proportional representation with strong parties that control nominations or even quota systems. Yet, the stickiness of institutions makes institutional reform a difficult target. Incremental reforms such as the adoption of term limits in many state legislatures have not been beneficial to women. Susan J. Carroll and Krista Jenkins find that in many states the dearth of women in the political pipeline meant that term-limited women were not replaced by other women.

The inadequacy of institutional explanations has led many scholars to seek out cultural and sociological explanations for women's slow political advancement. These explanations focus either on the voters and their willingness to support a female candidate or on the socialization of women and how these experiences inhibit women's efforts or desire to become a candidate for office. Research that focuses on voters points to the potential negative impact of gender stereotypes on voters' evaluation of candidates. Other scholars such as Barbara Palmer and Dennis Simon take a more macro-level approach. In their book, *Breaking the Political Glass Ceiling: Women and Congressional Elections*, they seek to identify the characteristics of districts that are more likely to elect women, for example, districts that are more ideologically liberal and more urban.

Scholars who view socialization as the primary culprit for women's underrepresentation in elected office focus on women's traditional place in the private rather than the public sphere and the status of women as the primary caregiver for children and families. It is well known that women who run for office are on average older than their male counterparts because they are more likely to wait until their children are older. House Speaker Nancy Pelosi personifies this trend. Elected in 1987, the 47-year-old Pelosi raised her five children before she capitalized on her credentials as a Democratic Party activist to win a seat in Congress. More recently, Jennifer Lawless and Richard L. Fox have focused on another feature of socialization, gender differences in levels of political ambition. Surveying women who hold occupations that serve as springboards for political careers, Lawless and Fox report that women are less likely than men to say they have thought about running for office and men are more willing to take the steps to run for office without encouragement from others. The persistence of sociological norms would suggest an entirely different set of reforms such as increased recruitment efforts aimed at women by parties and organized groups and educational programs designed to encourage young women to consider running for office.

Clearly, the potential causes of women's slow advancement into political office are numerous. Scholars need to more carefully identify the relative importance of the institutional, sociological, and cultural barriers to the election of women at all levels of government. A fuller and more nuanced understanding of these barriers will lead to more informed proposals for reform.

Of possible related interest: Chapters 26, **56**, **60**, **94**.

Suggested additional reading

Carroll, Susan J., and Krista Jenkins. "Do Term Limits Help Women Get Elected?" *Social Science Quarterly* 82 (2001): 199–203.

Lawless, Jennifer L., and Richard L. Fox. *It Takes a Candidate: Why Women Don't Run for Office*. New York: Cambridge University Press, 2005.

Palmer, Barbara, and Dennis Simon. *Breaking the Political Glass Ceiling: Women and Congressional Elections*. New York: Routledge, 2006.

63

IS AMERICA BECOMING
A MORE CLASS-BASED
SOCIETY?

Robert D. Putnam
Harvard University

Understanding the causes and consequences of large-scale social change has been a primary responsibility of social inquiry since the emergence of social science in the nineteenth century. Many social changes are so dramatic and visible that they come to be labeled "revolutions"—the industrial revolution, the democratic revolution, the women's revolution, the civil rights revolution, and even the internet revolution. Understanding major changes of this sort is important both because they encourage intellectual breakthroughs by social scientists and because they are important to our fellow citizens.

America may now be in the midst of another social transformation that deserves study. Over the last three or four decades social class differences in life chances have increased along several crucial dimensions. Most widely discussed is the growth in income inequality since the early 1970s, but this is not the only sign that class matters more now. In an era in which residential segregation by race and religion has been steady or even declining, residential segregation by social class has increased. In an era in which both religious and racial endogamy (the tendency to marry within one's religion or race) have declined, class endogamy has increased. Voluntary associations are less likely now to bring people from different classes together. And in an era in which the persistence of a racial "achievement gap" has occasioned much warranted concern, almost no one has noticed the growth of a class gap among white adolescents. Research currently underway suggests that over the last 30 years, among white children from upper-middle class backgrounds, civic involvement, social trust, self-esteem, parental attention, church attendance, academic self-confidence, and academic aspirations have all increased, whereas all these predictors of life success have declined among white children from working class backgrounds. All these changes suggest the possibility that (quite apart from continuing racial differences) social class in America may be becoming more caste-like, as children from the two sides of the tracks live increasingly separate and unequal lives.

If that conjecture were confirmed, it would mark an important change from America's historical class structure. America's social contract has traditionally countenanced inequality in outcomes in exchange for equality of opportunity, but that rough bargain may now be being broken. Thus, three fundamental issues arise:

- Is this conjecture about growing class segregation and class inheritance accurate, when tested more rigorously than I have yet done?
- If so, why? Some conservatives suggest that these trends may be the inevitable concomitant of increasing meritocracy, whereas progressives will wonder about more malign, structural influences.
- So what? Given the low salience of overtly class conflict in American history, it would be imprudent to expect class segregation or even class inheritance automatically to produce a class-based politics. Nevertheless, it would be even more imprudent to ignore the potential long-run social, political, and moral consequences of a system in which life chances are increasingly fixed at birth.

Of possible related interest: Chapters 41, 48, 55, 87.

Suggested additional reading

Neckerman, Kathryn M., ed. *Social Inequality.* New York: Russell Sage, 2004.

64

THE NAACP NOBODY
KNOWS

Rick Valelly
Swarthmore College

Why do the stakeholders in the National Association for the Advancement of Colored People (NAACP) participate in it in the ways that they do—and with what intended and unintended consequences within and beyond the organization itself? One would think that by now we would know the answers because there would have been a good political science study of the NAACP. It is, after all, almost a century old, plenty of time to arouse curiosity. Its centennial is just two years away from the time of this essay's composition. Also, it is one of the few truly federated national organizations with state and local chapters. Unlike many national organizations it is not based in Washington, DC—instead, its headquarters are in Baltimore. In that respect it is well suited for testing Theda Skocpol's claims about the cross-class, civic educational, and policy-implementing roles of federated organizations such as the American Legion and the black fraternal organizations (think here of the Prince Hall Masons) about which she and her co-authors have written recently.

Political science is a discipline that has long focused on formal and informal organizational life and behavior. Recognizing that robustly organized groups mobilize and convey political influence, political scientists have enjoyed puzzling over who organizes, why, and how—and who *doesn't* organize, why, and how. Simply by being there—and having talented lobbyists such as Clarence Mitchell with access to President Lyndon Baines Johnson and Senate leaders—the NAACP had productive influence.

Then, too, political scientists have had little trouble accepting Mancur Olson's elegant formulation of the collective action problem. Participation is a complex mix of costs and benefits for one thing. Who can afford the different mixes will say much about the extent to which Schattschneider's famous quip about the group system—that the "heavenly chorus sings with an upper class accent"—holds true. Simply by overcoming the collective action problem and surviving the NAACP long subverted the notion that only the powerful organize.

So, to repeat, it is something of a puzzle that there is no study of the NAACP. So far as I know there is not even a journal article by a political scientist that treats the NAACP.

Some of the problem may be the NAACP's apparent—but only apparent—stodginess. We now know from Aldon Morris's work on the localized nature of the civil rights movements that the protest organizations which captured the imagination of so many political scientists were actually spin-offs from NAACP chapters. But many persist in believing that "the movement" scooped the NAACP because, the story goes, it had been unconscionably incrementalist and timid.

Part of the lack of attention too is that there have been few incentives for a study of the NAACP. Instead there has been a welcome interest in the alternative of developing large-N and rigorously behavioral studies. Political scientists have turned with increasing sophistication and subtlety to nonelectoral participation and its arresting biases. Think of the path-breaking collaboration to study "voice and equality" among Henry Brady, Nancy Burns, Kay Schlozman, and Sidney Verba—or the work by Jeffrey Berry, Kay Schlozman and John Tierney, and Jack Walker on the dense interest-group universe that has emerged in Washington in the last 50 years. To put it another way, if anyone thought about studying the NAACP they may have worried that they would end up without a job and an unpublished, thick-descriptive bag of observations.

But on reflection it is easy to see that the NAACP is itself a large-N universe all its own. The number and vigor of its many national, state, and local parts have waxed and waned in ways that we know only in bare outline. What are the actual patterns? And what explains them? In pointing out these obvious questions I have returned full circle to where I began—and reiterated the puzzle and challenge that the lack of attention to the NAACP poses for the profession.

It won't be easy—and it will probably require a team. Also there isn't much of a nonsocial science literature on the NAACP. There are memoir-istic accounts, there are biographies of NAACP leaders, there are histories of key periods in the NAACP's existence, including a magnificent recent study, *The Ticket to Freedom*, by the German historian Manfred Berg. Also, there is a fine study by the legal scholar, Mark Tushnet, of the Legal Defense Fund's school desegregation campaign. But that's about it.

On the other hand, if you are looking for a model there is Maryann Barakso's sprightly and highly informative case study of an organization some people consider similar to the NAACP, *Governing NOW*. And, I have a dataset of NAACP membership figures for Southern states for the 1940s and 1950s collected from the (nonmicrofilmed) NAACP Papers at the Library of Congress.

To paraphrase Henny Youngman, take my dataset, please.

Of possible related interest: Chapters **86**, *87, 88, 98.*

Suggested additional reading

Skocpol, Theda. *Diminished Democracy: From Membership to Management in American Civic Life.* Norman, OK: University of Oklahoma Press, 2003.

65

AT THE INTERSECTION OF INEQUALITIES

Shauna L. Shames
Harvard University

Political equality is a fundamental tenet of democracy, and political scientists have long sought to understand the explanations for and consequences of its lack. Over the past four decades, important works in the American and Comparative subfields have contributed to our knowledge. We know, for instance, that inequalities in the political arena often stem from inequalities in the economic and social spheres. We know that inequalities seem to track membership in various types of identity-based groups. And we know that these inequalities on the whole appear to be persistent, rather than rotating; certain groups are nearly always advantaged and others disadvantaged.

What we do not yet know is how categories of identity intersect to produce more or less advantaged groups and group members. The prominence of inequalities at all levels of American life, and their implications for public participation, has been a running theme through recent American political science studies. Together, these works help to illuminate the necessary next step for our discipline: addressing the intersections of inequalities.

Contemporary feminist writings, particularly from women of color, speak to the power of intersectionality (see, e.g., works by Kimberlé Crenshaw, Angela Harris, and the Combahee River Collective). Inequalities, when layered, are not additive but multiplicative. Therefore, studying such inequalities individually misses a large part of the story. As Mary Hawkesworth demonstrated in a 2003 *APSR* study, U.S. Congresswomen of color undergo distinctive marginalization based on a process of "racing-gendering" that is about neither race nor gender alone. Previous studies of women in legislatures missed this process, she explains, because the literature has not considered that political institutions themselves produce and reproduce raced/gendered experiences. Only by focusing her lens on the interaction between racing and gendering in the 1996 welfare reform debates was Hawkesworth able to illuminate the particular forces operating to render invisible the Congresswomen of color, along with their work and policy priorities.

Such intersectionality is often prohibitively difficult to study. Each time we add in an axis of inequality (race, class, education, gender, religion, etc.), we divide our sample, reducing the amount of data available to draw conclusions. Employing interaction terms requires collecting yet more data; analyzing the intersection of all these types of inequalities would necessitate intensive data collection on groups notoriously difficult and expensive to study (the homeless, say, or small populations like disabled Latinas). Even after overcoming these hurdles, analysis of survey or roll-call vote data—and statistical methods more generally—can take us only so far. Dealing seriously with the complexities of intersecting identities necessarily triggers data difficulties like endogeneity, collinearity, and multiple causation. Despite sophisticated statistical methods, the standard goal of regression analysis (isolating the effects of individual variables) may not help (or indeed, may impede our ability) to fully understand the construction and functioning of hierarchies based on intersectionality. We must work to pair quantitative data with qualitative methods that help us frame and interpret results.

Such a question—how to study the intersections of inequalities—is part and parcel of a larger, perennial, social science question: how shall we study power? For we are, and should be, concerned with inequalities because of the power differential they imply. Power, however, is notoriously tricky to measure or even define. Power differentials create and sustain inequalities through complex mechanisms we have yet to understand. Then again, these mechanisms are themselves a product of inequalities. Endogeneity tends to rear its ugly head when we use statistical methods to study such cycles. Yet I venture to suggest that the production and reproduction of inequalities are indeed cyclical, and, worse, are based largely on the inequalities them-selves. As feminist political scientists have taken pains to point out, gender deeply shapes our understanding of power. Political scientists of color convincingly argue the same about race/ethnicity. If the ways in which we think about power are already steeped in power, if the very language we use reinforces existing inequalities, then we shall have to be careful indeed in our concept definitions, methods, and conclusions.

The study of power and politics, our discipline, is itself a site of politics and power. Political scientists are hardly immune to the operation of intersecting inequalities. In a recent essay in *Politics and Gender Journal*, Melissa Harris-Lacewell writes that black women political scientists offer stories and perspectives rendered silent in research by their white male colleagues. Power for these women, she explains, is more than an abstract concept. Their vastly different life experiences include personal and community-based experiences of race/class/gender discrimination and exploitation, leading them to formulate new research agendas, to focus on overlooked populations, and to ask questions in a different way than those who currently dominate political science. Such an understanding calls into question the value of ever studying gender, race, education, or class alone.

These are not easy questions: how do we define and study power? What is its role in creating and perpetuating inequalities? How do inequalities grow, build, and intersect? Can we as a discipline, itself a site of power relations and inequalities, objectively address these questions? Yet the challenge is precisely the point. Too many of the graduate students I know are content to work within accepted frameworks of research, using easily obtained data. This leaves us, as a discipline, in the situation of the proverbial drunk looking for his keys not where he dropped them, but where the street light shines brightest.

Taking seriously the power of intersectionality is of more than merely academic interest. Inequalities between the haves and have-nots are on the rise globally. In the U.S., inequalities persist along multiple axes, including (but not limited to): race, ethnicity, income, sex, gender, sexual orientation, religion, immigrant status, education, dis/ability, size, age, and more. The impact of these inequalities and their intersections on politics, policy, public life, and political science is yet to be fully understood. Using intersectionality as a lens for political science research will help us to study power more realistically and to better understand the inequalities that haunt our claims of democratic legitimacy.

Of possible related interest: Chapters **10**, **42**, 48, **61**.

Suggested additional reading

Cohen, Cathy J. *The Boundaries of Blackness: AIDS and the Breakdown of Black Politics*. Chicago, IL: University of Chicago Press, 1999.

Hawkesworth, Mary. "Congressional Enactments of Race–Gender: Toward a Theory of Raced–Gendered Institutions." *American Political Science Review* 97 (2003): 529–550.

Strolovitch, Dara Z. *Affirmative Advocacy: Race, Class, and Gender in Interest Group Politics*. Chicago, IL: University of Chicago Press, 2007.

66

THE PROFESSIONAL
CAMPAIGN

Ganesh Sitaraman
Harvard Law School

One of the great transformations in the American political realm is the professionalization of electoral campaigns. Presidential campaigns now begin over two years before the election, and speculation begins the day after an election. Campaigns spend hundreds of millions of dollars on mobilization and advertising. And entire industries of professional operatives and consultants have sprung up, always ready to begin the next campaign. Such constant campaigning is unknown in other countries. Our British brethren still begin political campaigns some 21 days before an election. Television advertisements at the constituency level are rare. And total costs are far less. The campaign is perhaps the most influential and important institution in the American political process, but our knowledge of political campaigns is at best rudimentary.

With a newfound willingness for qualitative studies, we must consider what we can learn from the nuts and bolts of the campaign. We must be willing to delve deep into the heart of the campaign in order to understand what drives campaign consultants. How do pollsters shape data analysis? What mobilization and organizational approaches do strategists and campaign managers adopt? How do strategy and tactics unite to influence and engage voters? How much does political commentary and spin determine the winners and losers? Are strategists and political journalists the new "bosses"?

Political philosophers too must reflect on what these various strategies say about the nature of American politics—does tacking to the middle imply a different understanding of democracy than mobilizing the base? Does our political language and strategy influence, purify, or corrupt our visions of the public good? Is the professionalization of the campaign necessary and beneficial?

The pervasive and significant influence of the professional campaign requires extraordinary attention of political scientists. Engaging these questions will bring political science back into the most dynamic parts of the political realm—and will lead to greater knowledge about politics itself.

Of possible related interest: Chapters 9, 47, **68**, 69.

Suggested additional reading

Thurber, James A., and Candice J. Nelson, eds. *Campaign Warriors: Political Consultants in Elections.* Washington, DC: Brookings, 2000.

Thurber, James A., and Candice J. Nelson, eds. *Campaigns and Elections American Style: Transforming American Politics.* 2nd ed. Boulder, CO: Westview Press, 2004.

67

WHAT POLITICIANS ACTUALLY CAN DO

A Modest Proposal for Reporting on Campaigns

Daniel Schlozman
Harvard University

I live in the People's Republic of Cambridge, whose foreign policy, a longstanding issue in local elections, has absolutely nothing to do with our AAA bond rating or our troubled schools. Our relations with Cuba may be a charming local quirk, but they open up a more basic point about explaining what matters in public life. Journalists, who more than political scientists explain politics to the public, ought to pay more attention to explaining what political science has told us as regards what the officials chosen in the contest can and will actually *do* in the job, as opposed merely to repackaging the candidates' positions and self-presentations.

Political scientists know a tremendous amount about what elected officials of varying stripe can—and cannot—get accomplished. When they report about public officials at work, journalists have learned many of our lessons: they report about how first-term members of Congress learn about their new jobs, or how lobbyists approach committees, or the ways that governors exercise power through appointments to boards and commissions. Yet, too rarely is that knowledge transferred from governing to seeking office. Rather, coverage even of the horse race too often degenerates into parroting and parsing claims not terribly germane to the office at hand.

Candidates face two temptations on which journalists should call them: they can seek to appear overly moderate; or they can exaggerate their influence. On the first score, a generation's work on polarization has shown that parties matter, and that the "independent fighter" is probably not. Even if candidates genuinely want to build bridges to the other party, the circumstances are stacked against them. Yet most voters aren't paying attention. The hope, therefore, is to teach the activists who are. One hopes they could learn something about what—in a rather bewildering system—

a variety of institutions actually do, and also about the compromises endemic to them: work on rules and bargaining has formalized this basic insight. As things stand, candidates grandstand too often unchallenged about problems that they (ought to) know they cannot solve, often debating ideological purity on matters far from the job's expertise. The more ideologically extreme the constituency, I think, the worse the problem. These are, to some extent, signaling mechanisms, designed for candidates to show voters their true colors. Fine, but that should be noted.

The second temptation applies particularly to Congress. Although they sometimes feign omnipotence when they campaign, members of the House are specialists; in local debates, candidates seeking open seats, therefore, should be asked about what committees they would seek to join, not simply about the details of their never-to-be-enacted healthcare bill. Or they should be asked about how they expect to act as legislators—not always apparent from their campaign style or home style. Will they orate on the floor or make deals behind closed doors? So, too, political science has much to teach about administration, lessons that the media ought to heed in campaigns as well as in covering the work of government. Given the way that dollars with strings attached flow from Washington to state capitols, candidates for governor should explain themselves as administrators. How will they staff agencies and authorities—with strong supporters (who risk insufficient independence) or with technocrats (perhaps devoid of vision)?

Because campaigns offer such a public arena for political science to explain its findings, they can serve as an important civics classroom for voters, and even for nonvoters. My modest suggestion probably does not ask journalists to learn anything new, merely to apply what they already know. And while I, like many of us, would wish for more coverage of issues and less about the horse race, my suggestion asks merely to reframe existing coverage. Whether changing journalistic practice would meaningfully affect participation or outcomes is, of course, another matter. However, if the distemper in American politics comes at least in part from activists' inability to accept the slow, ordinary business of government that follows from elections—with consequences such as the permanent campaign and politics by other means—then asking the journalists to reckon in campaigns with what elected officials can actually do seems like a good place to start.

Of possible related interest: Chapters **36**, **66**, **68**, 94.

68

ELECTIONS: FIVE RULES FOR COMMENTATORS

John Mark Hansen
University of Chicago

Modern political science has devoted more energy to the study of elections than to any other subject. The very earliest applications of multivariate statistics, by pioneers such as Harold Gosnell in the 1920s, investigated electoral behavior. The American National Election Studies, which date to 1952, are the longest continuous nongovernmental data collection enterprise in all the social sciences.

In that time, political scientists have learned a good many things that help scholars, journalists, pundits, and curious citizens to put the particulars of an election into a context for understanding. Although every election is different—the candidates change, the issues change, the times change, and the voters change—every election also fits within a regular pattern. The quality of election analysis would be much the better to recall five of the most significant regularities:

1. The most important influences on the outcomes of elections are already set by the time the nominees are selected. Many election analysts speak of several election "fundamentals": the baseline partisanship of the electorate, the condition of the nation's economy and foreign affairs, and incumbency. The baseline partisanship of the electorate—the proportions of voters who think of themselves as Republicans or Democrats—sets a limit on the performance of any candidate. It was easier for Democratic candidates to win elections in the 1960s, when Democrats outnumbered Republicans, than it is now, when partisanship is more closely balanced. The conditions of the nation's economy and foreign relations either aid or impede the two candidates.

Voters reward the party of the president for peace and prosperity and punish it for war and worry. Finally, the powers and allure of office are powerful electoral assets. Even in presidential elections, incumbents gain upwards of four percentage points on the strength of incumbency alone.

Taken together, the fundamentals place a close limit on election outcomes. Republicans stood little chance to win the White House in 1964, Democrats little chance in 1984, but 1960 and 1976 were bound to be close. After taking these major structural conditions into account, the safest course to anticipate the outcome is to disregard the horserace polls and ignore most of what happens in the actual campaign.

2. Voters only intermittently pay attention to campaigns, so most of what happens in a campaign has little effect on voters' choices. Voters make their decisions whenever they feel they have enough information to make a choice. For many, the decision is not very difficult. A majority of voters, sometimes as many as two-thirds, claim to have made up their minds by the close of the conventions. Others wait longer, stepping up their attention as the deadline, Election Day, draws near. At any given point in the campaign, the number of people attending more than lightly is very small. When asking what effect some event—an endorsement, a gaffe, a new advertisement—will have on the outcome of the election, the best answer is almost always "not much."

3. Despite intermittent attention, over the course of a campaign, voters learn a great deal about the candidates and the issues. For voters, the most important fact about the campaign environment is that the flow of information about the candidates and issues is two-sided. When elections are competitive—in the sense that the candidates are well matched in resources, which is always the case in presidential elections but often not the case in congressional elections—voters receive both positive and negative information about the candidates from the charges and counter-charges that issue from the campaigns. The balance between positive and negative information means that voters can evaluate any new information about a candidate relative to leanings they have developed from a large store of previously acquired information. Accordingly, the impact of new information, either positive or negative, is more limited the further the campaign progresses. In a competitive, two-sided-information environment, campaigns are not easily won with "smoke and mirrors."

4. The outcome of the election is seldom as much in doubt as the swings in the polls seem to indicate. Confronted by a pollster's demand for a choice, weeks before voters actually must make one, survey respondents report preferences based on considerations that most immediately come to mind. Still far from having to make a choice, voters still economize on attention, and so the considerations at hand are shaped by the current reports in the media. As voters settle down to the business of making a real choice, they acquire more information, which tends overwhelmingly to reinforce them either in their preexisting partisan allegiances—however

unattractive the party's nominee, in the fierce light of a decision he usually looks better than the alternative—or in their evaluations of the performance of the current administration. Until the end of the campaign, that is, the horserace polls are a better indicator of the content of the media coverage of the campaign than a predictor of the outcome of the campaign.

5. Most true electoral change is very slow. The tendency the day after the election is to believe that the world has changed. Winners like to believe it, and observers are happy to indulge them. To be sure, most elections mark a readjustment of the partisan balance in Congress or a turn in partisan control of the White House. But even a "landmark" election does not indicate or portend massive change in the electorate. Candidates succeed and fail having little to do with the quality of the campaigns they ran. Most election outcomes are the expression of momentary pleasure or fleeting frustration with the status quo. True change in the fundamental partisan orientations of the electorate—in party identification—changes on a secular time scale, over decades, as younger voters and new citizens take the place of older voters. Do not look to the last election to discern the direction of the nation. Look to the partisanship in formation in the rising generation of new adults and new citizens.

Of possible related interest: Chapters **30**, **34**, **66**, **67**.

Suggested additional reading

Green, Donald P., Bradley Palmquist, and Eric Schickler. *Partisan Hearts and Minds: Political Parties and the Social Identities of Voters*. New Haven, CT: Yale University Press, 2002.

Rosenstone, Steven J. *Forecasting Presidential Elections*. New Haven, CT: Yale University Press, 1983.

69

NEGATIVE ADS—CYNICAL PUBLIC?

Arthur Sanders
Drake University

We all hate "negative ads" in political campaigns. And the common wisdom is that they distort the truth, coarsen campaigns, alienate voters, raise levels of public cynicism, and harm our democracy. But careful, systematic scientific study by political scientists of both the content of such ads and the ways in which people process the information they receive from these ads shows us that such ads provide valuable information for citizens about candidates and issues, information that does, in fact, make them better-informed voters who are more strongly connected to the political process. In fact, there is much evidence to indicate that the emotional responses that these ads provoke and the information that they provide allow citizens to learn more from "negative ads" than from so-called "positive ads." Furthermore, the information and emotional connections that these ads provide draws at least as many citizens into the political system, as it drives away. This does not mean that there are not negative ads that are deceptive, misleading, or unfair. But the focus of the media on this limited subset of cases, or the piling together of these cases of deceptive ads into a broader condemnation of "the negativity" of campaigns, may be at least as responsible for the cynicism about our political system that concerns so many as the actual content of the ads we so quickly blame. Better understanding of what we know about negative ads by those in the media and by the public at large, would place these ads into a clearer context and make the positive attributes that political scientists have identified have an even healthier effect on our democratic processes.

Of possible related interest: Chapters **24**, **34**, **66**, **68**.

Suggested additional reading

Geer, John. *In Defense of Negativity: Attack Ads in Presidential Campaigns.* Chicago, IL: University of Chicago Press, 2006.

Lau, Richard, and David Redlawsk. *How Voters Decide: Information Processing during Election Campaigns.* New York: Cambridge University Press, 2006.

Marcus, George, W. Russell Neuman, and Michael Mackuen. *Affective Intelligence and Political Judgment.* Chicago, IL: University of Chicago Press, 2000.

70

INDEPENDENT ELECTORAL COMMISSIONS

Nahomi Ichino
Harvard University

Under what conditions is the independence of an electoral commission established and respected? Why and under what conditions do politicians or governments interfere or refrain from interfering in institutions that can award them political power with some degree of legitimacy?

Many countries in the developing world hold elections for president and other high offices, contested by politicians and political parties that have access to the means to capture those offices through fraud and intimidation. Only about half of the elections in sub-Saharan Africa since 1990 have been considered mostly free and fair, without irregularities that likely affected the outcome. In nearly one-quarter, the opposition engages in a partial boycott, and in nearly one-third, the losers refuse to accept the outcome. Common in these elections is the charge of an uneven playing ground, created by unequal access to media and state funds and an electoral commission under the influence of the incumbent party.

Electoral commissions are generally charged with voter registration, certification of the eligibility of candidates and political parties to contest office, and the organization of the election itself. They tabulate and certify voting results, decide whether to call for a run-off election, and declare a winner. At each of these stages, an electoral commission may favor one contestant over another and sometimes do so, disqualifying particular candidates or political parties and certifying the results of obviously problematic elections. More subtly, they may refuse to issue credentials to particular organizations that wish to send election observers, they may hire electoral officers who supervise the polling stations on the basis of political recommendations, or they may print ballots without serial numbers so that it is easier to stuff a ballot box. They may fail to purge deceased voters or multiple or under-age registrants from the voters register in incumbent government strongholds, or they may fail to assign enough polling stations or send enough ballot boxes and papers to pro-opposition areas. One only need to look at the presidential elections in Nigeria in 2007 and in Zimbabwe in 2008 to see the myriad of ways in which electoral commissions affect election outcomes. But, remarkably, given what is at stake, electoral commissions have served as imperfect but reasonably neutral rule-writers, competent executors, and unbiased referees in many other elections.

Our discipline has made significant progress in the analysis of how electoral rules and other formal regulations affect voting decisions and voter participation, as well as some of the factors that affect the adoption of particular rules. We have recently begun to study when political actors, in the context of these formal rules, try to affect voter behavior in their favor through vote buying and intimidation. Our understanding of who wins political office and how would be greatly improved by a complementary analysis of when such illicit activities are de facto permissible and of when these are replaced by political influence over the electoral commission and other centralized, less "retail" strategies of securing an electoral victory.

Of possible related interest: Chapters 25, 30, 66, 68.

71

WATCH OUT! THE UNITS YOU ARE COMPARING MAY NOT BE WHAT THEY USED TO BE

Philippe C. Schmitter
European University Institute

When Aristotle gathered data on the "social constitutions" of 158 Greek city-states, he set an important and enduring precedent for future comparativists. The apposite units should be from the same generic type of polity and at the same level of aggregation. Also, they should be more or less self-sufficient and possess a distinctive identity. Since then, almost all theorizing and empirical analysis in comparative politics has followed this model and focused on supposedly "sovereign" states whose populations shared a supposedly unique "nationality." It was taken for granted that only these "sovereign-national" polities possessed the requisite capacity for "agency" and, therefore, could be treated as equivalent for purposes of comparison.

Needless to say, large-N comparisons incorporating all United Nations member-states rested on this fiction—and they have rarely produced convincing findings since many of these 180+ units do not possess the requisite capacity for autonomous political action. Even area specialists working with geographically or culturally denominated subsets of countries in Latin America, Sub-Saharan Africa, the Middle East and North Africa, and South, South-East, or North-East Asia occasionally have had to face this issue of inference and external validity. Was Honduras in the 1950s when a substantial portion of its territory was owned by foreign banana producers "really" comparable with the much larger Brazil whose (then) major export resource, coffee, was in native hands? What is the utility of comparing the fiscal system of Kuwait that rests virtually exclusively on petroleum-derived revenues with that of Jordan that depends largely on foreign aid and its own citizens?

176

In the contemporary setting, due to differing forms of internal complexity and degrees of external interdependence, as well as the compound product of these two, it has become less and less possible to rely on the properties of sovereignty and nationality to identify equivalent units for analysis. No polity can realistically connect cause and effect and produce intended results without regard for the actions of others. Virtually all polities have persons and organizations within their borders that have identities, loyalties, and interests that overlap with persons and organizations in other polities.

Nor can one be assured that polities at the same formal level of political status or aggregation will have the same capacity for agency. Depending on their insertion into multi-layered systems of production, distribution, and governance, their capacity to act (or react) independently to any specific opportunity or challenge can vary enormously. This is most obviously the case for those national states that have entered into supra-national arrangements such as the European Union or signed binding international treaties such as those of the International Monetary Fund (IMF) or the World Trade Organization (WTO). Not only do they occasionally find themselves publicly shamed or even found guilty by such organizations, but they may regularly anticipate such constraints and alter their behavior accordingly. Moreover, many contemporary national polities have granted or been forced to concede extensive powers to their sub-national units and, in some cases, these *estados autonómicos, provinces, regioni, Länder, cantons, municípios,* and *communes* have entered into cooperative arrangements with equivalent units in adjacent national states.

I have been referring to "units of analysis" not "units of observation." Behavioralists in political science have relied virtually exclusively on survey data observed at the individual level to provide them with their microfoundations. When it comes to analysis, however, the collective context— usually, the characteristics of the national state within which the data were gathered—has often been brought to bear in explaining stable differences in individual level associations among variables. Hence, the social class or status of respondents as a predictor of their party preference might be expected to vary in strength from one polity to another—even though the overall direction of the relationship should be similar. While I am precluded by space constraints from developing the point further, I would argue that "complex interdependence" across the borders of national states has also affected the validity of using individuals as the micro-foundational units of observation. Its ever-increasing impact upon social interaction and economic organization has been such that persons or citizens have become a much less predictable "bundle" of diverse interests and opinions. In effect, individuals have become more individual (or "individuated" in the sociological jargon). Preference for any one interest or opinion comes to depend increasingly on the immediate context within which the choice is made, rather than some prior and stable ordering of them, whether rooted in national social structure, political culture, party ideology, or rational calculation.

From these observations, I conclude that comparativists need to dedicate much more thought than in the past to the collectivities they choose and to the properties these units of analysis supposedly share with regard to the specific institution, policy, or norm that is being examined. Try to imagine someone studying the extent of commitment to environmental protection across European polities without reference to the European Union where most of these policies are being made. Or another scholar comparing the human rights record of African states without taking into consideration the conditionalities posed by bi-lateral and multi-lateral foreign aid programs. I would admit that, in neither of these examples, should one presume that all variation in behavior or outcome can be explained by supra-national linkages. There still remains a great deal of difference that can only be explained by conditions within national polities, but exorcising or ignoring the external context in which these units are embedded would be equally foolish.

So, the increase in "complex interdependence" does not invalidate the enterprise of comparative politics, although it definitely makes it a more risky business. Even when the units chosen have been checked for equivalence in their capacity as actors, two other variables should be regularly and routinely taken into consideration: (1) integration; and (2) diffusion.

The former obtains when some or all of the units of analysis are members of an over-arching polity—regional or global—that can set norms, measure performances, and apply sanctions with regard to the specific institution or policy being compared. This used to be a property of empires—formal or informal, but in the contemporary world context these multiple levels of determination are often voluntarily accepted and virtually invisible.

The incidence of the latter is much more common and its effects well known. Sir Francis Galton raised the prospect of such a contamination of comparative research at a meeting of the Royal Anthropological Institute already in 1889! It refers to the likelihood that political units are observing each others' behavior and altering theirs accordingly—even in the absence of any supra-national political entity. The major contemporary difference is the emergence of so many transnational organizations—governmental and nongovernmental—that are in the continuous business of promoting such observations and evaluations at virtually all levels of society.

In both cases, the result at the level of association between "domestic" variables is likely to be the same, namely, attenuation. Collective outcomes will be more similar than in the past, even when there remains considerable variation in the "usual suspects" that formerly predicted much of the behavior at the level of national states and/or individual respondents. In other words, correlations in the dependent variable across units will

178

improve while those within them will decline. The obvious solution when it comes to drawing inferences should be to insert diffusion and integration across units as potential explanatory variables—much as one should test for the spuriousness of any observed relationship.

Of possible related interest: Chapters *10*, **15**, 57, 72.

72

DON'T STAY HOME

The Utility of Area Studies for Political Science Scholarship

Jorge I. Domínguez
Harvard University

What does or should an "area studies political scientist" do? Within the past two decades, this question has led at times to heated debates. For some, area studies research is at best the source of footnotes that more analytically oriented political scientists may employ fruitfully and effectively. For others, "political science" embodies pompous pretense in its own name and, at its worst, profoundly misrepresents politics as real human beings ordinarily understand it, experience it, and believe it. These two caricatures could be readily dismissed if they were to have no impact on careers, appointments, funding decisions, or collegiality within universities.

Area studies political science is not an oxymoron. It presumes that scholars interested in the study of politics somewhere would value the particularities of that "somewhere" as they frame the questions, hypotheses, and research instruments and procedures that they will employ. It equally presumes that they have read, pondered, internalized wherever appropriate, and otherwise learned in various ways from a wide array of fellow scholars who have worked in other "somewheres" with different research instruments and procedures and contrary hypotheses or analytic frameworks. Area studies political scientists seek to contribute to the analysis of the somewhere that has been the principal object of their research and also to the wider analytic and empirical study of comparative politics.

Harsh and unfair as many critiques of area studies research may have been, some scholars in that research tradition may have inadvertently caused their own self-isolation. They had emphasized the particularity or uniqueness of their research subject almost as if to build a barrier of scholarly "protectionism" to prevent external intrusion. Yet, in so doing, they also made many of their arguments subject to easy disconfirmation. Let me illustrate with reference to some research on Mexico.

Until the end of the 1980s, research on Mexico emphasized that the long-dominant party, the Institutional Revolutionary Party (PRI), was a "party without members." Only electoral fraud could explain support for the PRI, such scholars believed.

Similarly, until the end of the 1980s, the bulk of research on Mexico emphasized that the main opposition party, the National Action Party (PAN), which finally won presidential elections in 2000 and 2006, was a Roman Catholic party, such that religiosity was the key explanation for its mass base.

Finally, there was an unresolved debate among area studies scholars of Mexico with regard to how Mexicans may have thought about the main issues of the day. Some seemed to think that they simply did not; others averred that Mexicans worried strongly about such issues as corruption, electoral fraud, and poverty, and that a legacy of nationalism and revolution made them intensely hostile to the U.S.

Beginning in the late 1980s, scholarly survey research on Mexico became much easier, with various datasets available for analysis. It turned out that none of the area studies propositions summarized just above was accurate.

The PRI had considerable voter support in the late 1980s and through the 1990s and retained it even after it lost the presidency in 2000, thus winning thereafter many governorships, mayoralties, and seats in Congress. The interesting research question turned out to be why so many voters continued to vote for the PRI even though they understood that the PRI governments had often ruled badly.

Frequency of church attendance distinguishes PRI from PAN voters only rarely. The interesting research question is why the absence of religiosity distinguished voters who support the Party of the Democratic Revolution from both the PAN and the PRI. Even in this narrower circumstance, religion was rarely, if ever, among the more important explanations for voter behavior.

Mexicans focus on valence issues, much less so on positional issues. They worried about corruption, electoral fraud, and poverty, but none of those issues was a dominant explanation for voter behavior. Mexicans typically held the U.S. in high regard, even if at times (the 2000s) they strongly opposed the incumbent Bush administration. Mexicans showed that they were not unlike voters in other countries in their concern for the economy as a whole (sociotropic voting) and in their attention to "competence" as one way to distinguish between candidates.

From these findings, a research agenda emerges for area studies political science. A deep understanding of the particularities of a place matters; yet to have it requires both systematic data about citizens and systematic comparisons among countries. Focus first on questions of universal interest and applicability to enable scholars to demonstrate variation, for it would contribute to political science as a whole and to the study of a particular country—and it would make it easier to identify in what way was this country different from others. It turns out, for example, that Mexicans resemble "North Atlantic area" voters in their patterns of economic voting but differ in their patience for a misgoverning party such as the PRI, which they supported again and again over time albeit at declining levels. Mexicans were not unique in every respect but they did differ from less patient voters in other countries.

Area studies political scientists who work on Mexico would like others to join them in asking why voters in some but not all formerly authoritarian countries in Central and Eastern Europe and East Asia continued to support the parties heir to authoritarian regimes. Why is "voter patience" less common in North Atlantic democracies? Or, to put it in language that might be more familiar, why is partisan identification stronger or "stickier" in countries that seemingly never had "real" parties for most of their histories than in countries that have long had what for a while seemed strong parties that embodied timeless, "frozen" political cleavages?

This research also implies one important experience of which too few have taken timely notice: social science surveys of Mexicans, and citizens in many formerly authoritarian countries, have much higher response rates than surveys in the U.S. If you wish to study "the human condition," don't be just an "area studies political scientist" who works solely in the U.S.

Of possible related interest: Chapters 12, 34, 49, 75.

Suggested additional reading

Brady, Henry E., and David Collier, eds. *Rethinking Social Inquiry: Diverse Tools, Shared Standards*. Lanham, MD: Rowman & Littlefield, 2004.
Domínguez, Jorge I., and Chappell Lawson, eds. *Mexico's Pivotal Democratic Election: Candidates, Voters, and the Presidential Campaign of 2000*. Stanford, CA: Stanford University Press, 2004.

73

CAN WE REALLY BE HAPPY WITH THE STUDY OF COMPARATIVE GOVERNMENT?

Hans Daalder
Leiden University

For all its ancient lineage and wide-spread interest by academics and practitioners alike, the field of comparative government remains beset by unsolved problems. One is prejudice: too many think their own country "best." If not, its critics look for "better examples" to other countries, mainly the larger ones, which come to figure as "pattern states." Did not these larger countries traditionally inspire the best-known typologies used in comparative government writing such as the dichotomies of "presidential" versus "parliamentary government," "cabinet government" versus *"gouvernement d'assemblée,"* "P.R. systems" versus "plurality systems," "two-party systems" versus "multiparty systems," "winner-takes-all systems" versus presumed "consensual systems," etc.? Larger countries came to serve as measuring rods: whether positively for those reformers who sought to borrow specific institutions to make their own countries "better"; or negatively for those who sought arguments to resist unwelcome calls for change. Of course, our knowledge of other systems of government, rather than just the larger "pattern states," has greatly expanded. But the impact of this has remained limited: after all, it is difficult enough to know more than a few countries sufficiently well. And as the main instrument to make these countries better known is presentation in the widest known languages, there is considerable chance for misinterpretation: attempts to "translate" the specific experiences of a lesser-known country to an international public often fall victim to the political preconceptions of the country or countries "owning" the language concerned.

But there are other distortions. In our discourse of the working of different governments different criteria tend to slip in. To mention one example: those who advocate the "Westminster model" always emphasize values like single-party government and accountability through direct electoral choice, whereas advocates of multiparty government stress the value of genuine representation. Irrespective of whether such arguments are empirically true, this illustrates the presence of different norms, not easily brought in an unambiguous relation or hierarchy towards one another.

Of course, the shift from traditional comparative *government* to the study of comparative *politics* has tended to minimize the role of institutional arrangements. They are thought to be less important than really "decisive" societal features such as social structure, specific elites and groups, civic culture, rapid social change, and similar factors. Moreover, specific governmental institutions borrowed from another country often prove to work out very differently from the way they did in the original case—which confirms that they cannot be isolated from more general institutional arrangements or more important political and social elements.

Since World War II important new measures have developed for the comparison of different "political systems." Two stand out: (1) the revolution brought about by the wide-ranging comparative analyses of political and civic culture gave us such measures as trust in government, attitudes towards politicians and other actors, political participation, civic competence, political cynicism and the like; and (2) the comparative study of political performance which led to the collection of data such as economic growth, income distribution, wealth per capita, the role of welfare arrangements, or general social indicators such as health, infant mortality, life expectancy, levels of education, etc. Generally, of these two approaches the latter lends itself much better for widespread or even universal data collection, whereas the earlier category remains closer to more specific political environments. Yet, both approaches are likely to suffer from insufficient understanding of the specific governmental and political contexts from which data are drawn, and beg the question of the actual role of governmental decisions and policies.

Of course, we have long learned to reason in terms of overall "systems." Yet, can we be sure that interrelations between the many possible relevant factors in the working of political systems are taken into account, or, more pessimistically, really understood or even known? There is no lack of enthusiasm in the area of comparative studies. Yet one wonders whether such studies add up, and allow a real knowledge and true comparative evaluation of the working of today's numerous, yet highly diverse polities. Of course, rough classifications can be made on the basis of gross differences. Yet, paradoxically, this is less easy if one is to assess the working of specific institutions for countries seemingly more alike (e.g., stable modern democracies). Do we really give convincing answers to the older questions of the working and effect of different constitutional arrangements, let alone of the more specific institutions within these?

Perhaps, we need an Aristotle for the twenty-first century to bring order in the sprawling efforts of comparative government and politics!

Of possible related interest: Chapters 12, 15, 57, 71.

74

THE CONTINGENT FLAW OF MAJORITARIAN SYSTEMS

G. Bingham Powell, Jr.
University of Rochester

One approach to democratic government can be characterized as "majoritarian." It emphasizes the more or less direct election of strong executive governments that enjoy the power to carry out their campaign promises. This approach is appealing. It directly links the citizens and the policy-makers. It avoids rent-seeking in negotiating new governments. It exposes the incompetent and the untrustworthy to retrospective voter retaliation.

Yet, the majoritarian approach contains a serious flaw: majorities are rare. In elections that are unconstrained and offer multiple alternatives, voters almost never settle on a single party or candidate. Legislative votes are divided among multiple parties. If the executive is directly elected, she will often face legislative opposition. Even in countries using single-member district election rules, which depress the number of candidates because of the desire to avoid wasting votes or campaign resources, very few elections result in single-party voter majorities. (The U.S. is extremely unusual in this regard.) Most of the world's single-party legislative majorities emerge from various kinds of distortions in the vote–seat connection. Putting unfettered policymaking power in the hands of governments created through these processes means turning it over to representatives of a minority of voters. At best a plurality of voters elects a government; sometimes (in perhaps 10 percent of elections across a variety of countries) the winning minority is not even a plurality.

Is this a serious flaw for democracy? It depends on the distribution of citizens' preferences. In a relatively homogeneous society the supporters of different parties will, by definition, share fairly similar opinions. The substantive commitments of the parties will generally be fairly similar also. It won't make much difference whether we arbitrarily hand all the policymaking power to one of them, through operation of the election rules or pre-election coalitions, or require post-election negotiation. In either case the generally consensual preferences of the electorate will be matched with the commitments of the party(s) in the government. Under these circumstances the virtues of majoritarian arrangements in creating direct mandates and clarity of responsibility may be enjoyed without substantive cost. (However, there may be some loss of confidence in the political procedures, if parties winning little more than a third of the vote are regularly given complete policy control.)

But in a society with a polarized distribution of citizen preferences majoritarianism is highly problematic. In such a society citizens are deeply divided over policies. Giving unchecked governmental power to a minority may create policies that are quite distant from those preferred by majority or by other minorities. The tighter mandate connection only locks a citizen minority more closely to an unrepresentative government. Clearer responsibility highlights accountability for unpopular, but elected, policies. If polarization of preferences involves greater intensity of unhappiness among the losers, as often seems the case, the arbitrary creation of majorities is even more costly. This is the flaw of the majoritarian approach: its severity is contingent on the divisions in the society.

Of course, in a polarized society the representation of social divisions in the national assembly places a more serious burden on those who must negotiate. It is possible that negotiations may deadlock. Whether it is better to overcome deadlock through the arbitrary creation of majorities, if it cannot be overcome through negotiation, no doubt depends on how distasteful is the status quo relative to the alternatives. But the majoritarian approach eschews the possibility of encouraging policymakers to find accommodative solutions through creative negotiation.

Of possible related interest: Chapters 1, 32, 68, 92.

Suggested additional reading

Cox, Gary. *Making Votes Count: Strategic Coordination in the World's Electoral Systems*. Cambridge: Cambridge University Press, 1997.
Lijphart, Arend. *Patterns of Democracy*. New Haven, CT: Yale University Press, 1999.
Powell, G. Bingham. *Elections as Instruments of Democracy*. New Haven, CT: Yale University Press, 2000.

75

RELIGION AND POLITICS

Goldie Shabad
The Ohio State University

As a student of comparative politics, I have long been puzzled by the continued religiosity of Americans and the prominent role played by religion in U.S. electoral politics and in the public sphere more generally. I have recently had occasion to read widely on the subject, focusing on the U.S. as well as other parts of the world. I remain puzzled. In my view, there are significant and as yet unresolved questions about the complex and contingent relationships between religious politics, on the one hand, and modernization and democracy, on the other, that I think merit further attention by students of comparative politics. Here I will focus on just two sets of questions, which are by no means comprehensive.

The first set concerns the relationship between modernization and religious politics. It has long been held that modernization erodes religious beliefs and practices among mass publics, lessens significantly the role played by religion in the public realm, and mutes religiously based political conflicts. The "dechurching" of most advanced Western societies, together with the diminishing impact of religious divisions (be they inter-denominational or clerical–secular) on these societies' politics since the 1950s, appears to provide strong confirmation of the modernization thesis. And yet, there is the U.S., where religion plays a pronounced role in electoral politics and in the public sphere more generally. Is this another instance of American exceptionalism? If so, how can the American anomaly be explained? But other cases, apart from the U.S., also raise questions about the relationship between modernization and religious politics. For example, it would seem that, rather than eroding religious commitments, modernization in Iran under the Shah and in Turkey during the past two decades or so contributed to the politicization of religious cleavages— whether as a negative reaction to modernization itself or as a result of the resources and human capital that modernization provided to religious sectors to facilitate their political engagement. Consider, too, the different trajectories of Spain and Poland after democratization. Both are modern, urbanized societies with relatively educated populations. Both are Catholic.

From the late 1970s onward, Spain became a rapidly secularized society, in which the legalization of divorce, abortion, and same-sex marriage was contested but hardly became the stuff of sharp political divides. Poland, however, remains almost 20 years after it democratized a highly religious society in which church–state relations and the primacy of traditional Christian values in public life have been highly polarizing issues. What might a systematic examination of these cases and others tell us about the relationship between modernization and religious politics? What cultural, social structural, political, and institutional factors condition the linkage between the two?

The second set of questions has to do with the relationship between democracy and religious politics. As we all know, a highly controversial issue among social scientists, pundits, and policymakers concerns the compatibility of democracy with the doctrinal beliefs and practices of *particular* religions. Once upon a time it was Catholicism; now, according to Huntington and others, it is Islam. It is obvious that most Muslim-majority societies are not democratic. Is this because they are Muslim, or because of other characteristics these countries share in common? The management thus far of religious politics in newly democratic Indonesia, an overwhelmingly Muslim society, as well as the adherence to democratic practices by Turkey's governing Islamist-rooted Justice and Development Party, suggest that it is not Islam *per se* that is incompatible with democratic governance, but rather the interaction of Islam with other characteristics of Muslim societies that affect the emergence and sustainability of demo-cratic governance. It has also long been argued that religious-based con-flicts, whether between different faiths (e.g., India, Lebanon, the former Yugoslavia) or between sects or denominations within the same faith (e.g., Iraq, Northern Ireland) or between secular and clerical segments of society (e.g., Israel, the U.S.), pose serious challenges to democracy, because such conflicts often invoke mutually exclusive beliefs and social identities that are not easily reconcilable. Yet, we know that both the form and intensity of religiously based political conflicts, and thus the challenge that such conflicts pose, vary considerably among democracies. Why is this so? Is it the type of religious cleavage (interfaith, intra-faith, clerical/secular), and/or the extent to which the religious cleavage overlaps with other divisions, that matters? Are some kinds of political and institutional arrangements (electoral formats, party systems, constitutionally prescribed church–state relations) better than others at moderating religiously based political conflicts, regardless of the type of religious cleavage involved?

The persistence of unresolved questions about religion and politics is not due to the lack of attention paid to the issues I have posed here. Developments in both domestic and global politics during the past few decades have made the study of religion and politics, once relegated to the margins of the discipline, a focal point of political science across all subfields. For example, a few years ago Cambridge University Press initiated a series Cambridge Studies in Social Theory, Religion, and Politics. But much of the recent work that addresses these unresolved questions are either case studies that are not richly informed by theory or are large-N analyses in which religious faith is operationalized as a categorical variable (Western Christianity versus others, Islam versus others, etc.) and religiosity is measured by frequency of church attendance. Such studies raise questions about the generalizability of their findings or fail to explore the causal mechanisms that underlie the observed correlations. As a consequence, there are important conceptual and methodological issues that remain to be addressed in such a way as to allow comparative research on religious politics to proceed in a systematic and cumulative manner. I am agnostic by nature about which approaches, or combinations of approaches, might be most fruitful to study such complex issues but historical institutionalism, political sociology, and rational choice come to mind. What I am certain about, though, is that much more careful attention needs to be paid to how we conceptualize and measure the three pertinent components of religious phenomena: religious tenets, beliefs and practices at the individual level, and characteristics of religious institutions. What we also need to do is to conceptualize and measure more carefully the many factors—for example, socio-structural variables, cultural traditions, the constitutional status of religion, the extent to which partisan alignments are based in religious differences, the actions of political leaders—that might influence the nature of religious politics. Only then will we be able to understand variations in the relationship between religion and politics across time and space.

Of possible related interest: Chapters 2, 15, 53, **55**.

Suggested additional reading

Fetzer, Joel S., and J. Christopher Soper. *Muslims and the State in Britain, France, and Germany.* Cambridge: Cambridge University Press, 2005.
Kalyvas, Stathis N. "Commitment Problems in Emerging Democracies: The Case of Religious Parties." *Comparative Politics* 32 (2000): 378–398.
Norris, Pippa, and Ronald Inglehart. *Sacred and Secular: Religion and Politics Worldwide.* Cambridge: Cambridge University Press, 2004.

76

STUDY CHINA!

Roderick MacFarquhar
Harvard University

China preserved the same political system for some 2000 years, give or take a few bouts of disunity. The Roman Empire broke up and was never reunited; the Chinese empire broke up around the same time, but *was* reunited. Arguably, even the Maoist system was closer to the traditional one than to Stalin's. This unique longevity should surely command the attention of all political scientists. What was there in the Chinese political culture that permitted the continual rebirth of the system? Scholars who work on the American political system sometimes wonder why their methods and theories aren't adopted wholesale in comparative politics in general and Chinese politics in particular. But the singularity of the Chinese system suggests that maybe it should be the basis for the export of theory, rather than for imports. Instead of trying to apply sophisticated methodology constructed for research into, say, Congressional behavior patterns, maybe political scientists should drop preconceived notions and treat China as terra nova, strange, perhaps even exotic, but deserving of ground-up theoretical analysis.

Of possible related interest: Chapters 2, 72, 95, 96.

77

SOFT POWER AND THE FUTURE OF ASIA

Lucian W. Pye
Massachusetts Institute of Technology

In political science an illusion of progress is often evoked by merely introducing new, and hence fresh, words to replace old ones, but without any rigorous analysis of what is or is not new. Also the behavioral revolution in political science led to an emphasis upon empirical research and a discounting of normative issues, which had bulked large in traditional political science. These two problems of new terminology and the presumed superiority of empirical research over normative discourse arise with the recent popularity of Joseph Nye's concept of "soft power." At present, however, there is uncertainty over how much explanatory power can be given to the concept of "soft power," which seems to be answering a real need for new terminology, but which also seems to be a retreat from hard, empirically defined concepts of power and influence and a reemphasis upon normative dimensions of power.

Thus, in Asia we have a dramatic rise in Chinese influence and a decline in American power, all because of changes in the relative soft power of the two potentially hegemonic states. The American leadership role in both World War II and the Cold War gave Washington considerable soft power, but that power has been seriously eroded by the Iraq War. In the meantime, China which had been considered to be a revolutionary threat by most Asian states, has now been increasingly seen as a constructive neighbor.

The future of Asia will depend upon the fate of China's and America's soft power. The test will be which of the two will be seen by the other Asian states as having the strongest claim to leadership. Economic matters will have some influence as to the strength of each power's soft power, but the key to soft power lies more in the domain of values and normative considerations. In the competition to impress the Asian states with their soft power both China and the U.S. must strive to strike an acceptable balance between being a strong leader, and hence worthy of respect, and being too aggressive, and hence damage their soft power claims. At present

Beijing has some advantages as a newcomer to the world political stage, but with time the novelty of China's international involvement will wear off. The test will then be which has the greater appeal and hence the greater soft power. Asian leaders in their search for greater legitimacy will be involved in balancing features of their separate national political cultures with international standards of the modern nation-state system. That is to say, they must demonstrate that they are in tune with both their national histories and the modern international standards of state building.

It is easy to assert that the future of Asia will depend upon the playing out of the soft power of China and the U.S., but much more difficult to provide hard standards for measuring the actual levels of soft power. The problem is that as a discipline we are better at quantitative research about objective questions, and we are on less solid ground when it comes to evaluating normative issues. Thus we come back to our introductory remarks about the seductive power of new terms, and our limitations in normative matters. We may feel that we are making great progress by using the new concept of soft power, but in fact we can't get away from the strengths and weaknesses of the discipline. Our problem is not just that we need standards for measuring the relative strength of the Chinese and American soft power, but we need to know how the other Asian states are reacting to the soft power of China and the U.S. What impresses one government's leadership may not impress another's. This is particularly the case when it comes to subjective judgments about legitimacy and the moral basis of the claims to soft power. Each country needs to assert its distinctive cultural norms, but at the same time they need to feel that they are up to meeting international standards and thus show that they are a part of the modern world of politics.

Of possible related interest: Chapters 13, 76, 79, 97.

78

THE STUDY OF
INTERNATIONAL LAW

Jens Meierhenrich
Harvard University

The study of international law—in political science—is flawed. It is beset by a series of challenges that interfere with the explanation and understanding of (1) international legal institutions (e.g., international courts); (2) international legal processes (e.g., international legalization); and (3) international legal outcomes (e.g., international compliance). Frequently, answers to the question of how international law matters fall short. This contribution assesses the causes of these shortcomings, and suggests some cures.

I do not mean to suggest that political scientists have not advanced the study of international law. They certainly have made important contributions, first and foremost in the study of human rights regimes, treaty compliance, and dispute resolution in the World Trade Organization. And yet challenges remain.

A most important challenge relates to the fact that few political scientists have ever been exposed to international law. Some believe that political scientists can partially overcome this challenge by forming strategic alliances with international lawyers. Although interdisciplinary collaboration is clearly desirable, it is unlikely to be a sufficient response to the knowledge gap. On the contrary, I believe that political scientists, if they are serious about the study of international law, need to be specialists, and that sufficient expertise in international law is not as easy to acquire as is often presumed. I see a much greater need for training—doctrinal and applied—than is currently on offer.

It is important to recognize that *intra*disciplinary training (whether in law or political science) leaves scholars of international law on either side ill-equipped to *truly* comprehend the dynamics of this important phenomenon. A grounding in one discipline is—more often than not—anathema to explaining and understanding the practice of international law. This is evident in much of the leading scholarship on international law produced by political scientists. By far the greatest deficiencies can be found in the literature concerning the international ad hoc tribunals and the International Criminal Court. Even publications in leading journals are marred by erroneous interpretations of international instruments, misunderstandings of procedural and substantive law as well as random references to case law that misrepresent international jurisprudence.

It is a truism that the questions we ask determine the answers we get. Because political scientists tend to transplant research questions coming out of their own discipline to the domain of international law, many fail to identify the truly interesting questions of international law. The fact that research projects on international law in political science have been theory- and method-driven—rather than problem-driven—has had the unfortunate effect of scholars merely rehearsing stale research questions from international relations theory in a new domain (e.g., "What role for neorealism, neoliberalism, and constructivism in explaining the creation of the ICC?").

In an effort at capturing the methodological differences between legal and political science approaches to the study of international law, Robert Keohane several years ago distinguished between an "instrumentalist optic" and a "normative optic," and elucidated the deficiencies of each. In the intervening years scholars have made headway in reducing the cleavage of which Keohane spoke by using bifocal lenses. Moreover, by focusing on the concept of "legalization," Kenneth Abbott and others have sought to relate instrumental and noninstrumental explanations of international law to one another. But all is not well.

Let me introduce another distinction that illuminates a different, continuing challenge in the study of international law, namely the distinction between nomothetic and ideographic reasoning. In as far as political scientists have turned to the study of international law, a primacy of nomothetic reasoning has prevailed. The formal and quantitative study of international law is indispensable, of course. How else are we going to move toward generalization? Nonetheless, ideographic reasoning is critical as well, especially for moving from correlational to causal analysis.

Political science is ignoring the significance of qualitative research for the study of international law at its own peril. It is crucial to appreciate in this context that the kinds of ideographic reasoning at which the social sciences excel are qualitatively *different* from—and more sophisticated than—the descriptive (although often technically compelling) accounts of international legal institutions, processes, and outcomes typically produced by international lawyers. This is so because international legal scholarship continues to be dominated, in the words of Eric Posner and Jack Goldsmith, by an improbable combination of doctrinalism and idealism. Given this predicament, it is imperative for political scientists to substitute analytic narratives (perhaps along the lines sketched by Robert Bates, Barry Weingast, and their co-authors) for descriptive narratives in the study of international law—which brings me back to the issue of specialization.

At present, few political scientists are capable of developing such analytic narratives. Many simply lack the expertise and experience required for a subtle integration of nomothetic and ideographic reasoning in the study of international law. Professional training in law schools can only be a partial remedy, as few law schools offer adequate training in international law (due to the fact that the subject is deemed of secondary importance in the professional education of lawyers). The only way to obtain the skills necessary for making sense of international law is to practice it before analyzing it. Absent an extended exposure in an applied setting to, say, the inner workings of international courts and tribunals, any explanatory account of the choices justices make will remain impoverished. Conversely, any experience of the inner workings of international courts and tribunals that is not grounded in the methodology of the social sciences will remain just that—an insider's account of limited relevance to explanation and understanding.

What political science can bring to the study of international law, in short, is the methodology of the social sciences, which encompasses—aside from positive political economy—a rich tradition of comparative historical analysis (CHA). Such a contribution would be a boon to the study of international law, especially seeing that the prevailing lack of international law data necessitates data construction on a considerable scale. What international law can bring to the study of political science, in turn, is exposure to a third way of reasoning—legal reasoning. If political science as a discipline is serious about focusing on international law as a phenomenon to be explained—proficiency therein is a *sine qua non*. Downloading and coding international judgments and decisions is not enough for explaining and understanding international law. Technical capabilities are required—and must be acquired—to decipher them.

Of possible related interest: Chapters 9, **79**, 92, 93.

Suggested additional reading

Goldsmith, Jack L., and Eric A. Posner. *The Limits of International Law.* Oxford: Oxford University Press, 2005.

Merry, Sally Engle. "Anthropology and International Law." *Annual Review of Anthropology* 35 (2006): 99–116.

Simmons, Beth A., and Richard H. Steinberg, eds. *International Law and International Relations.* Cambridge: Cambridge University Press, 2006.

79

THE "SECOND IMAGE REVERSED" REVISITED

Robert O. Keohane
Princeton University

Almost 30 years ago, in a 1978 article in *International Organization*, Peter A. Gourevitch first discussed what he called "the second image reversed": the impact of international political and economic structure on domestic politics. Gourevitch argued that certain changes in the global political economy—such as the invention of the railroad and the steamship in the nineteenth century—had such profound effects that one could only understand what appeared to be *domestic* politics by understanding these systemic changes. Other examples are the impact of industrial revolution, with its emphasis on textile production, on the market for cotton and therefore on American slavery; the effects of World War I in Russia; the consequences of the Great Depression on the politics of Europe in the 1930s; and the implications of the Cold War for the politics of American and Soviet allies around the world.

We are now experiencing a vast set of changes in the world political economy that go under the loose rubric of "globalization." No aspect of globalization has more general implications than the rapid incorporation of formerly poor countries into the world economy. Particularly important and sudden is the rapid economic growth of China and India—with over a third of the world's population. Southeastern China has become the Workshop of the World over the course of the last 15 years, and India is the preferred English-language site for all sorts of services, outsourced from the U.S.—from call centers to computer programming. China has been growing at more than 10 percent per year, India at about six percent, with enormous consequences for the economies of the most advanced countries.

The effects of rapid growth in Asia are transmitted directly to the U.S. and Europe through increasingly inexpensive modes of transportation, as was also the case in the second half of the nineteenth century. Improvements in communications technology in both eras were even more dramatic—exemplified by the laying of the Atlantic cable right after the American

Civil War, and the creation and expansion of the internet since the beginning of the 1990s. In Thomas Friedman's evocative phrase, the world is becoming increasingly "flat." Nevertheless, it should be noted that as Robert Gilpin pointed out throughout his career, these transnational economic ties require a political structure—currently provided principally by the rules of the World Trade Organization, created as a result of negotiations among the major capitalist states and groupings.

The magnitude of these economic changes implies enormous political effects. Yet we have no systematic study of the effects on the advanced democracies of the rapid growth of China and India, and the corresponding transfer of many economic activities to these countries. How many of what may appear as the idiosyncratic features of Japan, the European Union countries, or the U.S. derive from these systemic changes? To what extent are the development prospects of Africa and Latin America conditioned as profoundly by the capabilities of India and China as they were in an earlier period by the dominance of the U.S. and Western Europe as markets and sources of capital?

Gourevitch emphasized in his article and subsequent book that a single global system could have divergent effects in different countries. The opening of agricultural lands in North America to European markets, through the railroad and the steamship, contributed in his interpretation to free trade and political liberalism in Great Britain, but to protectionism and militarism in Germany. Great Britain was an island without powerful hereditary landowners; Germany was located in the center of the European continent and had been traditionally dominated by the Prussian *Junkers.* There is nothing about the "second image reversed" orientation that predicts homogeneity or even necessarily convergence. New external pressures can be accommodated, as political systems adjust to a new location in an international division of labor, and in patterns of political–military relationships, or they can be resisted, as coalitions and party systems are "frozen" in place. The consequences for politics of a huge systemic change such as the rise of China and India are heavily mediated by the strategies pursued by the affected countries.

The situation now is complicated by the existence of a large number of multilateral organizations and international regimes that affect the integration of poor countries in the world political economy. There is every reason to believe that if the effects of the economic integration of poor countries are substantial, the rich countries (which dominate these organizations) may use multilateral institutions to moderate or shape these effects in their interests.

Until students of the joint field of comparative and world politics systematically study these issues, we will not know how profoundly the advanced industrialized countries are being affected by the entry of poor countries into the world political economy, or the extent to which we should interpret the activities of some multilateral institutions as a response to these changes.

The research program I am suggesting could engage students of comparative politics, specializing on any region or country in the world—including the U.S. The explanatory variable is the rapid growth in manufacturing and services in poor countries, especially China and India, since 1990. The dependent variables are many and various: there are lots of potential observable implications of the hypothesis that the effects of these changes are extremely important and extensive. Empirical work could systematically and comparatively explore the question: how serious and deep are the consequences of these changes for the economics and politics of countries—rich and poor—around the world? The implications of the answers for our understanding of the world of the twenty-first century would be profound.

Of possible related interest: Chapters 76, **78**, 80, 92.

Suggested additional reading

Gourevitch, Peter A. "The Second Image Reversed." *International Organization* 32 (1978): 881–912.

Wolf, Martin. *Why Globalization Works*. New Haven, CT: Yale University Press, 2006.

80

THE GLOBALIZATION GAP

James N. Rosenau
George Washington University

The sources, processes, and dynamics of globalization are woefully under-studied by political scientists. In particular, its political and cultural aspects are not probed nearly as much as seems desirable. As new electronic tech-nologies and greater flows of goods, funds, people, information and ideas shrink the world and as these developments generate various responses around the world, the need for probing investigations into the integrative and disintegrative underpinnings of global life intensifies accordingly. The U.S.'s tendencies to engage in unilateral actions abroad need to give way to policies designed to facilitate local institutions in other countries. To live in a globalizing world is to recognize that new centers of authority are being formed in every community and region elsewhere, giving rise thereby to a worldwide pattern in which decentralizing processes have become the central tendency at work in the world. Localization is no less salient as a global dynamic than globalization, and it may even be more powerful.

Of possible related interest: Chapters 57, 78, 81, 87.

81

CONGRESS AND THE SCOPE OF DEMOCRACY

Ira Katznelson
Columbia University

During the early 1940s, leading American scholars, among them Harold Lasswell and David Riesman, began to ruminate about the price that would be exacted for democracy if wartime emergencies were to become permanent. During the early Cold War, these anxieties became more prominent. Fierce democrats like Robert Dahl and C. Wright Mills considered how total warfare and the growth of enduring challenges to security threatened to erode the traditional distinction between commonplace political moments and unusual times of crisis. Their apprehensions bore directly on the standing of the legislature, the site of political representation, the hinge linking the population of citizens to the modern state, and thus the core of any liberal democracy.

Dahl cautioned in a 1953 volume on atomic energy he edited for *The Annals* that democratic theory had become circumscribed because traditional legislative prerogatives and processes are unsuitable in such areas of national security. Two years later, Mills' *The Power Elite* even more broadly depicted American politics as divided between subjects and policy disputes that are settled in Congress, and policy matters regarding war and peace that are decided mainly outside the legislature by a select few.

These colleagues were well aware that the breakdown of the majority of the globe's democracies in the heyday of Fascism, Stalinism, and other forms of authoritarianism and dictatorship had been instigated by political parties and social movements who thought that parliamentary government is inherently inadequate under conditions that require administrative dexterity and military force. Many mid-century students of American political behavior insisted that liberal democracy would remain vulnerable to such assaults unless realistic empirical scholarship could connect the study of institutions and action, including legislative politics, to normative concerns about democracy's range and capacity. How, they wished to know, does variation to the content of policy affect

200

the democratic process? What determines where decisions will be made? What happens when particular problems are emplaced outside the zone of normal democratic politics? How, in short, does the abstract notion of popular sovereignty actually operate across the full span of public policy?

These questions remain pressing, arguably now more than ever. Yet more than a half-century later, we know far too little about when or how the policy process falls into an ambit in which traditional theories of representative democracy do not work very well. Despite the centrality of Congress to such considerations, moreover, the congressional subfield has failed to focus on these challenges. The great disciplinary boom in congressional studies has not produced answers relating to whether or how much Congress gets to decide or oversee, or even, more basically, how different policy subjects of all kinds are distinctively handled in the legislature. Yet without such a research program efforts to address the scope of democracy are restricted to conjecture.

To be sure, political scientists once did make a start on developing some of the necessary tools. During the 1960s to the early 1980s, David Mayhew, Theodore Lowi, Aage Clausen, and other energetic students of American politics classified and coded public policies in order to test hypotheses dealing with how, in Congress, policy can make politics. They wanted to know which topics gain significance within the congressional process, and how the character of legislation can shape preferences, organize choices, and induce the formation of coalitions essential to lawmaking.

As it advanced, this literature regrettably became more narrow. Foreign affairs and national security matters largely dropped out of sight. In consequence, scholarship on the substance of representation came to be enclosed within the ambit of what Mills had labeled the middle level of politics, leaving unaddressed a determination of where the boundaries pertaining to decision-making are placed at different historical moments with respect to different issues. In probing how the content of policy can affect the dynamics of politics these writings thus advanced into promising terrain, but then sidestepped the quandaries that Lasswell, Riesman, Dahl, and Mills had attended about the breadth of congressional affairs and the contours of American democracy.

Even within its self-imposed limits, the focus on substance in legislative studies petered out by the 1980s, and not only for the want of good enough themes. Its categories for policy coding either were very abstract or too bulky. More important, this type of work did not identify mechanisms that could explain why or how a given policy might affect the locus and outcome of deliberation and decision. With these weaknesses, the scientific study of Congress soon left policy substance behind, and the American subfield moved even further away from the systematic agenda Dahl and Mills had projected in the 1950s.

As a result, the gap between what we need to understand and the instruments we possess has widened uncomfortably. With anxiety about the politics of security and fear again having come to the fore, we badly need pertinent research that can, once again, bring the relationship of Congress and the scope of democracy to the fore. This will require a return to the charged questions of our discipline's mid-twentieth-century leaders, underpinned by fresh methods of policy classification and analysis. For if studies about politics in the U.S. remain taciturn about these considerable issues without adequate tools and habits of practice, they will remain eerily and disturbingly quiet.

Of possible related interest: Chapters 21, 41, **88**, **100**.

Suggested additional reading

Dahl, Robert A. "Atomic Energy and the Democratic Process." In *The Impact of Atomic Energy,* edited by Robert A. Dahl. *The Annals of the American Academy of Political and Social Science* 290 (1953): 1–6.

Lasswell, Harold. "The Garrison State." *American Journal of Sociology* 46 (1941): 455–68.

82

"FREE ASSOCIATION"

Traveling Ideas and the Study of Political Equality

Nancy L. Rosenblum
Harvard University

The past few decades have been a renaissance for political philosophy: Rawls and Habermas, theories of multiculturalism, neo-republican thought and deliberative democratic theory. Every one of these strains reflects more than the ounce of optimism about human welfare, enlightenment, and freedom that is necessary to motivate political theory at its critical and constructive best. So it is not surprising that proud theorists reaffirm the orthodoxy that political theory sets the questions that political science investigates. The influence proceeds in one direction, on this view. True, theorists sometimes concede that their principles are constrained by common understanding of institutions and behavior, stability and efficiency. But that falls short of genuine reciprocity: political theorists' avowed resource is not political science but history or metaphysics, moral psychology or the internal dynamics of philosophical argument.

I want to illustrate this orthodoxy, and then temper it by indicating the fruitful "free association" of ideas as they travel back and forth between theorists and social scientists on the subject of political equality.

Political equality is a central element of democratic theory; it encompasses analysis of the dimensions of political equality—a complex idea, the foundational moral and political reasons for valuing its several facets, the political activities to which it applies (voting, advocating, deliberating, etc.) and its significance for specific institutions as well as for democracy overall. Some of political theory's claims are not amenable to empirical study: the intrinsic importance of political equality rooted in the notion of equal worth (so that failure to insure equal voice is by itself a palpable indignity, a show of disrespect) for example. Many other aspects invite study. The value of participation (and thus for equal, universal participation) for individual moral development, for example, is taken up by empirical studies of its effect on information, a sense of efficacy, and attention to the public good. Most commonly, political scientists draw on the strand of democratic theory that understands participation as "voice" and evaluates the connection between communication of interests and opinions and political outcomes. Empirical work demonstrates that politically active citizens have different interests and priorities than inactive ones, and that the voices of the poor are relatively unexpressed, attended to, or acted on. Political scientists' criteria of political equality and their motivation to investigate the conditions under which a particular aspect of equality is realized or not rests on borrowed ground, just as the orthodoxy about political theory leads us to expect. Political scientists seldom follow theorists and set political equality in the context of a fully developed substantive ideal of democratic citizenship, but they often acknowledge their sources in historical or contemporary democratic theory. In some instances, of course, they cite or invoke political theory ritualistically, paying it a sort of lip service; they are not always explicit about what aspect of political equality they have chosen to study and why; the criteria of political equality may be simplified to make them operational. But this does not undermine the larger intellectual picture: political theory's conceptual analysis of political equality and the moral reasons for its significance are meat for social science.

Now to temper this picture by considering an example of ideas traveling in the reverse direction. In recent studies, political scientists including Verba and his co-authors have demonstrated that men and women are *recruited* into active citizenship, including voting. They uncover a strong relation between the motivation and capacity to participate and being asked to participate. They show that recruitment goes on in formal and informal groups. This is a genuine addition to our understanding of political inequality: people without associational ties, lacking membership or affiliation, are less likely to be recruited and thus to participate.

Brought to light by survey research and confirmed by network theory and studies of civil society, the significance of associational life for political equality has reverberated in political theory. Consider five examples of the impact of the empirical finding of "recruitment" into participation as it travels to political theory.

First, the finding that associational membership is depressed owing to the relative isolation of men and women who are unemployed, for example, or who live in violent neighborhoods adds to political theory's menu of the elements of disadvantage and deprivation. It provides an additional, democratic justification for distributive justice: association as a condition of political equality.

Moreover, encouraged to see political equality in terms of institutionalized connections, political theorists propose regulative ideals of

association. If associations directly or indirectly promote democratic participation, an elementary question reappears in new guise: should the
associations from which citizens are recruited into participation be internally
democratic themselves, congruent with democratic principles and practices?
Does the connection to political capacity and motivation justify elevating
the participatory effects of association over other reasons for voluntary
association? After all, association is inseparable from other goods—convictions, cultural identities, status, salvation, demonstrations of competence,
exhilarating rivalry, and so on—apart from democratic citizenship.

Moving beyond regulative ideals of association, theorists consider
whether associations should be publicly recognized and supported by means
of taxes or subsidies if they represent major social interests, or are internally
democratic and other-regarding, or foster certain forms of organization
and practices of deliberation. Against advocates of a public policy of
"associational equality," others caution that government may be even more
powerful as patron than sovereign, that recognition and support configure
as well as stimulate voices, that associations may be more official artifact
than voluntary. They are skeptical about trusting official public judgments
as to what constitutes a healthy structure of group life, and find support for
skepticism in empirical studies of the complex, often benign participatory
effects of even undemocratic and illiberal associations.

Of course, the significance of association for political equality brought
to light by political science has encouraged theorists to recover historical
antecedents (Hegel, Tocqueville, the British pluralists) and to bring to the
surface buried aspects of the much-mined philosophy of Rawls or Habermas
or postmodernist thought. Attention to this facet of political equality has
also reshuffled divisions within political theory. Associations turn attention
beyond procedural equality and past the legally structured institutions of
elections, but the inequality of membership and availability for participation is not an artifact of general background economic inequality either.
A fertile middle ground positively invites a fresh mix of theoretical
perspectives. There is, for example, an entry for constructivism: after all,
the connection between association and recruitment to participation does
not assume that voice is "there," latent and in need of communication.
Associations are only sometimes formed for advocacy and participation;
often voices emerge unpredictably from groups formed for nonpolitical
purposes. Like women's groups in the 1970s, they *become* advocacy groups,
recasting what counts as matter of political interest in the process and
constituting as well as expressing voices.

In a short time, the theme of political equality, participation, and association has risen in importance in both political theory and political science.
The back and forth travels of these ideas are unmistakable in the arguments
and bibliographies of scholars of every stripe. These reverberations have
shaped new questions, guided empirical work, sharpened concepts, and

generated regulative ideals about political equality. It makes vivid the importance of traveling ideas and underscores our own professional reasons to recruit and promote open and fluid "free association."

Of possible related interest: Chapters 10, 43, 50, 83.

83

TO PARTICIPATE OR DELIBERATE—IS THAT THE QUESTION?

Dennis F. Thompson
Harvard University

Is participation compatible with deliberation? Here is a question to which both political theorists and political scientists should wish to have an answer, but which neither alone can answer satisfactorily. Empirical answers may challenge normative theory, but in turn the theory poses further questions. The best method for finding the right answer would integrate normative and empirical approaches more closely than is common in the discipline today. That method would also recognize that theorists should ultimately decide what the answer means.

Among democratic theorists, the turn toward deliberative theory in recent years has not displaced participatory theory. Although elitist versions of deliberative theory look with suspicion on citizen involvement in decision making, most deliberative democrats favor greater participation by citizens, if not in the deliberation itself then at least in judging the deliberation in which representatives engage. Rather than transcending participatory theory, many deliberative democrats see themselves as extending it. To the standard list of political activities in which citizens participate—voting, organizing, protesting—they add deliberating. At the core of deliberation is the practice of mutual justification—giving reasons that one's fellow citizens could accept as the basis for fair terms of cooperation. Citizens should adopt this practice to make decisions not only about policies but also about processes. Citizens should deliberate about how to participate.

The most common empirical challenge to deliberative theory takes the same form as the most common challenge to participatory theory. These theories are unrealistic, critics say, because most citizens are not political animals. They are not inclined to participate or deliberate, and are not good at either when they do it. But this critique has never impressed normative

207

theorists. It misses the point: theory challenges political reality. It is not supposed to accept as given the political reality that political science purports to describe and explain. It is intended to be critical, not acquiescent.

The more penetrating (and ultimately more constructive) empirical challenge seeks to show that the values that a theory prescribes conflict in practice. The theory falters not because democracy fails to realize its principles, but because one of its principles cannot be realized without sacrificing another one of its principles. Such a conflict is especially disturbing if the principles define essential goals of the theory, and are equally indispensable to its justification. Trade-off techniques and pluralist approaches offer no ready solution.

A democratic theory that combines participatory and deliberative principles is a case in point. Some recent empirical research suggests that the more citizens deliberate, the less likely they are to participate. Specifically, the more they discuss politics with people whose views differ from theirs, the less likely they are to engage in political activity. Some studies find that the deliberation may encourage participants to take more extreme positions. But other studies give deliberative democrats hope. Deliberating citizens come better to appreciate views of their opponents, show greater tolerance for legitimate differences of opinion, and are more prepared to make reasonable compromises. Yet these deliberative benefits come at a high price. The moderate attitudes that deliberation helps produce also weaken some of the most powerful incentives to participate. Opponents come to seem less like enemies; mobilizing to bring about their defeat appears less urgent. Unlike citizens who talk mostly with like-minded compatriots, deliberating citizens find themselves cross-pressured, their views more often challenged than reinforced. They may be less moved to take political action.

This conflict between participation and deliberation does not of course express a universal law. We do not yet know how general the conflict is— under what specific conditions it is more or less likely to arise. Is the conflict more likely to occur in discussions about certain kinds of issues? Is it more common in discussions among ordinary citizens than among political leaders? Is it more frequent in informal interactions than in formal institutions? Can forums for deliberation be structured in ways to avoid or mitigate the conflict? Some available research bears on these questions, but political scientists have much more work to do before democratic theorists would be ready to abandon their commitment to affirming both of these values. The empiricist's answer to the theorist's general question in this way prompts the theorist to ask more specific questions. The theorist needs the answers in order to evaluate how serious the conflict of values is, and what steps are worth taking to overcome it.

Political scientists may have some answers, but they do not have the last word. Even if the participation and deliberation conflict in significant ways, we still have to decide which value should have priority, or which combination of the two values is optimal. That decision depends significantly on considerations that are not primarily empirical—such as conceptions of human dignity and understandings of the fair terms of social cooperation. It is the theorist who must ultimately determine the nature and significance of any conflict. That is not as arrogant as it may sound if we keep in mind that as citizens we should all be theorists. To be sure: theorists who are well informed by empiricists. We need to know facts, but we cannot avoid making judgments about the fundamental values that our democracies promote or—more often—fail to promote.

Of possible related interest: Chapters 11, 13, 45, **82**.

84

UNDERSTANDING DEMOCRACY AS A COMPLEX ADAPTIVE SYSTEM

Louise K. Comfort
University of Pittsburgh

What are the most effective means for balancing equity and efficiency in democratic societies?

A major threat to U.S. democracy is the increasing discrepancy between the very rich and the very poor. While the fundamental values of a democratic society are based on the principles that all people are created equal before the law and that each person deserves basic respect and dignity, the reality of the market economy has produced a growing discrepancy between those who have stable economic resources and those who do not. This serious discrepancy creates conditions of inequity and injustice that are compounded by differences in race, sex, education, age, and ethnic background. Although the law clearly states that all citizens are equal and that discrimination based on race, sex, age, ethnicity, or disability is prohibited, economic and social structures have evolved in practice that inhibit citizens born in unequal conditions from overcoming these limitations. These persistent barriers to individual development erode the capacity for community development, and the nation is left with a growing underclass that undermines the vision and norms of a democratic society.

While the last century saw many efforts to address the disparity in income and opportunity for different groups within the U.S. society—minorities, women, children, elderly—these efforts did not solve the problem and often erred on the side of inefficiency. The primary focus of landmark legislation such as Aid to Families with Dependent Children (AFDC), in effect from 1935 to 1997, Aid to Disadvantaged Children (Elementary and Secondary Education Act, Title 1) implemented in the 1960s as a means to redress poverty, and the Comprehensive Employment and Training Act, implemented in the 1970s to broaden access to reliable employment, relied on economic redistribution and regulation to ease the disparities in equity among social groups. Too often, these mechanisms, based on flawed assumptions regarding the initial conditions of the target groups, created dependencies instead of the expected personal growth, as shown in the painful legacy of intergenerational dependence of families on welfare that became the public image of the AFDC.

Finding the appropriate balance between equity and efficiency in a democratic society is an old problem, but it deserves fresh examination and re-conceptualization of the dynamics that drive social interaction in a democratic framework. Experience from the last century shows that economic redistribution alone is not the solution, but the link between individual development and the design of public policy to support it is not well understood. Learning and responsible action cannot be mandated, but creating arenas of action that enable individuals to engage in constructive social activities and develop skills needed for effective communication and problem-solving is essential for collective action. The task is to identify what types of information individuals need at what stages in their lives and what types of practice in decision-making contribute to the development of responsible citizens who manage their own lives with minimal dependence and maximum benefit for the public good.

Reframing the problem of balancing equity and efficiency in public policy, I suggest four areas of inquiry that focus on the role of information in stimulating individual development and informed collective action. Such inquiry assumes the capacity for public investment in an information infrastructure to support not only individual growth, but also the search and exchange of information to create and communicate new meanings that bridge individual growth with community development and sustainable democratic practice.

1. Democracies require the development of basic skills in communicating needs, knowledge, and social values among the citizenry as well as the capacity to envision the public good.
2. Meeting basic economic needs, while essential for individual and community growth, captures only a part of the equation for building sustainable democratic societies.
3. The increasing size and complexity of democratic societies require a different conceptual model of democracy as an evolving complex adaptive system.
4. The methods of communication, coordination, and collective action essential for democratic self-governance can be developed most effectively through public investment in a sociotechnical infrastructure that supports an iterative process of action, feedback, and learning for individuals and organizations.

Each of these premises warrants further exploration in developing the logic of democratic action. Communication between individuals, within groups, and among groups is the basic function underlying collective action. The increasing rate of communication and the resulting ease, frequency, and range of communication among multiple individuals, groups, and organizations supported by current technologies has created a rapidly changing profile of political/social/economic interactions in democratic societies. This profile is at once hopeful and troubling. The basic task of initiating social change is how to design constructive processes of communication and feedback within and among social groups without stifling the creative individual expression that supports self-organization and adaptation among the groups and between the groups and their environment.

The increasing rate, scale, and intensity of communications among political, economic, and social groups have generated a complex set of interactions that does not fit previously identified models of organizational or political analysis. Understanding this emerging set of relationships represents a fundamental problem in organizational design that requires a fresh examination of the interactions between technical infrastructure and skills required for communication, changes in organizational structure and processes to reflect different audiences, varying degrees of access to information from public agencies, and a process of identifying and correcting error in this ongoing public dialogue. It is endemic to building a democratic society.

If the balance between equity and efficiency lies in enabling citizens to develop skills for self-organization and self-development within a structure of mutual respect, reciprocity, and law, the design, investment, and implementation of public policy needs to be refocused in a substantially different manner. The focus shifts to achieving self-control, lessening the burden on public agencies, and enabling a more dynamic pattern of search, exchange, collaboration, and continuous learning among the diverse groups and citizens of the nation. Processes of integration and incorporation of differences, leading to new and more creative visions of the public good, lessen the reliance on mechanisms of public control, as citizens gain capacity to manage their own affairs.

Of possible related interest: Chapters 10, 52, 86, 94.

Suggested additional reading

Lempert, Robert J., Steven W. Popper, and Steven C. Bankes. *Shaping the Next One Hundred Years: New Methods for Quantitative, Long-Term Policy Analysis*. Santa Monica, CA: Rand, 2003.

Ostrom, Elinor. *Understanding Institutional Diversity*. Princeton, NJ: Princeton University Press, 2005.

Young, Iris Marion. *Inclusion and Democracy*. Oxford: Oxford University Press, 2002.

85

THE PUBLIC ROOTS OF PRIVATE ACTION

A New Look at Voting Costs

Susan B. Hansen
University of Pittsburgh

Thanks in large part to the pathbreaking research by Sidney Verba and his colleagues, we now know much more about why people do or do not participate in politics. The "private roots of public action" have been plumbed in depth, and personal resources (education, income, social skills) have been shown to have a huge impact on the amount and types of political actions individuals undertake.

We have also learned more about how the social and cultural context influences individuals' choices, and how contacts by political parties, co-workers, churches, or labor unions can impact political interest and involvement. Verba and his co-authors showed how involvement in African-American churches added considerably to the political knowledge and activism of people whose minority status and lack of education might otherwise have kept them out of the public arena. Even participating in a public-opinion survey can increase one's likelihood of voting.

However, a major agenda for future research is the impact of increasing costs and barriers to voting. As the Brennan Center for Justice recently observed, "Voting is at the heart of our democracy. But, unfortunately, defects in election administration and outright vote suppression efforts keep many Americans from voting each election year." In the aftermath of the 1965 Voting Rights Act, the 24th Amendment banning poll taxes, Motor Voter laws, and growing opportunities to vote by mail or by using absentee ballots, one might have assumed that previous financial or institutional barriers to voting no longer carry much weight. But the 2000 election served as a major wake-up call to problems with access to the polls and the growing impact of felon disenfranchisement.

We have learned that even if one were able to cast a ballot, it might not be counted, whether the problem was hanging chads, voting-machine malfunction, butterfly ballots, or faulty records at the polling place. Many of these problems were also evident in the 2004 elections, and according to a 2005 report by the General Accounting Office, were especially prevalent in minority and democratic precincts.

The Help America Vote Act of 2002 attempted to remedy some of these problems, to fund updated voting equipment, and to provide for computerization of voter records. It also called for "provisional" ballots to be provided if someone's registration or voting qualifications were challenged at the polling place. But even if such provisional ballots were available, most of them are never counted. Although millions of dollars have been spent to upgrade voting equipment, computerized touch-screen voting without a required paper record has left open the possibility of fraud. Computerization of voter records has also led to widespread purging of both eligible and ineligible voters from the rolls.

Amid growing allegations of voter fraud and concern over illegal immigration, several states now require photo identification or other proofs of citizenship or residence at the polls. In April 2008 the U.S. Supreme Court, in *Crawford v. Marion County Election Board*, upheld Indiana's law requiring a government-issued photo identification in order to vote. The 5–4 decision cited the "potential" for voter fraud, and rejected the argument that the cost of obtaining photo identification constituted a new form of poll tax.

Political scientists therefore need to move beyond the "private roots of public action" and reconsider the public roots of private action. We must investigate the social and political consequences of the increasing legal, financial, and administrative barriers to voting. If credible evidence of voter fraud is indeed found, as many Republicans are claiming, appropriate remedies should be implemented in order to restore public faith in democratic elections. But what if such "remedies" have a disproportionate impact on poor, elderly, or minority voters, as many Democrats allege? Clearly we need to learn much more about the complexities of our system of elections, where the major administrative and financial responsibilities rest with state and local officials who are often elected or appointed by partisan methods. And we also need to learn more about how the limited personal resources of poor or minority citizens interact with the legal or administrative requirements necessary for fair and efficient elections.

In 1957, Anthony Downs' *Economic Theory of Democracy* introduced many political scientists to a cost-benefit analysis of voting. We again need to pay more attention to voting costs and to how well-intentioned reforms may have altered individuals' calculus about the act of voting.

Of possible related interest: Chapters 22, 56, 74, 87.

Suggested additional reading

Gillman, Howard. *The Votes that Counted: How the Supreme Court Decided the 2000 Presidential Election*. Chicago, IL: University of Chicago Press, 2001.

Manza, Jeff, and Christopher Uggen. *Locked Out: Felon Disenfranchisement and American Democracy*. New York: Oxford University Press, 2006.

Overton, Spencer. *Stealing Democracy: The New Politics of Vote Suppression*. New York: W.W. Norton, 2006.

86

ON THE FREE RIDER PROBLEM

Jane Mansbridge
Harvard University

Our collective failures to deal with crises in the environment and elsewhere are often based in a failure of political will. But that failure in will is itself based in part in an intellectual failure. Since the 1950s, our world has had the intellectual tools to understand collective action problems, with their embedded free rider dynamics. Most political scientists are aware of these dynamics, which constitute the major argument for government. But most citizens and journalists do not yet grasp the central idea.

The logic of collective action is, I believe, as important as the logic of supply and demand. If better and more widely understood, it would have the potential for explaining when governments must act and when they can (or should) do nothing. Economists often describe the goods that create a collective action problem as having three properties: being nonexcludable, jointly supplied, and nonrival. This formulation has not done much to advance the public's grasp of the issue. We can explain the problem to the public better if we focus on only one of these properties, nonexcludability. That is, once the good has been brought into being, those who have not contributed to its production cannot be excluded from its benefits. (We could explain the problem even better if we had a better term.)

The characteristic Hobbesian reasons for government involve the nonexcludable goods of protecting a nation from foreign enemies and maintaining domestic law and order. Robert Nozick once suggested that private security forces, paid for by each individual, could solve this nonexcludability problem, but no one has taken this suggestion seriously. It is more efficient to defend the country and to provide law and order collectively. When these goods are collectively provided, however, those who do not volunteer to help provide national defense, and those who do not voluntarily obey the law (or voluntarily sanction those who do not) benefit as much from the outcome as those who volunteer. Large numbers of other goods, including roads, education, and environmental controls, have the same characteristic of nonexcludability. In a highly interdependent large-scale world where the social sanctions of a small group are relatively ineffective, most of those goods require governmental collective action, that is, collective action backed by coercion (either the threat of sanction or the actual use of force).

In an earlier era, the laws of supply and demand were not well understood. Today when a price goes up most college-educated people ask, "Has supply fallen? Has demand risen? Or is some group exerting power over the market?" We expect supply and demand to produce market equilibria that are efficient and could even be just if the distribution of buying power were just. When governments pass laws legislating prices and wages, we expect that, whatever the benefits, that legislation will probably generate inefficiencies as well as widespread temptations to violate the law, at least in the absence of strong countervailing norms such as those that sometimes develop in a national emergency.

Only when as many people understand the logic of the free rider problem as understand supply and demand will we be able to address effectively the collective action problems in the environment.

For years, I have begun classes with a collective action problem. In the version of the problem I present, I act as a "common pool" that will double the resources of the people present without any effort on their part. Each person chooses, anonymously on a folded piece of paper, whether to give me $0 or $100. Whatever I receive, I double and return equally to all. In this situation, it pays each individual to contribute nothing and benefit from an equal return based on the others' contributions. But the less the members of the group contribute, the less they can benefit from my capacity to double their resources. All other things equal, the polity in which every individual contributes will do better than the polity in which some individuals do not. But in the absence of strong internal norms or external coercion, such benign outcomes (presuming for the moment that the ends to which the collective action is directed are benign) also tend to "unravel." If some have not contributed in the first round, more will fail to contribute in the second round (not wanting to be taken for suckers), and after three or four rounds practically no one will contribute.

A common pool of this sort is much like a fishing ground where fish reproduce, a commons where grass renews itself, or a society in which law and order facilitates economic transactions among strangers. Without coercive collective action, the fishing ground will be fished out, the commons will be overgrazed, and law and order will break down. Most citizens realize in a general way that they need governments to solve such problems when the scale is large enough to make social coercion ineffective, just as before economists developed the laws of supply and demand, most people realized in a general way that when crops failed the price of wheat would rise. But neither citizens nor the journalists who inform them on a

217

daily basis have the intellectual tool of the collective action problem to help them single out nonexcludable goods as requiring governmental action.

If this one finding—central to political science although developed in another field of the social sciences—were more widely understood, our profession might be able to help citizens in democracies move beyond a deep, inchoate anger at the very existence of government to a more nuanced understanding of where government is most needed and how to make its necessary work more just.

Of possible related interest: Chapters 36, 68, **87**, 92.

Suggested additional reading

Hardin, Russell. *Collective Action.* Baltimore, MD: Johns Hopkins University Press, 1982.

Olson, Mancur, Jr. *The Logic of Collective Action.* Cambridge, MA: Harvard University Press, 1965.

Ostrom, Eleanor. *Governing the Commons: The Evolution of Institutions for Collective Action.* Cambridge: Cambridge University Press, 1990.

87

TIME AND ACTION IN THE TWENTY-FIRST CENTURY

Anya Bernstein
Harvard University

Political scientists should apply the collective action problem to how Americans spend, allocate, and organize their time. As a result of the collective action problem, individuals have few incentives to work for social changes which would benefit everyone, not just themselves. The effect of the collective action problem can be seen locally, when parents don't participate in an effort to increase school funding, and it can be seen globally, when people don't get involved in efforts to stop global warming. Why should I decrease my carbon emissions when my SUV-driving neighbor is going to benefit just as much as I will from my efforts?

People who work for social change tend to have more money, education, and time than those who don't. However, Verba, Schlozman, and Brady (p. 303) show that, in contrast to money and education, spare time is relatively well distributed across the population. This means that there is less class bias with regard to time than money, which is good for those seeking to equalize political participation. But it also reminds us that the time crunch that affects people at both ends of the economic spectrum, from professionals working long hours to hourly workers who need two jobs to support themselves, has a huge impact on political engagement. As we strive to compete in a global economy, many Americans don't have time to fight the cable bill, to say nothing of demanding changes in environmental policies, or making changes in their own patterns of consumption.

But the twenty-first century demands political involvement as never before. And while efforts have been launched to reengage the young and the poor, little attention has been paid to the fundamental constraint of time and to its relationship with nonaction. If the twenty-first century is not going to go down as the greatest collective-action debacle in human history, we need to think about how to help people find the time to be civically, as well as economically, engaged.

Of possible related interest: Chapters 46, 63, 80, **86**.

Suggested additional reading

Olson, Mancur, Jr. *The Logic of Collective Action: Public Goods and the Theory of Groups.* Cambridge, MA: Harvard University Press, 1965.

Verba, Sidney, Kay Lehman Schlozman, and Henry E. Brady. *Voice and Equality: Civic Voluntarism in American Politics.* Cambridge, MA: Harvard University Press, 1995.

88

THE ORGANIZATION "GAP" IN POLITICAL SCIENCE

Joseph LaPalombara
Yale University

The centennial issue of the *American Political Science Review* (Volume 100, November 2006) serves as a reminder that we political scientists, with rare exceptions, do not pay much theoretical or research attention to the organizations (*as organizations!*), that are the most immediately involved in the political process. Of the 20 most-often-cited articles discussed in that issue, only two (i.e., March and Olsen on organizational theory, and Polsby on institutionalization phenomena within Congress) would qualify as addressing the following question: how do the organizations that are most directly involved in the political process of any country actually operate, and why is this so?

References by political scientists to the work of James March seem curiously abstract, in that they are rarely matched by empirical research that illuminates why and through what processes institutions germane to the political process come into existence; what rules are fashioned to govern the internal and external behavior of these institutions; how these rules work in practice; and how, over time, these rules and behaviors are interpreted, modified, or replaced.

This is what March and a few others (like Herbert Simon), for several decades, have been urging political scientists to do, but with very limited success. As a result, their seminal theoretical work has had considerably more purchase in the other social sciences. Dramatic evidence of this attention to organization is quickly gleaned, for example, from the pages of The Handbook of Organizational Learning and Knowledge (edited by Meinolf Dierkes et al.).

Our profession's mid-century concentration on the participatory "inputs" into the political process, and our more recent shift of attention to systemic "outputs" of policies, have strongly reinforced the scant attention that political scientists pay the "black box" of the governmental process itself. In both instances, scholars continue to make many assumptions about the transformation of "inputs" into "outputs." Few of these assumptions, sometimes masqueraded as "inferences" are supported by empirical evidence as to what actually happens, and why, in legislative halls, executive offices, judicial chambers, and, above all, in the governmental and bureaucratic offices of any political system.

This neglect of the organizational dimensions of politics is equally true of those emanations of civil society, such as political parties and interest groups, which are intimately involved in the making, the interpretation, and the implementation of public policies. In all cases, however, empirical studies of outstanding quality remain relatively scarce items in our discipline.

The extreme paucity of strong theoretical formulations, followed by empirical work on organizations, is especially troublesome in the case of political parties and legislatures. They are, after all, the formal institutions most immediately associated with democratic political systems. In the case of political parties, arguably the nerve centers of representative democratic systems, there is almost nothing of recent vintage in our discipline that follows on lines of inquiry in the tradition of earlier writers like Michels, Ostrogorski, Gosnell, Merriam, and a few others.

This situation is clearly limned in an article by H.L. Riker that appears in the centennial issue of the *APSR* mentioned earlier (Vol. 100, 2006, 613–619). He notes that, in the first decades of the discipline's history, a scant 10 percent of party-centered articles that appeared in political science journals paid attention to *any organizational aspect* of these important political entities. In recent years, even that scant number has been reduced by 80 percent! One might actually be led to believe that internal workings of these organizations are essentially irrelevant to how it is they actually behave.

The obvious consequence of this failure to theorize and to test theoretical formulations regarding the actual workings of governmental and other politically relevant institutions is that political science seems to know least about that concerning which political scientists should be most expert and knowledgable. Thus, the postwar revolt against older formalisms took modes of inquiry that, however valid they might be regarding the "inputs" or "outputs" of governments, illuminated precious little regarding the intricate processes that convert the first category into the second. In short, several decades following the so-called "behavioral revolution" in our discipline, we remain largely in the dark, or tied to untested impressions, regarding how the "authoritative allocations of values" takes place in any political system.

It was not always thus. Leading exponents of the "Chicago School," for example, did probe the internal workings of America's political parties. Two of its distinguished leaders (Charles Merriam and Harold Gosnell) not only confirmed much of what Michels and Ostrogorski had written a couple of decades earlier; they showed that the oligarchic control of American political parties placed these organizations, and through them, the governments of the U.S., at the service of special economic interests.

Another member of that group, Herbert Simon, with others, attempted at mid-century to lead the discipline to more sophisticated theoretical empirical approaches to the workings of public bureaucracies. And a third major figure who briefly graced the University of Chicago's political science group, A.F. Bentley, was literally sent into academic exile because he wrote a book, *The Process of Government* (1908), that boldly challenged the then prevailing notions as to how the policymaking and policy-implementing processes worked in practice. They pleaded largely in vain.

It may turn out that the "New Institutionalism" in political science research will bring about a treatment of state institutions as "arenas" within which, as Bentley once noted, conflicting groups compete for control of the institutions themselves, and of their outputs. This change might bring some of the discipline's members back to the study of *power*, a murky concept to be sure, which does not, for that reason alone, deserve to be excised from the discipline's vocabulary, or its theory-building and theory-testing activities. In any event, there are sufficient important landmark studies in the discipline's history that would provide important guidelines as to how to proceed to reduce a serious gap that other political scientists have in the past also recognized.

Of possible related interest: Chapters 64, **81**, 89, *100*.

Suggested additional reading

Dierkes, Meinolf, Ariane Berthoin Antal, John Child, and Ikujiro Nonaka, eds. *Handbook of Organizational Learning and Knowledge*. Oxford, UK: Oxford University Press, 2003.

Gross, Bertram. *The Management of Organizations*. Glencoe, IL: Free Press, 1964.

March, James G., and Herbert A. Simon. *Organizations*. New York: Wiley, 1958.

Panebianco, Angelo. *Political Parties: Organization and Power*. Cambridge, UK: Cambridge University Press, 1988.

89

THE SUDDEN BIRTH OF STICKY INSTITUTIONS, 1890–1915

Gerald Gamm
University of Rochester

Consider Brookline. As the *Boston Globe* wrote in 1906, the town "has triumphantly repelled all the attempts that have been made to annex it to the great metropolis that virtually enfolds it." Indeed, as historians agree, Brookline's repeated refusals in the late nineteenth century to consolidate with Boston represented the first signal that cities would now face stout opposition to their continued growth by annexation. With Brookline in the late nineteenth century, the independent suburb was born.

Or consider the American Political Science Association. The Association was founded in 1903, in an era when the social sciences assumed their modern forms. Nascent political scientists had recently created two journals—*Political Science Quarterly* (1886) and *Annals of the American Academy of Political and Social Science* (1890). With the founding of the Association, they soon created a third: the *American Political Science Review*, which began publication in 1906.

Or consider Harvard, which in 1890 combined the Faculty of the College with the Faculty of the Lawrence Scientific School to establish the Faculty of Arts and Sciences. Only a few years before, under the leadership of President Charles Eliot, had Harvard begun to offer graduate training in the College, transforming a small, elite undergraduate school into one of the nation's first great research universities. Or consider A. Lawrence Lowell, who with his appointment in 1897 as a part-time teacher, became the first member of the faculty whose work was devoted entirely to the study of government. Or consider the Government Department itself, which was founded in 1910 by President Lowell.

Within a single generation—roughly spanning the period from 1890 to 1915—modern America was born. The independent suburb, the organized discipline of political science, and the American research university all emerged in this age.

In the centuries preceding 1890, there was great ferment in the organiz- ing structures of American life. This ferment was evident everywhere, but nowhere more clearly than in the nation's political institutions. Senators before 1890 had not yet invented the position of floor leader, relying for guidance instead on a myriad of experimental institutions that came and went, ranging from powerful presiding officers to ad hoc steering committees. Members of the House of Representatives had not yet realized the advantages gained from a strong speaker, who could lead the majority party in its battles with the minority. The national parties themselves knew nothing except a narrative of creative destruction and reorganization, with their history littered with Jeffersonian Republicans, Federalists, Whigs, and a plethora of minor parties. And the president was oftentimes weak relative to Congress, with no inclination to appeal to the population for support.

Then came the period 1890–1915. Arthur Pue Gorman invented the position of floor leader when he was in the minority in the Senate during the 1890 fight over the Federal Elections Bill, and the Democrats have had a floor leader ever since that year. Republican senators established the position of floor leader in 1913, and both parties had created the position of whip by 1915. In the House, Thomas Reed consolidated majority power in the speakership in 1890, then in 1910 the House took its modern form, with majority rule tempered by strong committees. The modern presidency emerged full-blown with Theodore Roosevelt, who began addressing the public and seeking its support for legislation immediately after taking office in 1901. And the 1896 realignment represented the first time that both major parties survived intact, even as they reshuffled supporters and changed their policy priorities. Also in the 1890s, American voters began their long disengagement from electoral politics, ending at that time their once-ecstatic embrace of the voting booth, the political rally, and the torchlight parade.

For those living in 1890–1915, innovation was everywhere. The majority and minority leaders of the Senate, the structure of the House, the president "going public," the stability of two political parties, the disenchantment of voters: all of this was new, all of this was foreign. When Speaker Reed began to count nonvoting members for a quorum in 1890, James Morgan (D, MS) rose in fury to denounce the speaker's action as "unconstitutional and revolutionary." It was, indeed, a revolutionary age. The automobile and airplane grew up alongside the suburb. New York's Metropolitan Museum of Art, Boston's Symphony Hall, the new home of the Library of Congress, and Widener Library all opened their doors in the same era that the *American Political Science Review* began publication and Lowell delivered his first lecture.

But the revolution proved brief, and these institutions proved to be remarkably sticky. Looking back over a century's time, it is clear now that the convergence of changes and institutional organization in 1890–1915 established the contours of modern America. Of course, innovation did not end. But institutional innovation since 1915 has largely taken place within the framework established in that brief era. (Even the greatest social transformation of twentieth-century America, the revolution for civil rights, was undoing an institution, Jim Crow, which took form in 1890–1915.) The American political, intellectual, and cultural world in 1915 looked dramatically different from the world of 1890—much more different, in fact, than the institutions of the early twenty-first century are from the institutions of 1915. It was the governmental institutions established in 1890–1915 that led the United States to victory in two world wars and the Cold War, to the Moon, and into the computer age. It was a Congress, a presidency, and a party system, along with suburbs and cities and research universities that had all taken shape in the late nineteenth and early twentieth century.

Why so much changed, so quickly, in 1890–1915 is the obvious question. But at least as interesting is the matter of why these institutions, which had been adapting and transforming themselves in fundamental ways for centuries prior to 1890–1915, have not undergone such fundamental change since that era. Why did a myriad of institutions grow suddenly sticky at the turn of the last century? Frederick Jackson Turner was prescient in identifying the end of "the frontier in American history" in 1893, but only now can we see that the frontier stage of the nation's institutional development had been lived in Cambridge and Brookline and Washington and New York as much as in the hinterlands. While scholars have examined many of these institutional changes in isolation, we lack a unifying explanation both for the great changes in 1890–1915 and the enduring stickiness thereafter. Not only might there be value in analyzing this set of changes in American institutions, but in considering other places and other periods in history when institutional innovation crests then subsides.

Of possible related interest: Chapters 4, 22, **88**, 97.

Suggested additional reading

Jackson, Kenneth T. *Crabgrass Frontier: The Suburbanization of the United States*. New York: Oxford University Press, 1985.

Ross, Dorothy. *The Origins of American Social Science*. Cambridge: Cambridge University Press, 1991.

Schickler, Eric. *Disjointed Pluralism: Institutional Innovation and the Development of the U.S. Congress*. Princeton, NJ: Princeton University Press, 2001.

90

THE EMERGING FIELD OF
EDUCATION POLICY

Paul E. Peterson
Harvard University

In the rapidly developing field of education policy, new findings of policy significance are emerging at an increasingly rapid rate. Although some of the new findings remain controversial, multiple studies provide surprisingly strong support for the following propositions:

- Variation in school expenditures is very weakly correlated with student performance, even when student background and many other factors are taken into account.
- Although a student, in one year, will learn a year's worth of additional material from a good teacher (top quartile) than from an ineffective teacher (bottom quartile), whether or not a teacher has the appropriate credential (state certification that a particular program of study has been completed) is unrelated to teacher quality.
- After kindergarten and first grade, reduction in class size (within the range typically observed) has little impact on student performance.
- In the U.S., school choice innovations are more likely to enhance the academic performance of African-Americans than that of white students.
- When students are evaluated by means of an external examination, the impact on their performance in high school is significantly improved.
- Civic participation and civic mindedness is little affected by whether students attend a public or private school.

Many public policies in the U.S. are based on beliefs and assumptions contradicted by these six findings. If and when the propositions stated above become the conventional wisdom, significant, beneficial policy consequences are to be expected.

The rapid development of this field has occurred for reasons that resemble those that spurred progress in the study of public opinion and citizen participation in the decades immediately following World War II. Progress in both fields was generated by political, theoretical, methodological, and technological changes occurring at a specific historical moment.

Political. In the early sixties, citizens' expectations of their government were rising rapidly, causing institutional strains in developing and developed nations alike. Scholars searched for explanations for the politics they were observing. Today, the policy elites and the public at large have both come to appreciate the importance of educational institutions for economic growth and for the mitigation of social inequality, while, at the same time, discontent with the quality of public schools has intensified.

Theoretical. In the early sixties, academic foci in political science shifted from institutions to individuals, behaviors, and processes. Today, scholars in several social science disciplines (economics, political science, policy analysis, and sociology) have returned to the study of political institutions, including those that affect the generation of human capital.

Methodological. In the period following World War II, an increasing number of political scientists began using statistical techniques to identify and interpret the attitudes and behaviors of a large number of political participants. However, the data upon which they relied was largely observational, not experimental. Now it has become possible to test policy-relevant propositions by means of experimental or quasi-experimental research designs (identification of natural discontinuities, regression discontinuity analysis, propensity matching, fixed effects analysis, etc.), facilitating the identification of causal relationships. Significantly, it has proven feasible to apply these new methodological tools more extensively in the field of education policy than in many other areas of political science.

Technological. It has been said that scientific innovation is more influenced by technology than any or all of the three factors discussed above. Certainly, that was true of the study of citizen participation, which found its bearings when survey research techniques were able to generate vast new bodies of information about the opinions and activities of ordinary citizens. Today, a similar upsurge of information is occurring in the field of education, as a vast amount of new data about student performance and school characteristics is being generated by numerous government agencies. Given the extraordinary advances in computer technology, it is now cost-effective to analyze the hundreds of thousands, even millions, of observations that are now being generated.

For these reasons, one can expect in the coming years a continuing flow of surprising findings with significant implications for school policies. Education research, after floundering for decades, appears to be entering a golden era.

Of possible related interest: Chapters 23, 96, 99, 100.

Suggested additional reading

Chubb, John E., and Terry Moe. *Politics, Markets, and America's Schools.* Washington, DC: Brookings Institution Press, 1990.

Howell, William, and Paul E. Peterson. *The Education Gap: Vouchers and Urban Schools.* Washington, DC: Brookings, 2006.

Jencks, Christopher, and Meredith Phillips, eds. *The Black-White Test Score Gap.* Washington, DC: Brookings Institution Press, 1998.

91

AMERICAN POLITICS AND THE NOT-SO-BENIGN NEGLECT OF CRIMINAL JUSTICE

Traci Burch

Northwestern University

> Today, however, we have to say that a state is a human
> community that (successfully) claims the monopoly of the
> legitimate use of physical force within a given territory. . . .
> Like the political institutions historically preceding it, the
> state is a relation of men dominating men, a relation
> supported by means of legitimate (i.e. considered to be
> legitimate) violence. If the state is to exist, the dominated
> must obey the authority claimed by the powers that be.
>
> (Max Weber, *Politics as a Vocation*, 1921)

Well established among political theorists is the idea that government
exists to provide security for its citizens. Although governments have taken
on many other functions such as redistribution, the primary responsibility
of government remains protecting citizens from outsiders and each other.
The subfield of international relations studies extensively the efforts of the
United States and other countries to defend their residents from external
threats. However, Americanists largely have neglected to study how the
U.S. protects its citizens domestically, ceding much of the study of U.S.
criminal justice policies to sociologists and criminologists. This oversight
is surprising given the fact that according to the Bureau of Justice Statistics,
U.S. governments spent nearly $193 billion on law enforcement, courts,
and corrections in 2005, and employment in these areas has doubled since
1980.

Ignoring such a major activity of American governments at all levels
prevents us from understanding many aspects of politics because the
criminal justice system touches American politics in ways that implicate

nearly every area of study. For instance, scholars of American Political Development might explore the rapid growth of federal and state criminal justice bureaucracies designed to process, supervise, and institutionalize large numbers of citizens; the maintenance of these bureaucracies also informs long-standing debates in federalism, state politics, and urban politics. Those behavioralists who study campaigns and elections, public opinion, or agenda setting may find that crime and criminal justice issues are central to their understanding of policy preferences and elite framing. Likewise, scholars of individual behavior have learned from the policy feedback literature that government actions can affect the power, resources, and participation rates of citizens; this finding is no less valid for convicted individuals and their families. Recognizing the impact of criminal justice on American political institutions and behavior is most pressing for those of us who study minority politics because it means that we can no longer ignore the dramatic increase of arrests, convictions, and supervision borne by black communities and black men in our theories, surveys, and case studies.

Inequalities such as these matter for political outcomes, and scholars in the American subfield need to pay more attention to criminal justice, its unequal application, and its unintended effects. Notable works by Lawrence Bobo and Devon Johnson, Jeff Manza and Christopher Uggen, Marie Gottschalk, Tali Mendelberg, and others have examined the role of crime and criminal justice in shaping political behavior, public opinion, campaigns, and policy preferences; however, much more remains to be done with respect to thinking about the relationship between crime policies and politics. Failing to consider this important topic will have consequences for our ability to understand American politics both now and in the years to come.

Of possible related interest: Chapters 18, 47, 81, 88.

Suggested additional reading

Gottschalk, Marie. "Black Flower: Prisons and the Future of Incarceration." *Annals of the American Academy of Political and Social Science* 582 (2002): 195–227.

Manza, Jeff, and Christopher Uggen. *Locked Out: Felon Disenfranchisement and American Democracy*. New York: Oxford University Press, 2006.

92

LAW OR POLITICS?

H. W. Perry, Jr.
University of Texas at Austin

Law or politics? The question seems straightforward when posed "Are we to be a government of laws or men?" Or "Does Nation X operate under the rule of law?" In reality, the question of the relationship between law and politics is a profound and difficult one. How should a commitment to the rule of law shape or constrain politics and political behavior, especially the behavior of legal actors? How and in what ways does it? Is the outcome of *Bush v. Gore* the result of law, politics, or some complicated interaction between the two? Despite the centrality of issues related to the interaction of law and politics to the disciplines of political science and law, neither is as far along as we would hope in answering the normative and descriptive questions.

Normative theorists, especially those who wrestle with the philosophy of law, have made progress trying to distinguish law and politics, but formal definitions are ultimately not very helpful, especially to the political scientist. If, for example, politics is defined as "the authoritative allocation of values," law would simply be a form of politics. Normative concerns regarding law and politics run the gamut from questions about the proper organization of governments to the liberating versus repressive nature of law. The most common debates, however, center on constitutions, constitutionalism, and the role of judiciaries. An old and prominent example is the debate over the "countermajoritarian dilemma." Notwithstanding many efforts to explain away the dilemma, especially by legal academics, the normative problem remains. It continues to be a very important question to ask to what extent a constitution, especially one enforced by an unelected, unaccountable judiciary, should limit the decisions of democratic processes. The question is still relevant for the U.S., Great Britain, and the European Union, but it is of surpassing importance to many developing democracies. Do judiciaries reinforce liberal democratic values better than democratic institutions, or is such reinforcement contingent on many factors, including how judges see their roles? Political science ought to have more to say about this than it does. To do so, however, requires a *sophisticated* understanding of the actual behavior of individuals and governing institutions. Despite progress, our answers are still simplistic, especially when compared to other areas of political science.

Compare the law and politics question with questions about representation. There are varying normative and theoretical positions on representation, but we are quite sophisticated at understanding how representation works in the U.S. Congress. We have good research on how members of Congress think about representation, and we have good research that shows how they behave. We have progressed to see how behavior and normative positions mesh. Our answers are not dichotomous: trustee or instructed delegate. Rather, we know that politicians often see themselves as both, and we have a good sense of when and why they act as one or the other or in combination. Relatedly, we have become very sophisticated at understanding when and how rules and structures constrain and alter behavior and outcomes. Moreover, we can address theories about representation not only because we have a good grasp of how U.S. institutions work, but also because we know a great deal about how different systems affect representation; for example, presidential versus parliamentary, single member versus multimember, federal versus unitary, etc. By any measure, the level of sophistication as to how legislators, or executives, or voters make decisions is far superior to our understanding of how judges make decisions.

Massive amounts of research on judicial behavior have enabled us to predict behavior, but we still do not have a very good handle on how law and politics interact when it comes to the decision-making of judges or other legal actors. If the rule of law means anything, surely it means that judges must have some fidelity to the law that will constrain them. We know that law is often sufficiently indeterminate such that it rarely dictates answers. Even two judges who are dedicated to an impartial application of the law might come out differently. We also know that Democratic judges are likely to behave differently from Republican judges. Nevertheless, for the law to have a meaningful distinction from politics, it must constrain pure partisan behavior or individual predilection. Much research in political science suggests that the law provides little restraint. The most extreme forms suggest that appeals to the law or methods of interpretation are nothing but ex post facto rationalizations. This completely political understanding of legal decision-making flies in the face of all claims about the constraining nature of law that judges claim governs them. If that is so, how could they do their jobs with a straight face? To accept a premise that judicial decisions are nothing but the assertion of political preferences masquerading as law would suggest either that there is a grand conspiracy on the part of judges to be disingenuous, or that they are so profoundly dense that they have no insight into their own behavior. Of course as social scientists, we would not accept that law meaningfully constrains politics just because it is a dominant myth or because judges say so. However, the fact that there is another academic discipline, law, that accepts the idea that law should and often does constrain political behavior is noteworthy. Of course there are huge debates in the legal academy on this issue as well. Legal realism has been around for over 80 years and critical legal studies for at least 20. But most legal academics scoff at dominant understandings of judicial behavior by political scientists. As a political scientist, I can be highly critical of the legal academy on some terms, but it gives me some pause to say that there is an entire academic discipline and profession that rests on false premises. We know that an undue belief in judges being constrained by the law is a myth, but we also have reason to believe as with many other professions that professional norms and socialization matter in ways that would counteract the sheer assertion of preferences by judges. Compared to our more sophisticated understandings of the behavior of legislators, executives, bureaucrats, or even tinhorn dictators, our understandings of judicial behavior are wanting.

One development aiding advances in public law is increased interest in comparative questions. Comparative political science is particularly attuned to context. So, for example, a comparative perspective would start from the premise that emerging democracies come out of unique political histories and face varying circumstances. This understanding might call for very different answers about the degree to which we would want to constrain majorities by a constitution, the degree to which we would want to vest power in courts, and the extent to which judges should be made politically accountable. Political scientists should be the first to realize this. Compared to their legal academic colleagues who globe trotted to set up new constitutions, they did. The problem is that comparative scholars rarely cared about judicial institutions, and public law scholars disproportionately focused on the U.S. With some exceptions, until recently there has been little interest in developing a deep understanding of legal culture and how judges make decisions outside the U.S. Comparative public law is blossoming. Coming to understand law in different contexts may push us past some of the debates in public law where we have seemed to polarize or stall. In sum, as we look forward, the most important question for the future of public law scholarship is a very old one: the interaction of law and politics.

Of possible related interest: Chapters 6, **78**, 79, 93.

Suggested additional reading

Murphy, Walter F. *The Elements of Judicial Strategy*. Chicago, IL: University of Chicago Press, 1964.

93

WHAT IS PUBLIC POLICY?

Catherine E. Rudder
George Mason University

Political science needs to reconceptualize what is meant by the term *public policy*. Political science textbooks, reflecting disciplinary consensus, use a very constrained definition of *public policy* that focuses on government statements and activities: The composite of laws, rules, regulations, and actions *of government*, taken together, is characterized as public policy. Government, in this case, is used generically to mean any legally constituted branch, level, or agency of government. The *of government* part of the definition is presumably what makes the policy *public*. Hence under this conception of public policy, decisions made by private entities, like the Financial Accounting Standards Board or the American Petroleum Institute, cannot, by definition, be a matter of public policy regardless of how much of an impact they have on the general public.

Few scholars in the field of American politics have tried to grapple with public decision-making that occurs outside government, as Grant McConnell, who coined the phrase *private government*, did in 1966 in his seminal but neglected *Private Power and American Democracy*. More recently, international relations scholars have been highlighting the fact that much international public policy is made in the partial or complete absence of government, but often with national governmental actors involved. Despite these developments, political science has yet to incorporate nongovernmental policymaking into a full-fledged reconsideration of what constitutes public policy. Reality has outrun definition.

Why have the changes in contemporary politics not been adequately reflected in the public policy field? The answer may lie partially in the difficulty of agreeing upon which policy issues legitimately fall within the sphere of public concern or, more specifically, under what circumstances some or all of the public deserve a voice—perhaps even a deciding voice—in matters that the discipline has defined and seen either as *private* or as a matter of expertise. So, for example, under traditional ways of thinking, closing a plant in a one-company town, or selecting accounting standards, or deciding the number of consecutive hours a medical resident should be allowed to work in an emergency room are all *private* decisions based on claims of private property rights, expertise, and private self-governance, respectively. To suggest that private entities make public decisions is to confront several serious difficulties, including the charge of trying to renew an apparently long-settled ideological controversy over what is private.

The question of the right of the public to be represented in certain "private" decisions raises a host of practical questions, ranging from *who is the public* to *how can the public be represented*—questions confronted by the Internet Corporation for Assigned Names and Numbers, for example, when it unsuccessfully tried to represent the entire world in its decision-making. Without the convenient link to *government* involvement in a decision, how is it possible to identify a public policy decision?

Political scientists should care about this issue not only for practical reasons, that is, because reality has outstripped conceptualization, but also for normative ones. Abraham Lincoln asserted the unique American experiment to be one of government of, by, and for the people. What are the consequences for this national experiment when public policy is being made by private actors whose actions are not necessarily *of, by, or for* the people?

One must question, for example, whether policy decisions made by a private group of subject-matter experts are value-neutral or whether such decisions reflect an epistemic bias that may lead to unbalanced public policy. As Giandomenico Majone has observed, if a group of experts on nuclear energy were asked whether more reactors should be built, the answer would likely reflect the particular training, conceptual frameworks, and life choices that have been made by these nuclear scientists. Similarly, the Financial Accounting Standards Board, the nonprofit group that sets U.S. accounting standards, can be expected to make decisions that flow from accounting principles even if those decisions ultimately lead to the elimination of defined benefit pension plans or to the elimination of retiree health benefits for millions of Americans. When public decisions are made by professional organizations, such as the American Medical Association, under the banner of self-regulation, one can expect serious conflicts of interest to arise sometimes; what is good for a profession and what would benefit the public are not always congruent. Subject-matter experts are not necessarily, nor are they likely to be, public policy specialists, that is, skillful in refining and enlarging views in a way that may lead to second-best technical policy but that endeavors to represent the needs, concerns, and interests of the general population rather than those of the experts.

Until recently, the field of political science has described a society in which civil society, the market, and government each exist as unique and separate categories with clearly defined roles to play in the life of the nation. In reality, this was never the case. With the movement away from governmental regulation and toward self-regulation, however, and with the growing importance of international rule-making regimes, this simplification has become increasingly problematic. To overlook these blurred lines is to miss a large part of the reality of policymaking that truly is public.

Of possible related interest: Chapters 8, 22, 60, 100.

Suggested additional reading

Cutler, A. Claire, Virginia Haufler, and Tony Porter, eds. *Private Authority and International Affairs*. Albany, NY: State University of New York Press, 1999.

Mueller, Milton. *Ruling the Root: Internet Governance and the Taming of Cyberspace*. Cambridge, MA: MIT Press, 2002.

Weimer, David L. "The Puzzle of Private Rulemaking: Expertise, Flexibility and Blame Avoidance in U.S. Regulation." *Public Administration Review* 66 (2006): 569–582.

94

NOTE TO POLITICIANS

Forget the Silver Bullet!

Kay Lehman Schlozman
Boston College

> There is always a well-known solution to every human
> problem—neat, plausible, and wrong.
> (H.L. Mencken, "The Divine Afflatus")

When it comes to the way American politicians deal with complex problems, H.L. Mencken's observation is too often on target. A contemporary political scientist might come up with a far less quotable truism: "There are always a number of solutions to every problem—some of them neat, some of them plausible, and all of them partial." The problems that public authorities in America address on a long-term basis rarely have a single cause. Complex problems require multi-pronged solutions. Nevertheless, politicians search for the silver bullet that has the virtue of being financially practical, ideologically congenial, or easily collapsed into a sound bite. That single solution is, of course, doomed to disappoint.

As an illustration, consider an enduring regularity—which, to many, is not a "problem"—the pay gap between men and women who are in the workforce full time. While there are, not surprisingly, methodological disputes among those who adduce systematic evidence to explain this phenomenon, there is reason to conclude that multiple factors contribute to the continuing gender disparity in wages. Some of them can be grouped loosely under the rubric of human capital deficits: the fact that, compared to their male counterparts, women who are in the workforce full time, year round show, in the aggregate, a deficit with respect to both the educational credentials needed for the most demanding and remunerative careers and, because they may take time out of the workforce to raise children, seniority and experience. Other explanations of the gender gap in wages can be grouped loosely under the rubric of discrimination. There is strong evidence that, in many occupations, women are not hired, rewarded, or promoted on the same terms as men having similar human capital endowments with the result that, in any particular occupation, the most prestigious and highly paid positions tend to be held by men. Moreover, many occupations are gender segregated and, all things equal, those with a high proportion of female workers are less well paid; with other factors taken into account, as the proportion of female workers in an occupation rises, its wages fall.

Given the complex origins of the gender gap in pay, other than mandating the exact same pay for all workers no matter how many hours they work, no matter how hard they toil, no matter how skilled or experienced they are, no single social or economic change, and certainly no single policy innovation, would close it completely. Parity in pay between men and women depends, for example, upon myriad private decisions by individual women and men in what and how long they study and how they arrange to manage their households and care for their children; upon decisions in corporate board rooms and human resources departments about policy with respect to such matters as pregnancy and family leave, the handling of sexual harassment, and the assignment of employees to particular job titles as well as upon decisions about which particular individuals to hire, promote, and recommend for employee training programs; and upon government policies with respect to such matters as day care, pregnancy, and family leave, or the enforcement of anti-discrimination laws. Substantial change with respect to any one of these would have an impact on the pay gap, but no single development can be expected to produce gender equality in pay or even to reduce the disparity very substantially. In fact, over the last generation various developments ranging from the passage of Title VII of the Civil Rights Act of 1964 and Title IX of the Educational Amendments of 1974 to women's decisions about their educational preparation, career choices, and workforce attachment have reduced the pay gap by about two-fifths.

Nevertheless, public officials who care about the pay gap—and there are not very many of them—are unlikely to embrace the whole range of social, economic, and policy changes that might, taken together, make a real difference. Instead, they are likely to call attention to a much narrower set of solutions that fit the ideology and pocketbook: summarizing the problem as, on the one hand, originating entirely in market decisions made by individuals or, on the other, arising entirely from discriminatory practices.

This pattern of selective focus repeats itself for many other issues with complex origins. Rates of violent crime? One side emphasizes mandatory sentencing. The other stresses gun control. Energy needs? The answer is drilling for oil in the Arctic Refuge. Or is it conservation? Academic achievement deficits in the public schools? There are cheerleaders for school vouchers and advocates for higher teacher salaries. More recently, the conversation has been broadened to argue that even together these policies will fail unless attention is paid not only to schools but also to the lives of the young—including early childhood education, children's health, and after-school activities.

Why do politicians so frequently fix on a single solution? Ordinarily, the preferred, though partial, solution is the one—among the options that can be easily communicated to the electorate in a sound-bite world—that articulates with other normative and policy commitments and that is not offensive to other, more deeply held, values. Yet the refusal to eschew the silver bullet not only impedes the solution of complex problems but contributes to political and partisan polarization in contemporary American politics. In short, wouldn't it be nice if politicians understood what political scientists, like all social scientists, know? We live in a multi-variate world.

Of possible related interest: Chapters **60**, 62, 84, 99.

Suggested additional reading

Kingdon, John W. *Agendas, Alternatives, and Public Policies*. 2nd ed. New York: Longman, 1995.

Stone, Deborah. *Policy Paradox: The Art of Political Decision Making*. New York: W.W. Norton, 1997.

Tetlock, Philip E. *Expert Political Judgment: How Good is it? How Can We Know?* Princeton, NJ: Princeton University Press, 2005.

95

REDISCOVERING
COMPLEXITY AND
SYNTHESIS

Bear F. Braumoeller
Ohio State University

International relations scholarship has benefited in many ways from having adopted the epistemologic orientation of the hard sciences, with its focus on theorizing and the derivation and testing of hypotheses. Even if that orientation were to be supplanted tomorrow—by, say, a more descriptive model, or one that rejects rigid hypothesis-testing—its emphases on careful measurement, rules of inference, and replicability would surely live on.

From the point of view of theorizing, however, the hard-science model has had at least one deleterious effect: it has embedded in the minds of international relations (IR) practitioners the prima facie assumption that theories are made to be tested against one another, period. Whether embedded in the titanic "paradigm wars" of the 1980s and 1990s, the long-simmering rational choice controversy, or the more recent constructivist challenge to orthodox IR theory, this bedrock premise has closed off avenues of thought that had previously been both fruitful and fascinating. The main avenues of thought that I have in mind are the complementary ones of theoretical complexity (elaborating scope conditions and interactions within theories) and theoretical synthesis (merging two or more theories to form a unified and more comprehensive whole).

The dialogue among paradigms provides a nice illustration of this point. Originally, theoretical paradigms such as realism and liberalism were adopted in an attempt to make the unmanageable complexity of international politics more tractable. By "bracketing" (or ignoring) other variables, IR scholars could better focus on the internal logic of theories that implicated power or preferences (or meaning) in the study of human behavior. In a discipline that increasingly emphasized theory-testing, however, this temporary theoretical convenience was transformed into ossified ontology. Realists argued that the world was made of units that were usefully differentiated *only* by their relative capabilities, and testing a realist explanation against an X-ist explanation became standard, even expected, in dissertations and journal articles.

What, then, was to become of John Herz's *Political Realism and Political Idealism,* a book that attempted to understand how the reality of power politics could be reconciled with the human desire to transcend it? Or Arnold Wolfers' essay, "The Pole of Power and the Pole of Indifference," which offered a different answer to much the same question? Both are thought-provoking, learned, and insightful. Neither is standard fare, or anything like it, in graduate orals reading lists. Their insights seem nearly forgotten. As it happens, I found both on the shelves of used-book stores, and the price of the two combined would just cover a latte at my local coffee shop.

To be sure, there are occasional recrudescences of this sort of contextual, synthetic thinking. William Zimmerman's essay on "Issue Area and Foreign-Policy Process," Brian Pollins and Randall Schweller's article on "Linking the Levels: The Long Wave and Shifts in U.S. Foreign Policy," and Emerson Niou and Peter Ordeshook's "'Less Filling, Tastes Great': The Realist-Neoliberal Debate" surely deserve mention. And to give credit where it is due, Robert Keohane's earlier paradigmatic work in particular seeks to build on realism, and Alexander Wendt's constructivism admits a necessary "rump materialism" (though the anatomical analogy hardly gives it pride of place). But the inexorable pull of the theory-testing premise has led subsequent developments in both paradigms toward differentiation and away from synthesis. Socialization also tends to work against synthesis: scholars working primarily within one paradigm who attempt it are likely to be chastised for theoretical impurity (see e.g., Andrew Moravcsik and Jeffrey Legro, "Is Anybody Still a Realist?").

At the same time, advances in statistical methodology are opening a back door to thinking about synthesis and complexity. What are hierarchical models, Boolean models, and simple multiplicative interactions, if not models of context? What are endogeneity biases and selection effects, if not an indicator that another theory must be incorporated? (And what, if we face up to our darkest fears, *isn't* at least potentially endogenous in the study of IR?) Still, these issues tend, like heteroskedasticity, to be treated as a nuisance to be eliminated, rather than an opportunity to formulate a richer and more satisfying description of social reality.

A broader epistemological orientation, one that encompasses synthesis and complexity as well as theory-testing (and, I would add, descriptive inference and interpretation, but that's for another essay) would sooner or later raise a host of questions that merit discussion. When, for example, are theories so poorly specified that synthesis would be counterproductive? Which kinds of theories should be tested against each other, and which are better candidates for synthesis? (Is ontological incommensurability, in other words, an obstacle or an opportunity?) How severe is the tradeoff between our desire for parsimony and the greater demands of understanding more complex theories? Or, to put the question in its broadest form: how do we best incorporate synthesis and complexity into our understanding of IR?

Admittedly, my assessment of the importance of this research agenda deserves a disclaimer: my research on the methodology of causal complexity, and my substantive work synthesizing dyadic theories of conflict with a systemic theory of politics (itself a synthesis of structural and domestic theories), clearly make me a less than unbiased observer. While my work in those areas has been quite rewarding, it has also increased my appreciation of the number and difficulty of the questions that must be answered if complexity and synthesis are to be addressed in a serious way.

Of possible related interest: Chapters 77, 83, 94, **96**.

96

WHY?

Kenneth A. Shepsle
Harvard University

Post-war, mid-twentieth century developments in political science, mainly of a methodologic flavor, transformed a discipline prone to historical narratives and descriptive tomes into a social science. We learned to count, measure, and generally to identify regularities and give precision to otherwise imprecise observations. But we forgot, for quite a long time, how to ask "Why?" And even in those cases where we did, it was often as an afterthought. The real triumph was the identification of empirical patterns in data, not explanations of them.

"Why?" is the question to which we political scientists should devote more of our intellectual labor. Explanations for empirical regularities, carefully derived from clearly articulated premises, are the gold standard to which we should hold ourselves. Robin Farquharson in his *Theory of Voting* (Yale, 1969), quoting the mathematician C.A. Coulson, put it thus. He suggested that the use of mathematics in application to a social or physical problem involved three steps: "i) a dive from the world of reality into the world of mathematics; ii) a swim in the world of mathematics; iii) a climb from the world of mathematics back into the world of reality, carrying the prediction in our teeth." An explanation for him (and for me) is a (set of) sufficient condition(s), better yet necessary and sufficient condition(s), characterizing "how the world works."

The modeling tradition in political science and political economy has provided an antidote to a thick empirical focus to our research, but it is hardly a fully satisfactory one. Ranging from microeconomics to canonical rational choice theory, game theory, behavioral decision theory and agent-based modeling, there are growing signs of interest in building a skills-set to engage why-questions and provide explanations qua mechanisms to account for empirical regularities. The fact that nearly all PhD political science programs in major research universities offer training in modeling is hopeful. Each new generation of political scientists comes armed with both methodological and theoretical tools their teachers can only envy. If persuasion and conversion are blunt and only partially effective instruments of intellectual change, then it will be generational replacement that is the principal vehicle for moving us along toward answers to why questions. ("Scientific progress occurs one death at a time" as they say.)

The behavioral revolution produced a methodological transformation of political science. In its zeal for precise measurement and the development of tools with which to analyze the data thus produced, however, it threw some babies out with the bath water. Attention to explanation is one of these.

Of possible related interest: Chapters 9, 53, **95**, 97.

Suggested additional reading

Laver, Michael. *Playing Politics: The Nightmare Continues.* New York: Oxford University Press, 1997.

Shepsle, Kenneth A., and Mark S. Bonchek. *Analyzing Politics: Rationality, Behavior and Institutions.* New York: W.W. Norton, 1997.

97

PATH DEPENDENCE

Peter A. Hall
Harvard University

What is path dependence and what are its implications for the study of politics? In recent years, few concepts have risen to more prominence. The Google search engine identifies 379,000 references to the term and Google Scholar yields 18,100. But analysts assign it many different meanings and clear definitions are rare.

Douglas Puffert's elegant formulation describes path dependence as "the dependence of economic outcomes on the path of previous outcomes, rather than simply on current conditions." But what is the difference between "previous outcomes" and "current conditions" and how can the former have causal effect in the present if not through the latter? In an article for *Theory and Society*, James Mahoney argues that "path dependence characterizes specifically those historical sequences in which contingent events set into motion institutional patterns or event chains that have deterministic properties." Should chains of developments, however, be described as path dependent only if their initiating events are contingent, that is, not amenable to systematic explanation? Margaret Levi claims that "path dependence has to mean, if it is to mean anything, that once a country or region has started down a track, the costs of reversal are very high." Subsequent inquiries into the costs of reversal have been revealing, but does this definition capture the full range of causal processes seemingly referenced by the concept? There is strong agreement in the literature that the concept of path dependence describes an important set of phenomena, but agreement on precisely what those phenomena are has been elusive.

In some respects, the notion is a venerable one, already visible in Marx's claim that "the tradition of all the dead generations weighs like a nightmare on the brain of the living." He was not simply saying that "history matters" but advancing precise claims about how it matters. In recent years, the term has been used to explain why market competition does not always produce efficient outcomes, notably because of increasing returns to adoption and network externalities. The basic intuition behind path dependence is familiar to game theorists and historical institutionalists alike: choices made in the past can bias current choices so thoroughly as to rule out many

246

courses of action. Comparing these two approaches, however, reveals one of the unresolved issues: what features of the social, economic, or political world give developments in the distant past such influence over subsequent actions? Most analysts presuppose some sort of ether that carries the imprint of the past into the present, whether in the form of institutions, prevailing ideas, or what Tocqueville termed habits of the heart. But we need to know more about the relative role played by each type of factor.

If the concept of path dependence is confusing, why use it at all? One answer is that images of causal processes in the political world have changed since the days when political outcomes were explained largely as the product of socioeconomic factors operating with the same causal force in all times and places. Compare contemporary analyses of transitions to democracy with older, hydraulic images of democracy as a response to socioeconomic pressures.

Variations in explanatory taste provide another answer. Explanations couched in terms of current conditions do not always have much purchase over phenomena that are the product of long chains of historical development. In principle, one can explain national variations in the generosity of social spending by reference to national variations in the character of benefit systems, but many may prefer to go on to ask why those benefits systems were developed in the first place and never reduced—inquiries that take one into the realm of path dependence.

However, I think the central appeal of the concept of path dependence lies in the acknowledgment it accords context effects, namely conditions cumulating over time in each place that alter the local effects of a common causal factor, such as an economic shock or a shift to the political right. Where interaction effects of this sort are important, similar causes have different effects across space and time, turning history into a branching tree whose forks supply the most familiar metaphor for path dependence. The concept points to instances in which common shocks increase, rather than diminish, the differences across nations or regions—a phenomenon political science is beginning to recognize, along with equifinality, its mirror opposite.

The implication is that we need better conceptualizations of how path dependence operates and more methodological sensitivity to the possibility that it might be operating. This calls, not only for the type of "disciplined configurative inquiry" that Sidney Verba described in his famous 1967 article for *World Politics* on the dilemmas of comparative research, but for building interaction effects more fully into our statistical models and paying closer attention to their residuals. These are worthy challenges for the new generations of scholars working in the field.

Of possible related interest: Chapters 71, 84, 89, 96.

Suggested additional reading

Mahoney, James. "Path Dependence in Historical Sociology." *Theory and Society* 29 (2000): 507–548.

Pierson, Paul. "Increasing Returns, Path Dependence and the Study of Politics." *American Political Science Review* 94 (2000): 251–267.

Thelen, Kathleen. "Time and Temporality in the Analysis of Institutional Evolution and Change." *Studies in American Political Development* 14 (2000): 102–109.

98

SEARCHING FOR A
POLITICS OF SPACE

Jennifer Hochschild
Harvard University

Political science would benefit from a more systematic study of the politics of space, analogous to recent work on the politics of time. Consider a few analyses of time: Stephen Skowroneck, like Samuel Huntington and Albert Hirschmann, has written on "the tendency for politics to cycle over broad spans of time." Paul Pierson and Kathleen Thelen, in contrast, both analyze the linear projection of time through history, such that sequences of events, conditions at starting points or crucial junctures, and slow-moving but powerful trajectories all shape political structures and possibilities. David Mayhew, however, declares a pox on all their houses. In deconstructing the best-known Americanist claim about political change over time, electoral realignment theory, he insists that "any partitioning of electoral history into regular spans of time is likely to rub up against reality and fail" in the face of contingency, short-term strategies, and opportunistic valence issues.

This is a fascinating and useful debate; we need an analogous consideration of the politics of space. A few elements could include:

- "Attention to the politics of scale—the processes by which scale is constructed," in the words of Susan Clarke. How are boundaries around small, medium-sized, and large entities created and changed? When, how, and why do large entities (say, a country) subdivide? When do small entities (city states or European countries) get absorbed into a larger unit (national state or European Union)? How does politics change in a location when it subdivides or gets absorbed? What sorts of politics do changes in boundaries permit, encourage, and forbid? Samuel Beer's analysis of the invention of American federalism, and Alberto Alesina's and Enrico Spolaore's dissection of "the size of nations," provide a fine start here.
- Attention to relations between units of different size. Larger units usually dominate smaller ones and use their scale to extract resources.

But when, how, and why do smaller units occasionally exercise power over larger ones? What is the appropriate division of labor among units of different scales? Scholars such as Robert Dahl and Peter Katzenstein have written elegant books on size and democratic governance or trade policy, and the concepts of subsidiarity or localism frame useful analyses. But we lack a systematic theory to tie together research on links among large and small political units.

- Attention to the scale of political activity. Political calculations and interactions presumably change as actors move from direct engagement in small groups to communication with millions of citizens through the media or some other aggregative mechanism. How are concepts of democracy, participation, or authority rethought as one moves from a room to a community to a country to an international organization? Do small cities or states conduct political business differently from large ones, or does institutional structure override size? Scholars ranging from Jane Mansbridge and Diana Mutz on face-to-face interactions to Larry Bartels and Robert Hackett on national and international political communications provide a wealth of material for developing a theory of political scale.

- Attention to interactions among units close to or far from one another. Poverty in cities is intimately, perhaps causally, connected to inequalities between cities and suburbs; as Douglas Rae argues, "Being able to choose where is a more powerful instrument for deciding what and how one's family will live than anything else." Immigration from a neighboring nation generates a different commitment to and from the host country, and a different form of nativism, than does immigration from a distant nation, as Christian Joppke and Gallya Lahav have shown. A collapsing regime near one's own country might generate a different sort of political response than a regime collapse on the other side of the globe.

- Attention to political strategies that revolve around scale. When and why do activists seek to expand the scope of conflict, as E. E. Schattschneider advised; when do they prefer subsidiarity or localism? Who promotes federalism and decentralization, or national oversight and centralized governance? Does the slogan, "think global and act local" have any real political content? Compare, for example, the activities of environmental movements seeking to clean up the local park with those focused on a nation's nuclear testing or the world's global warming; are there general lessons to be derived therefrom?

- Attention to the imperatives of space. Rae argues that American cities developed as they did not only because they were near good harbors or navigable rivers, but also because AC electric currents worked better over wide areas than did DC currents and because inventors developed trains on fixed rails before cars that could choose their path. David

Laitin and colleagues argue that civil wars can be partly explained by the presence of mountains or swamps. Did natural boundaries such as rivers and mountain ranges in Africa shape the history of European colonization and its effects on nation-building and contemporary governance? Scholars such as David Lublin and Dewey Clayton, as well as the U.S. Supreme Court, have compared physically compact or bounded electoral districts with those gerrymandered to permit election of representatives of scattered but politically important interests. Are there broad principles here; is there a generalizable politics of geography or topography?

A list of bullet points is far from a theory. But it hints both at ways to bring together extant literatures that are now unconnected, and at untrodden pathways of analytic development. As that sentence suggests, it is hard to write without spatial metaphors; maybe we should move from metaphor to research program.

Of possible related interest: Chapters 31, 52, 58, **71**.

99

THE QUESTION OF
RELEVANCE

Joseph S. Nye, Jr.
Harvard University

Political scientists should devote more attention to unanswered questions about how our work relates to the policy world we live in. A survey of articles published over the lifetime of the *American Political Science Review* found that about one in five dealt with policy prescription or criticism in the first half of the century, while only a handful did so after 1967. As journal editor Lee Sigelman observed in the centennial issue, "if speaking truth to power and contributing directly to public dialogue about the merits and demerits of various courses of action were still numbered among the functions of the profession, one would not have known it from leafing through its leading journal."

As citizens, academics might be considered to have a normative obligation to help to improve policy ideas when they can. Moreover, such engagement in the policy debates can enhance and enrich academic work, and thus the ability of academics to teach the next generation. As Ambassador David Newsom argued a decade ago,

> the growing withdrawal of university scholars behind curtains of theory and modeling would not have wider significance if this trend did not raise questions regarding the preparation of new generations and the future influence of the academic community on public and official perceptions of international issues and events. Teachers plant seeds that shape the thinking of each new generation; this is probably the academic world's most lasting contribution.

Yet too often, scholars teach theory and methods that are relevant to other political scientists, but not to the majority of their students sitting in the room before them.

One can argue that while the gap between theory and policy has grown in recent decades and may have costs for policy, the growing gap has produced better political theory, and that is more important than whether it is relevant. To some extent the gap is an inevitable result of the growth and specialization of knowledge. Few people can keep up with their subfields, much less all of social science. But there are costs as well as benefits if we become more elegant and less relevant. There is a danger that political science will say more and more about less and less. This is the question to which we should pay more attention. As Robert Putnam put it in his APSA presidential address, "simple questions about major real-world events have driven great research. Worrying about the same 'big' issues as our fellow citizens is not a distraction from our best professional work, but often a goad to it."

Even when academic political scientists supplement our usual trickle-down approach to policy through students and professional journals with articles in policy journals, op-eds in newspapers, blogs, and consulting for candidates or officials, we now find many more competitors for attention. Some of these transmission belts serve as translators and additional outlets for academic ideas, but many add a bias provided by their founders and funders. They are very heterogeneous in scope, funding, ideology, and location, but universities generally offer a more neutral viewpoint. In addition, journalists, public intellectuals, nongovernmental organizations, trade associations, private contractors, and others are involved in providing policy ideas. As Ernest Wilson points out in *PS*, while the pluralism of institutional pathways may be good for democracy, many of the non-university institutions have narrow interests and tailor their policy advice to fit particular agendas. The policy process in democracies is diminished by the withdrawal of an academic community which has more impartial agendas and more rigorous intellectual standards.

Stephen Walt has argued in *The Annual Review of Political Science* for "a conscious effort to alter the prevailing norms of the discipline." Departments should give greater weight to real-world relevance and impact in hiring and promotion decisions, and journals could place greater weight on relevance in evaluating submissions. Universities could facilitate interest in the real world by giving junior faculty greater incentives for participating in it. Since many young academics are (understandably) risk averse, that would require greater toleration of unpopular policy positions. One could multiply such useful suggestions, but young people should not hold their breath waiting for them to be implemented. If anything, the trends in academic life seem to be headed in the opposite direction. That is the central un-answered question to which I think political science should devote more effort.

Of possible related interest: Chapters 81, **88**, **90**, **100**.

Suggested additional reading

Nye, Joseph S., Jr. "Studying World Politics." In *Journeys through World Politics: Autobiographical Reflections of Thirty-Four Academic Travelers*, edited by Joseph Kruzel and James N. Rosenau, 199–212. Lexington, MA: Lexington Books, 1989.

Putnam, Robert. D. "APSA Presidential Address: The Public Role of Political Science." *Perspectives on Politics*, 1 (2003): 249–255.

100

CAN (SHOULD) POLITICAL SCIENCE BE A POLICY SCIENCE?

Kenneth Prewitt
Columbia University

Political scientists know more about the general workings of politics than any other expert groups. What they know is relevant to improving political practice—on topics ranging from designing fair election regimes to recognizing instabilities in security alliances.

If this is so, why ask the question that titles this note? Because relevant knowledge is not necessarily used knowledge. It would be instructive to frame an agenda for research that explained the conditions under which political science theory and findings were used to improve political practice and public policy.

Political science might start by systematically examining the probable outcomes depending on the strength of scientific evidence available to a given policy choice and the strength of the political forces working to prevent or advance the policy. "Smoking causes cancer" worked its policy influence when the science was too compelling to allow the limited political opposition from the tobacco industry to prevail. In contrast, early uncertainties in the science of global warming allowed a strong, broad political opposition to postpone a policy response, and then to reframe warming in ways beneficial to interests that initially had denied it. These instances from biology and atmospheric science have counterparts in the social sciences. Educational psychologists document a causal connection between teacher quality and early learning, yet a policy application makes little headway where teacher unions are strong. In contrast, the same scholars documenting the importance of early invention found an easy policy opening as the nation rushed to pre-school programs. Strong science/weak science and strong politics/weak politics is a two-by-two table that, if systematically examined, could point toward a theory of the use of scientific knowledge in policy process. Political science is well suited for this examination.

Alternatively, we might compare political science with the other social sciences. We might learn that the influence of political science on political matters is comparatively less than the influence of economists on economic practice or sociologists, at least when in evaluation mode, on social policy or educational psychologists on school reform. If this pattern of comparative influence were indicated, is it because there is something intrinsic to political science that lessens its influence? I suspect there is. Politics, or statecraft more generally, is jealously guarded by the people who make their livelihoods in it. The people of power to whom political science must speak about this or that procedural improvement—say, a responsible two-party system, thresholds for representation in multi-party systems, campaign finance—are not inclined to admit that someone brings an expertise superior to what they have accumulated experientially.

It may be that procedural improvements are less amenable to targeted policy advice than advice based on a more generalized explanation of how politics works. Political science could help policymakers see why a majoritarian strategy is so often trumped by interest group politics. It is probable, however, that the political insiders will always believe their knowledge of how politics actually works to be more reliable than the pages of the *APSR*, even when their knowledge is a second- or third-hand version of what earlier appeared on those pages—mad scribbling about concentrated costs and diffuse benefits is a classic case of Mertonian obliteration by incorporation.

Perhaps the foregoing paragraphs have misspecified the research question. It should not be whether specific findings bear on specific improvements. It should, rather, move to a much higher level of abstraction—the realm of ideas. Woodrow Wilson's *Congressional Government* argued for strengthening executive power and administrative expertise at the expense of messy, corrupt legislative politics. His hope for an Age of Administration merged into the rise of Progressivism. Graham Wallas, in *Human Nature in Politics*, worried that a public motivated by fears and phobias could not act dispassionately in the political realm. This reoccurring worry about the excesses of democracy finds its most mature expression in the elite theory of democracy articulated in Joseph Schumpeter's influential *Capitalism, Socialism and Democracy*. Conservative theorists calling into question the efficiencies of a regulatory state is another oft-cited example of the power of research-derived ideas in the political realm. Or, in another domain, Harold Lasswell's developmental construct of the garrison state, though ahead of its time, is highly relevant to today's debates about the enlargement of executive power.

These cursory paragraphs do not pretend to answer the question posed in the title, only to argue that it should be asked. Since its beginnings in the late nineteenth century American political science has been two closely linked projects: a *science project*—deeper understanding of political behavior, relationships, institutions, etc.; and, a *nation-building project*—strengthen democracy, protect national security.

Research that pays attention to the linkage between these two projects is in short supply. The obligatory final paragraph in research articles, "someone should pay attention to my findings because they have policy relevance," hardly passes the test of serious inquiry into the conditions under which social science knowledge improves policy and practice. Many of us—certainly the editors of this volume and the remarkable scholar it honors—believe that such serious inquiry will demonstrate that in interacting with policy and practice, our discipline both strengthens its scientific foundation and influences, for the better, what it investigates.

Of possible related interest: Chapters *81, 88, 90,* **99**.

Suggested additional reading

Katznelson, Ira. "Policy History: Origins." In *The International Encyclopedia of the Social and Behavioral Sciences,* edited by Neil Smelser and Paul Baltes, 11541–547. Amsterdam: Elsevier, 2001.

Lasswell, Harold D. *"Policy Sciences."* In *The International Encyclopedia of the Social Sciences*, edited by David Sills, 181–189. New York: The Free Press, 1968.

Prewitt, Kenneth. "Political Ideas and a Political Science for Policy." *Annals of the American Academy of Political and Social Sciences* 600 (2005): 14–29.

APPENDIX: CONTRIBUTORS

John Aldrich, Pfizer-Pratt University Professor, Duke University, cannot remember the first time he met Sidney Verba, but it was a dozen years ago that he discovered that poker is actually not a competition but a setting for "sit-down" comedy.

James E. Alt, the Frank G. Thomson Professor of Government at Harvard, recalls his first encounter with Sid's wit and sense of decency 30 years ago, when Sid offered him a junior job at Harvard. Upon being declined, Sid had the grace to express agreement with the decision, earning undying respect and affection.

Kristi Andersen, Laura J. and R. Douglas Meredith Professor of Teaching Excellence in the Department of Political Science at the Maxwell School at Syracuse University, met Sidney Verba when she was a graduate student at the University of Chicago and he served as a member of her dissertation committee. Since then, she has enjoyed dinner and good conversations with him at approximately 394 professional conferences.

Ana Barbič worked with Sidney Verba on the cross-national project on public participation (1968–72) and joined his data elaboration team at the National Opinion Research Center (NORC) (1969/70), which resulted in the grant of SPSS to the University of Ljubljana. She is a professor at the University of Ljubljana and a founder of the field of rural sociology in Slovenia.

Larry M. Bartels has been learning from Sidney Verba's work for the past 30 years and recently served with him on the American Political Science Association's Task Force on Inequality and American Democracy. He is the Donald E. Stokes Professor of Public and International Affairs at Princeton University.

Robert H. Bates, the Eaton Professor of the Science of Government at Harvard, got to know Sid Verba only when they became departmental colleagues—even though he had long read and admired Sid's work.

Anya Bernstein models her own teaching and advising after Sidney Verba, her dissertation Chair, and has found herself repeating to her students what he told her after every one of their meetings: "So what are you waiting for? Go do it!" She is a Senior Lecturer and Director of Undergraduate Studies in the Committee on Degrees in Social Studies at Harvard.

Jeffrey M. Berry got to know Sid Verba at various events sponsored by the Department of Government at Harvard. He is the John Richard Skuse Professor of Political Science at Tufts University.

Katja Boh worked with Sidney Verba on the same project as Ana Barbič. After being a professor of sociology at the University of Ljubljana in the first decade (1991–98) of the independent state Republic of Slovenia, she served as a Member of Parliament, a Minister of Health, and the Ambassador of Slovenia in Vienna.

Henry E. Brady, Director of the Survey Research Center and the Class of 1941 Monroe Deutsch Professor of Political Science and Public Policy at the University of California, Berkeley, has not yet graduated from the life-long seminar with Sidney Verba that began as a graduate student at Massachusetts Institute of Technology (MIT) in the mid-1970s at a joint Harvard-MIT seminar organized by Sidney and Walter Dean Burnham. Along with fellow student, Kay Schlozman, Brady is planning to continue his enrollment in Verba's seminar—if he keeps his grades up.

Bear F. Braumoeller of the Department of Political Science at the Ohio State University, was a colleague of Sidney Verba's for the better part of a decade at Harvard University. Despite repeated attempts, he was never able to pry any information out of Verba, then the University Librarian, regarding the coveted secret faculty offices in the depths of Widener Library.

Traci Burch, Assistant Professor of Political Science at Northwestern University and a Faculty Research Fellow at the American Bar Foundation, is the latest in a long line of political scientists who began their careers as Sidney Verba's research assistant. She hopes that her future career will be as illustrious as those of the other members of this privileged group.

Barry C. Burden exchanged ideas and poker winnings with Sidney Verba during their seven years together at Harvard. He is Professor of Political Science at the University of Wisconsin.

Nancy Burns recalls that the only time she asked Sidney Verba when he was planning to retire was when he called to recruit her to graduate school in 1986; throughout their many years of working together, the question never again came to her mind. She is Warren E. Miller Professor of Political Science at the University of Michigan.

David Butler has been a Fellow of Nuffield since 1951. He attended early Almond/Verba conferences on both sides of the Atlantic.

Andrea Louise Campbell, Hayes Career Development Associate Professor of Political Science at MIT, heard the legend of Sidney Verba as a Harvard undergraduate in the 1980s; met the man through graduate advisor, Henry Brady, in the 1990s; and had the pleasure of serving with him on the Harvard faculty in the 2000s.

David E. Campbell first met Sidney Verba in 1996 as a greenhorn grad student in Harvard's Government Department. He is now the John Cardinal O'Hara, C.S.C. Associate Professor of Political Science at the University of Notre Dame.

Daniel Carpenter, Professor of Government and Director of the Center for American Political Studies at Harvard, has known Sidney Verba for only eight years but has secretly kept tapes of all of his jokes, hoping for the rights to them when Sidney moves to California.

Louise K. Comfort met Sidney Verba as a junior research associate on the Civic Culture study at Princeton University in January, 1959, and has continued a lifetime friendship with Sidney as mentor and colleague over all these years. She is Professor and Director of the Division of Public and Urban Affairs at the Graduate School of Public and International Affairs, University of Pittsburgh, and Principal Investigator of the Interactive, Intelligent, Spatial Information Systems (IISIS) Laboratory.

Philip E. Converse first met Sidney Verba more than 40 years ago in Norway, where they were both attending a Stein Rokkan international conference, and later collaborated with him on a little book for the 1972 presidential campaign entitled *Vietnam and the Silent Majority: The Dove's Guide*. He is Distinguished Professor-Emeritus, University of Michigan, and Director-Emeritus, Center for Advanced Study in the Behavioral Sciences at Stanford.

Hans Daalder, Emeritus Professor of Political Science at Leiden University, first met Sidney Verba when a select group of scholars met in 1966–67 at the Center in Palo Alto to work on the ambitious, but still unfinished, Smaller European Democracies project. During Sid's two-year European interlude in the early 1970s he saw to it that the Netherlands was included in the seven-nation political participation project, whilst Norman Nie "burned" the Leiden computer night and day to develop SPSS.

Russell Dalton unfortunately did not meet Sidney Verba in person until midway through his career, but as a struggling assistant professor he was fortunate that Verba wrote a positive letter in his tenure case (Thanks Sid!). He is now a professor of political science at the University of California, Irvine.

Rodolfo O. de la Garza, the Eaton Professor of Administrative Law and Municipal Science at Columbia University and Vice-President for Research of the Tomas Rivera Policy Institute, first met Sidney Verba in 1989–90 when they both were directing national surveys of political attitudes and behavior. In response to his query about how to direct major team projects, Verba said, "The first thing I would do is change my name to Abraham Abromowitz."

Michael X. Delli Carpini did not encounter Sidney Verba in person until he was a faculty member at Rutgers in the early 1980s, but he first "met" Sidney Verba as a graduate student when he read, and was influenced by, *Participation in America*. He is currently the Dean of the Annenberg School for Communication at the University of Pennsylvania.

Jorge I. Domínguez is the Antonio Madero Professor of Latin American Politics and Economics and the Vice Provost for International Affairs at Harvard University. Sid Verba was the Department Chair at the time when he became a tenured professor at Harvard; they have been friends and colleagues for 30 years.

Morris P. Fiorina, the Wendt Family Professor of Political Science at Stanford University, first met Sid when he was recruited by Harvard in 1981. He and wife, Mary, look forward to many more dinners with Sid and Cynthia in Mono City, California (a suburb of Lee Vining).

Michael L. Frazer is an assistant professor of Government and Social Studies at Harvard University. He had the misfortune not to arrive at Harvard until 2007, when Sidney Verba was entering retirement.

Jeffry A. Frieden, Professor of Government, Harvard University, has depended upon the kindness of Sidney Verba ever since he came to Harvard—intellectually, personally, humoristically, and financially (at the poker table).

Gerald Gamm still smiles at the memory of his senior year in 1985–86, sharing newly discovered census documents and unrolling maps in Sidney Verba's office in Wadsworth House, and he remembers just as happily the day he took the Verbas and the Shepsles for a tour of Roxbury and Dorchester's churches, synagogues, and neighborhoods. He is Associate Professor of Political Science and History and Chair of the Political Science Department at the University of Rochester.

Claudine Gay has benefited from Sidney's scholarly advice and professional support for 15 years, first as a graduate student and later as a colleague at Harvard. She is a Professor of Government at Harvard University.

Peter A. Hall recalls being unable to answer the first question asked at his oral general examinations in May 1977 by Sidney Verba, with whom he studied comparative political behavior the previous year. He is currently Krupp Foundation Professor of European Studies at Harvard University and is still trying to answer that question.

John Mark Hansen is the Charles L. Hutchinson Distinguished Service Professor in Political Science and the College and the Dean of the Social Sciences at the University of Chicago. He first met Sidney Verba in 1984 while a graduate student, when Professor Verba, in typically generous fashion, came forward at a conference to compliment Hansen's remarks on a paper delivered by one of Verba's former students.

Susan B. Hansen first met Sidney Verba when she was a student in his Comparative Politics seminar at Stanford University. She later followed him to the National Opinion Research Center at the University of Chicago to work on the Participation in America project, on which her dissertation *Concurrence in American Communities: The Response of Local Leaders to the Community Political Agenda* (Stanford, 1972) was also based. She is currently Professor of Political Science at the University of Pittsburgh.

Hugh Heclo was a colleague with Sidney Verba in the Harvard Government department during the 1980s. He is currently Robinson Professor of Public Affairs at George Mason University.

D. Sunshine Hillygus is the Frederick S. Danziger Associate Professor of Government and Director of the Program on Survey Research at Harvard. As Sid's junior colleague, Sunshine has been the recipient of his sage advice and witty one-liners since 2003.

Jennifer Hochschild has learned from and been influenced by Sidney Verba's work since she was an undergraduate at Oberlin College several decades ago, and one of her proudest moments occurred when she became his colleague. She is Henry LaBarre Jayne Professor of Government, Professor of African and African American Studies, and Harvard College Professor at Harvard University—and a member of the Brookline Political Science Association.

Nahomi Ichino met Sidney Verba in the Department of Government at Harvard University where she is an assistant professor.

Torben Iversen first met Sid Verba in 1994 upon joining the Harvard Department of Government as a lecturer. He is now the Harold Hitchings Burbank Professor of Political Economy in the same department.

Lawrence R. Jacobs was first drawn to Sidney Verba when he read *The Civic Culture* as a graduate student and later became a deep admirer when he chaired the APSA Task Force on Inequality and appreciated Sidney's remarkable contributions. He is Mondale Chair at the University of Minnesota's Department of Political Science and Humphrey Institute and Director of the Institute's Center for the Study of Politics and Governance.

Christopher Jencks has been Sidney Verba's colleague at Harvard on and off since 1974, and from 2000 to 2006 they collaborated on a study of the diverse consequences of rising economic inequality in the USA. He is currently the Malcolm Wiener Professor of Social Policy at the Kennedy School of Government.

M. Kent Jennings first encountered Sidney Verba, the author, when, just beginning his career, he ran across Verba's stimulating work on small groups; he literally cannot remember the first time that Verba, the author, assumed human form though he suspects it was at some conference where Verba was making his trademark perceptive and witty comments. Jennings is Professor of Political Science at the University of California, Santa Barbara, and Professor Emeritus at the University of Michigan

Philip Edward Jones joined the Verba-Schlozman-Brady juggernaut in 2006 as a research assistant, and later a co-author. He is a PhD candidate in Harvard's Department of Government.

Michael Jones-Correa recalls that, in 1994, Sidney Verba chaired the search committee that hired him for his first job out of graduate school, thus ensuring both his gainful employment and his start as a bona fide political scientist. He is now Professor of Government at Cornell University.

Jane Junn met Sidney Verba in the late 1980s while working on the Citizen Participation Study, and has learned many things from him —among them the distinction between the categories of shlemiel, shlimazl, and shmegegge. She is Associate Professor in the Department of Political Science and the Eagleton Institute of Politics at Rutgers University.

Ikuo Kabashima, Professor Emeritus of Japanese Politics at University of Tokyo and former Vice-President of the International Political Science Association, was a student and co-author of Sidney Verba. His nonsocial science undergraduate training, combined with social science graduate training as a student of Sidney Verba's, has enabled him to conduct research using FMRI.

Ira Katznelson arrived at the University of Chicago in 1974, having just missed the colleagueship of Sidney Verba, but not his profound influence on that department and the larger discipline. Presently, Katznelson is

Ruggles Professor of Political Science and History at Columbia University.

Nannerl O. Keohane greatly admired Sid Verba's work on comparative politics as a graduate student at Yale; over the years they have become friends and colleagues and collaborated most recently on the Harvard presidential search. She has served as president of two institutions (Wellesley and Duke) and now teaches political philosophy at Princeton.

Robert O. Keohane, now Professor of International Affairs at Princeton, has followed Sidney to various universities, including Harvard, where they became friends and co-authors—even though he maintains that he has never caught up with Sidney intellectually. He tries to follow Sidney's advice never to write about a country he hasn't at least flown over.

Gary King has known Sidney Verba for more than two decades as a friend, colleague, co-author, and member in good standing of the Brookline Political Science Association. He is the David Florence Professor of Government, and the Director of the Institute for Quantitative Social Science, at Harvard University.

Casey A. Klofstad was honored to have Sidney Verba as the Chair of his dissertation committee while earning his PhD at Harvard University (2005). He is currently an Assistant Professor of Political Science at the University of Miami.

Anton Kramberger was inspired by Almond and Verba's book, *The Civic Culture*, as a student in the 1970s, which encouraged him to research political sociology topics ever since. He is Professor of Sociology and Social Science Methodology at the University of Ljubljana.

Joseph LaPalombara is the Arnold Wolfers Professor Emeritus of Political Science and Management of Yale University. His life has been enriched by over a half-century of professional and personal friendship interactions with Sidney Verba.

David C. Leege, though influenced by Sidney Verba's earlier works, first interacted closely with him around 1993 in the lead-up to *Voice and Equality*. Leege is Emeritus Professor of Political Science, University of Notre Dame, and co-edits a book series called Cambridge Studies in Social Theory, Religion, and Politics.

Jan Leighley couldn't find a political participation panel at a professional meeting for the first 10 years of her career that did not include Sidney Verba (as well as Kay Schlozman and Henry Brady); everything she knows about paper presentations she learned from the best. She is Professor of Political Science at the University of Arizona.

Arend Lijphart first met Sidney Verba in the 1960s when they were teaching at, respectively, the University of California, Berkeley, and Stanford University, and worked closely with him during 1994–95, when Verba was President and Lijphart President-Elect of the American Political Science Association. Lijphart is Research Professor Emeritus of Political Science at the University of California, San Diego.

Roderick MacFarquhar, Leroy B. Williams Professor of History and Political Science and Professor of Government, has known Sidney Verba since arriving at Harvard in 1984. For the six years while MacFarquhar served as department Chair, Verba occupied the neighboring office and was his most valued source of sage advice and the author of wonderful lyrics for his farewell party.

Thomas E. Mann, Senior Fellow and W. Averell Harriman Chair in Governance Studies at The Brookings Institution, first met Sid Verba while on the staff of the American Political Science Association. He has been an avid student of Sid's ever since.

Jane Mansbridge remembers that Sidney Verba left the University of Chicago for Harvard just as she became an Assistant Professor at Chicago, but he graciously gave her a reading of her first book, in which she had used some of his and Norman Nie's survey questions, and ushered her into the warmth of his friendship. She is currently the Adams Professor at the John F. Kennedy School of Government at Harvard University.

Harvey Mansfield, Kenan Professor of Government at Harvard, was a classmate of Sidney Verba (Harvard '53) and has enjoyed his company as colleague in the Harvard Government Department since his arrival. He reports that on every occasion when they discuss a point, either they agree or Verba wins.

William C. McCready, Vice-President, Academic & Nonprofit Research, Knowledge Networks, first met Sid at NORC and, as the lab director at Northern Illinois University, later worked with Sid on the fieldwork for the participation project with Professors Brady and Schlozman. He recalls Sid's kindness to students and considers Sid to be a consummate academic gentleman of the old school—both civic and civil to an extraordinary degree.

Eileen McDonagh, currently Professor of Political Science at Northeastern University and Visiting Scholar at the Institute for Quantitative Social Science (IQSS) at Harvard University, met Sidney Verba in 1968 while struggling to finish her PhD dissertation as a graduate student in the Government Department at Harvard. Little did she know then that the instant interest and compassion he showed would be something she could count on—and has counted on—for decades to come.

Jens Meierhenrich first encountered Sidney Verba in 2005 when the latter engaged him in a discussion about methods—preferred methods of book storage in the offices of the newly built Center for Government and International Studies. He is Assistant Professor of Government and of Social Studies at Harvard University.

Eric Nelson has known and admired Sidney Verba for over 10 years. He is currently Assistant Professor of Government at Harvard University, and was until recently a junior fellow in the Harvard Society of Fellows.

Norman H. Nie, Director of the Stanford Institute for the Quantitative Study of Society and Research Professor of Political Science at Stanford University, met Sidney Verba as an entering graduate student at Stanford in the fall of 1964. This career- and life-altering encounter produced several books, numerous articles, and a friendship that now spans more than four decades.

Pippa Norris, the McGuire Lecturer in Comparative Politics at Harvard University, has been walking in Sidney Verba's footprints for as long as she can remember. Her latest publications are *Driving Democracy* and *Making Democracy Deliver* (an edited report for the United Nations Development Programme).

Joseph S. Nye, Jr. is University Distinguished Service Professor at Harvard University. For four decades, he has admired Sid Verba as a friend, colleague, department Chair, and fellow member of more university committees than he cares to remember.

Philip Oxhorn has known Sidney Verba since 1982, when he began his doctoral studies at Harvard, and was later privileged to benefit from his insights while writing a doctoral dissertation on political opposition in Chile's slums during the 1980s. He is currently an Associate Professor in the Department of Political Science at McGill University.

Benjamin I. Page, the Gordon Scott Fulcher Professor of Decision Making at Northwestern University, has been learning from Sidney Verba ever since he started graduate school at Stanford in 1965 but has never mastered Sidney's jokes, especially those involving rabbis.

H. W. Perry, Jr., especially appreciated Sid's willingness to stop and ooh and ahh so convincingly over the newest baby pictures and Sid's role in creating a civil culture that included an abundant generosity with his colleagues and students when he served as an assistant and associate professor in the Harvard Government Department. Perry is now is an associate professor in the Department of Government and in the School of Law at the University of Texas at Austin.

Mark A. Peterson reveled in the humor, grace, and intellect of Sidney Verba when they were colleagues and they co-taught at Harvard University in the 1980s and 1990s. He is now Professor of Public Policy and Political Science at the University of California, Los Angeles (UCLA) School of Public Affairs.

Paul E. Peterson, then an assistant professor at the University of Chicago, discovered what it was to be a true intellectual the night Sidney Verba left a party to write down an idea for his book, *Vietnam and the Silent Majority* (1970). In recent years he has greatly profited from the fact that his position as Henry Lee Shattuck Professor of Government at Harvard University allows him to have an office immediately adjacent to Professor Verba's.

John R. Petrocik, Professor and Chair at the University of Missouri-Columbia, mumbled hello to Sidney Verba in September of 1970 as an entering graduate student at the University of Chicago. They were only occasional collaborators after he left to spend almost 25 years at UCLA, but Sidney's influence on how he thought about politics, research, and the scholarly enterprise never waned.

Gerald M. Pomper first met Sidney Verba when they were graduate students and neighbors in married student barracks at Princeton and has shared thoughts, talks, and tales of their children for half a century. He is Board of Governors Professor of Political Science (Emeritus) at Rutgers University.

G. Bingham Powell, Jr., met Sidney Verba at Stanford in 1964 and persuaded him to serve on his PhD dissertation committee. He is currently Marie C. and Joseph C. Wilson Professor of Political Science at the University of Rochester.

Kenneth Prewitt, now the Carnegie Professor of Public Affairs, Columbia University, first benefited from Sidney Verba's career advice in the early 1960s, and has returned repeatedly to it as he has wandered at the career boundaries between political science and other venues: "Seems a bit far-fetched, but should be O.K. if you keep in mind that if the science isn't right, none of the rest of it will be."

Robert D. Putnam, Peter and Isabel Malkin Professor of Public Policy at Harvard, has been the beneficiary of Sidney Verba's guidance for nearly half a century. *The Civic Culture* sparked Putnam's first interest in political behavior; Verba was the anonymous (and cautiously positive) reviewer of Putnam's first book manuscript; Verba recruited Putnam to the Harvard faculty with the aid of a timely cannoli in the North End; and over the ensuing years Sid and Cynthia gently honed Bob and Rosemary's appreciation for foreign films.

Lucian W. Pye is Ford Professor of Political Science Emeritus at MIT and past President of the American Political Science Association. He co-edited with Sidney Verba *The Citizen and Politics*, essays in honor of Gabriel Almond.

James N. Rosenau, University Professor of International Affairs at the George Washington University, first met Sidney when he moved to Princeton in the 1960s.

Nancy L. Rosenblum is a political theorist and the Senator Joseph Clark Professor of Ethics in Politics and Government at Harvard University. She is a consumer of Sid Verba's work, a beneficiary of his insight into the psychology of colleagues, and her poor memory makes her the perfect, eternally appreciative audience for his jokes.

Catherine E. Rudder is a professor in the School of Public Policy at George Mason University. As Executive Director of the American Political Science Association, she had the delightful experience of working with Sid when he was president.

Arthur Sanders began receiving thoughtful guidance from Sidney Verba as a graduate student at Harvard in 1979 and has continued to seek and receive his advice all these years since. He is currently Professor and Chair of the Department of Politics and International Relations and Director of the Honors Program at Drake University.

Virginia Sapiro has admired Sidney Verba and his work since 1974 when she was studying for her prelims. After more than 30 years in the Department of Political Science at the University of Wisconsin, Madison, she is now Dean of Arts and Sciences and Professor of Political Science at Boston University.

Anne Sartori has known Sidney Verba since 1993, when she became his research assistant and he gave her an intellectual home away from home. She is Associate Professor of Political Science at Northwestern University.

Eric Schickler was Sidney Verba's colleague at Harvard from 2003 to 2006 and a member of the Brookline Political Science Association. He is Professor of Political Science at the University of California, Berkeley.

Daniel Schlozman is told that he met Sidney Verba when he was a few days old and Sidney delivered a poem ("Who was the bravest in the lion's den?/ Who was the boldest of the frontier men?") in honor of his arrival. He is a PhD candidate in the Government Department at Harvard, and Sidney is a member of his dissertation committee.

Kay Lehman Schlozman began laughing at Sidney Verba's jokes as graduate student at the University of Chicago and has continued to do so throughout a research collaboration that has lasted more than three decades. She is J. Joseph Moakley Professor of Political Science at Boston College.

Philippe C. Schmitter first met Sidney Verba at the University of Chicago where they were colleagues from 1969 to 1972. Currently, Schmitter is a professor emeritus of political and social sciences at the European University Institute and a recurring visiting professor at the Istituto Italiano di Scienze Umane in Florence and the Central European University in Budapest.

Bill Schneider was a student and colleague of Sidney Verba at Harvard University in the 1970s. Since 1991, he has been CNN's Senior Political Analyst.

Goldie Shabad, Professor in the Department of Political Science at the Ohio State University, has never forgotten her long ago dissertation defense at the University of Chicago when Sid, her thesis advisor, asked her, "So why should we care about political equality?" Ever since, the "so what" question has informed her work and has been the first question that she asks of her dissertation advisees.

Byron Shafer, then Andrew W. Mellon Professor of American Government at Oxford University, first met Sidney Verba when the latter agreed to come and talk about his work and interests, a challenge that he repeatedly met. When Shafer became Glenn B. and Cleone Orr Hawkins Chair of Political Science at the University of Wisconsin, Verba graciously moved the same show to Madison, thereby exchanging drizzle for snow.

Shauna L. Shames was the footnote-checking slave for Sidney Verba on *The Private Roots of Public Action* in 2000, when she was an undergraduate. She is now a PhD candidate in American Government at Harvard University and has graduated to the exalted position of research assistant.

Kenneth A. Shepsle first met Sidney Verba in the spring of 1985 as the two stood on the patio of the Center for Advanced Studies in the Behavioral Sciences gazing at the Stanford campus below, with Sid describing how horrible, in comparison to Harvard, it would be to have to live "down there." Taking Sid's advice (and the Harvard offer), Shepsle is the George Dickson Markham Professor of Government at Harvard.

Ganesh Sitaraman is the Public Law Fellow at Harvard Law School. He first encountered Sidney Verba in 2001 as a first-year undergraduate in a course on representation, equality, and democracy and, then, enjoyed Professor Verba's company and mentorship for the next three years while serving as his research assistant.

Kenneth Stehlik-Barry first got to know Sidney Verba in 1991 when they were transitioning from the keyboard to that frisky little mouse in their efforts to coax knowledge from the Citizen Participation Survey data using the latest version of SPSS. He is a Principal Analytics Consultant at SPSS Inc. by day and a political scientist as time permits.

Michele Swers is an Associate Professor in the Department of Government at Georgetown University. During her time as a graduate student at Harvard, Dr Swers greatly benefited from Sidney Verba's mentoring and friendship.

Katherine Tate, University of California, Irvine, met Sidney Verba in 1988, when she was recruited from the University of Michigan to join the Department of Government at Harvard University as a faculty member from 1989 to 1993.

Dennis F. Thompson has participated and even occasionally deliberated with Sid Verba in the politics of the Government Department and the University for the past twenty years. Thompson is the Alfred North Whitehead Professor of Political Philosophy.

Carole Jean Uhlaner, Political Science, University of California, Irvine, received her best academic advice when told, winter of her first year in graduate school at Harvard, to take the seminar offered by newly arrived (from Chicago) Professor Verba. The seminar was followed by work as a research assistant, a dissertation, and years of friendly interaction, discussion, and dinners, during which "Professor Verba" became "Sid."

Rick Valelly was gently shepherded by Sidney Verba (and Amy Bridges and Harry Hirsch), during his dissertation years, 1979–84. He is currently Professor of Political Science at Swarthmore College.

James Q. Wilson, a retired Harvard and UCLA professor, recruited Sydney to the Harvard Government Department and taught introduction to American government with him for several years.

John Zaller, a professor of Political Science at UCLA, met Sidney Verba on an unsuccessful job interview in 1983 and has been an admirer ever since.

Ary Zolberg is the Walter Eberstadt Professor of Political Science and Director of the International Center for Migration, Ethnicity, and Citizenship at the New School for Social Research. Thanks to a number of shared tastes and the coincidence of having daughters with similar names (Erika and Erica), he and Sidney Verba became good friends as colleagues at the University of Chicago.

SELECTED BOOKS BY SIDNEY VERBA AND CO-AUTHORS

Small Groups and Political Behavior. Princeton, NJ: Princeton University Press, 1961.

The Civic Culture: Political Attitudes and Democracy in Five Nations. Princeton, NJ: Princeton University Press, 1963 (with Gabriel A. Almond).

Participation in America: Political Democracy and Social Equality. New York: Harper and Row, 1972 (with Norman H. Nie).

The Changing American Voter. Cambridge, MA: Harvard University Press, 1976 (with Norman H. Nie and John R. Petrocik).

Participation and Political Equality. Cambridge: Cambridge University Press, 1978 (with Norman H. Nie and Jae-on Kim).

Injury to Insult: Unemployment, Class, and Political Response. Cambridge, MA: Harvard University Press, 1979 (with Kay Lehman Schlozman).

The Civic Culture Revisited. Boston: Little Brown, 1980 (edited with Gabriel A. Almond).

Equality in America: The View from the Top. Cambridge, MA: Harvard University Press, 1985 (with Gary R. Orren).

Elites and the Idea of Equality. Cambridge, MA: Harvard University Press, 1987 (with Steven Kelman, Gary R. Orren, Ichiro Miyake, Joji Watanuki, Ikuo Kabashima, and G. Donald Ferree, Jr.).

Designing Social Inquiry: Scientific Inference in Qualitative Research. Princeton, NJ: Princeton University Press, 1994 (with Gary King and Robert O. Keohane).

Voice and Equality: Civic Voluntarism in American Politics. Cambridge, MA: Harvard University Press, 1995 (with Kay Lehman Schlozman and Henry E. Brady).

The Private Roots of Public Action: Gender, Equality, and Political Participation. Cambridge, MA: Harvard University Press, 2001 (with Nancy Burns and Kay Lehman Schlozman).

SELECTED MATERIAL
ABOUT SIDNEY VERBA

Sniderman, Paul. "Sidney Verba: An Intellectual Biography." *PS: Political Science and Politics* 27 (1994): 574–9.

Wilcox, Clyde, and Keiko Ono. "Sidney Verba's Voice." In *Maestri della Scienza Politica*, edited by D. Campus and G. Pasquino. Bologna, Italy: Il Mulino, 2004.

Articles from *The Harvard Crimson* (available at http://www.thecrimson.com/archives.aspx):

Milov, Sarah, "Pen and Paper Revolutionaries: The Academic's Academic," March 18, 2004.

Zhou, Lulu, "Library Chief to Close the Books," September 27, 2006.

Crimson Staff, "Scholastic Maverick," October 3, 2006.

INDEX

transition, political *see* democratization
trust 4, 13, 14, 44, 64, 89, 119, 157,
184, 185, 205
Turner, Frederick Jackson 226
Tushnet, Mark 160

Uggen, Christopher 231
unions 77, 99–100, 102, 213, 255; *see
also* labor
United Nations 80, 176

values 16, 17, 57, 68, 71, 72, 78–80,
112, 113, 119, 123–5, 127, 140–2,
183, 188, 191, 208–209, 210, 211,
232, 240
Verba, Sidney 1, 5, 49, 50, 51, 67, 73,
76, 101, 103, 104, 110, 115, 135,
137, 139, 140, 141, 160, 204, 213,
219, 247, 257
Vietnam war 49, 72
violence 13–15, 128, 152, 204, 230,
239
voluntary associations *see* associational
life
voting 16–17, 22, 47, 50, 52, 62, 67,
68, 69, 75–7, 78, 79, 82–4, 87,
101, 105, 106, 108, 111, 115–16,
118–20, 135, 137–39, 142, 155,
165, 167–8, 169–71, 172, 174–5,
185–6, 203, 204, 207, 225, 233; in
comparative perspective 2–3, 5,

181–2; costs of 213–215; swing
voters 87, 119; turnout 4, 70–2,
75, 101, 106, 123; voting rights 3,
101, 148–49, 213

Walker, Jack 160
Wallas, Graham 256
Walt, Stephen 253
Walzer, Michael 6
war 11, 47–8, 52, 55, 80, 116, 124,
134, 169, 200, 251 *see also* civil
war; Cold War; Iraq; Vietnam war;
World War I; World War II
Weber, Max 6, 7, 230
Weingast, Barry 194
Wendt, Alexander 242
Wilson, Ernest 253
Wilson, Woodrow 256
Wolfers, Arnold 242
World Trade Organization 177, 193,
197
World Values Survey 127, 141
World War I 72, 196, 226
World War II 52, 57, 115, 126, 135,
148, 184, 191, 226, 228

Yeltsin, Boris 19–21
youth *see under* age
Yugoslavia 12–13, 115, 188

Zimmerman, William 242